UNDERSTANDING
DIGITAL SIGNATURES

Understanding Digital Signatures

Establishing Trust over the Internet and Other Networks

Gail L. Grant

McGraw-Hill, Inc.
New York · San Francisco · Washington, D.C.
Auckland · Bogotá · Caracas · Lisbon · London
Madrid · Mexico City · Milan · Montreal · New Delhi
San Juan · Singapore · Sydney · Tokyo · Toronto

Library of Congress Cataloging-in-Publication Data

Grant, Gail (Gail L.)
    Understanding digital signatures : establishing trust over the
Internet and other networks / Gail Grant.
       p.   cm.
    Includes index.
    ISBN 0-07-012554-6
    1. Computer security. 2. Computer networks—Security measures.
3. Data encryption (Computer science)
QA76.9.A25G72 1997
658.4'78—dc21   97-39998
                                                            CIP

McGraw-Hill

A Division of The McGraw·Hill Companies

1 2 3 4 5 6 7 8 9 0 DOC/DOC 9 0 2 1 0 9 8 7

ISBN 0-07-012554-6

The sponsoring editor for this book was Scott Grillo, the editing supervisor was Bernard Onken, and the production supervisor was Pamela Pelton. It was set in Vendome ICG by Kim Sheran of McGraw-Hill's Professional Book Group composition unit, Hightstown, N.J.

Printed and bound by R. R. Donnelley & Sons Company.

McGraw-Hill books are available at special quantity discounts to use as premiums and sales promotions, or for use in corporate training programs. For more information, please write to the Director of Special Sales, McGraw-Hill, 11 West 19th Street, New York, NY 10011. Or contact your local bookstore.

This book is printed on recycled, acid-free paper containing a minimum of 50% recycled, de-inked fiber.

CONTENTS

Chapter 5   Uses of Public Key Systems   57

              Justification   58
              Public Key Buckets   60
              Identification   61
              Securing Communication   62
              Application Integration   63

Chapter 6   Identification and Authentication   65

              GE Research Center   66
              GTE   69
              Hewlett-Packard   70
              Liberty Financial Companies, Inc.   72
              State of Massachusetts   77
              QSpace   80
              USWeb   83

Chapter 7   Securing Communication   85

              Ultramar Diamond Shamrock   87
              Mellon Bank   89
              PrimeHost   90
              Wells Fargo   92

Chapter 8   Application Integration   95

              CyberCash   96
              E-Stamp   98
              NetDox   101
              Open Market, Inc.   104
              United States Postal Service   106

Chapter 9   Secure Electronic Transaction Protocol   109

              Business Situation   110
              How SET Works   112

Contents

Contents

PREFACE

Digital signatures is one of the most difficult technologies for anyone to understand, whether one has a technical computer background or not. For the businessperson this difficulty is especially daunting, because some of the words that are used to describe this technology—keys, certificates, signatures—are different enough from their physical counterparts to make grasping the subject even more difficult. Add to the mix unfamiliar terms like *asymmetric cryptographic methods, key pairs* and *message digests,* then stir in the infrastructure necessary to make it all work, and you have a great recipe for confusion.

Nevertheless, understanding is critical; the dream applications possible over the Internet require strong authentication and privacy. While the executive who signs the purchase order for "certification authority" services or products doesn't need to know all the algorithms involved, that person does need to understand how such technology works in broad terms, and what the implications are for his or her business. He or she needs to understand the issues involved in committing to this technology, and how the business can mitigate the risks and reap the rewards.

If digital signatures are so complex, why not use something simpler? Because using simpler technology means either increased overhead or additional risk. Nothing else available today is robust enough for broad-scale usage. If you want to have confidence that the person sending you an order for a million widgets isn't a hormone-driven hacker getting their latest thrill, you need digital signatures and certificates, or "digital I.Ds" that vouch for that person's or corporation's identity.

Understanding digital signatures requires a great deal of thought, but it can be done in small, digestible bites. This book is an attempt to carve digital signatures—and the infrastructure that is needed to truly trust them—down to manageable portions that any business executive can digest.

Organization

This book is divided into five parts. Each section builds upon the topics discussed in previous sections, but has been written to allow the more advanced reader to skip over known material to the sections most pertinent to him- or herself. The first part defines the problem space and the technology used to solve the problem. The second part explains how companies are using (or planning to use) the technology. The third part explains the issues from a business, legal, and technical standpoint. The fourth part lists the companies offering products that implement the technology, and the fifth and final section looks at some of the future possibilities of usage.

GAIL L. GRANT

ACKNOWLEDGMENTS

Many people helped with the creation of this book. I'd like to thank reviewers Kawika Daguio, Maureen Dorney, Mack Hicks, Paul Kocher, Chuck Miller, Mark Radcliffe and Pete Yeatrakas for their helpful comments on the manuscript, my editor, Scott Grillo for all his help/ encouragement, Loel McPhee for assistance/support, and Bernie Onken for his guidance during production. Several people contributed to the content of the case studies and product review section. Many thanks to:

- Bruce Bernstein for assistance with the GE Research Center case study.
- John Burnham for assistance with the Certco product review.
- Karen Cantu for assistance with the GTE case study.
- Stanley Choffrey for assistance with the U.S. Government case study.
- Steve Crocker for assistance with the CyberCash case study.
- Maureen Dorney of Gray Cary Ware and Freidenrich for permission to include Appendixes II and III.
- Scott Dueweke for assistance with the IBM product review.
- Ike Eze for assistance with the Qspace case study.
- Tim Gage for assistance with the xcert product review and help finding case studies.
- Dan Greenwood for assistance with the Commonwealth of Massachusetts case study.
- Milton Howard for assistance with the E-Stamp case study and product review.
- Catherine Kniker for assistance with the Liberty Financial case study and the BBN product review.
- Tim Knowlton for assistance with the Wells Fargo case study.
- Gary Lefkowitz for assistance with the Atalla Corporation product review.
- Andrew Morbitzer for assistance with the Cylink product review.

- Becky Repka and Gina Jorasch for assistance with the VeriSign product review and Becky's help finding case studies.
- Thomas J. Smedinghoff of McBride Baker & Coles for permission to include Appendix IV.
- Jeremy Stieglitz for assistance with the RSA product review.
- Dan Todd for assistance with the USWeb case study.
- Win Treese for assistance with the Open Market, Inc. case study.
- Nate Tyler for assistance with the NetDox case study.
- Michael Valentino for assistance with the Entrust product review.
- Erica Vanderhoof and Mike Shirer for assistance with the GTE CyberTrust product review and Erica's help finding case studies.
- Joe Wackerman for assistance with the USPS case study.
- Rebecca Young for assistance with the Premenos case study.
- Phillip Zakas for assistance with the PrimeHost case study.
- Robert "Hobbes" Zakon of MITRE for permission to include Appendix I.

Special Acknowledgment

A special thanks goes to Mack Hicks of Bank of America, who helped me to understand security requirements from a banking perspective, and Allan Schiffman of Terisa Systems, who so patiently explained to this crypto-neophyte what cryptography was all about, how it worked, and some of the multitudinous, nefarious ways that people can do nasty things to poorly designed security mechanisms. Without their tutelage over the years, this book would not have been possible.

COPYRIGHTS AND TRADEMARKS

All products, names, and services are trademarks or registered trademarks of their respective companies.

Atalla: NetArmor™, Paymaster™, SignMaster™, WebSafe™
BBN: SafeKeyper®
Certco™, Multi-Step Signing™
CyberCash™
CyberTrust™ Certification Authority
Entrust®
E-Stamp Internet Post Office™
E-Stamp Postage API™
E-Stamp Soho™
IBM Advantis™
IBM WorldRegistry™
Microsoft Internet Explorer™ 4.0
Microsoft Internet Information Server™
NetDox™
Netscape Enterprise Server™
Netscape Navigator™ 3.0
NetSure℠
Open Market Secure Webserver™
Open Market Transact™
Premenos:Templar™
RSA: S/PAY™, S/MAIL™, S/MIME™, BCERT™, BSAFE™, JSAFE™
Security Dynamics: SecureID™
SecureWeb Documents™
Sun: Java™
Terisa: SecureWeb Payments™

PART 1

Background and Definition

How did we get to the point where digital signatures are needed to enable people to conduct business over the Internet? What is the problem that this technology solves? How does this technology work? These are the questions that the first section answers.

We start with a brief review of the Internet and how it has grown and evolved, looking specifically at the areas that relate to the need for digital signatures. Then we explore how security requirements are met in the real world, and why that fails in the networked world. The technology is then laid out in simple terms, showing the evolution from early systems to those that provide digital signatures. The section closes with a look at the infrastructure required to make the technology work.

CHAPTER 1

Background

The Internet is growing at a phenomenal rate—from **5642** computers (mostly in the U.S.A.) in **1983** to over **16.1** million systems in **174** countries or regions in January **1997**. There are more Internet-connected computers today in Ecuador than there were in the whole world in **1984**. At least **12** computers are added to the Internet every minute, minimum. All these numbers are minima, because many computers with access to the Internet are not visible for counting. If the growth of the Internet were to continue at its current rate, in less than ten years there will be more computers on the Internet than people in the world.

Figure 1-1

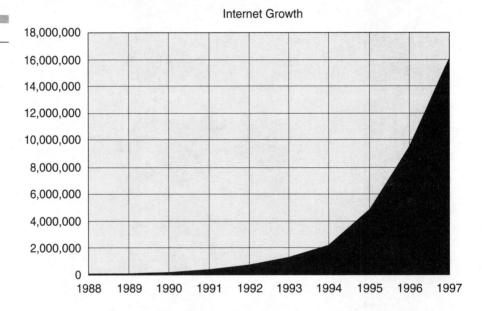

Internet Growth

What is the cause of this explosive growth? Applications and opportunity. Until the early 90's, the Internet access interface was a blinking cursor. That's right, just a blank screen.

You had to know:

- The name or address of the computer you wanted to access.
- Which "application" you wanted to use to connect to the computer.
- If you were accessing a file, you had to know both the name of the file and the directory in which it resided.

None of these programs have user-friendly, obvious names that come easily to mind. You just had to remember that telnet would allow you to log into a system, ftp would allow you to transfer files, etc. Needless to say, this did not encourage nontechnical folk to use the Internet. Only the technical *gnostikoi,* the elite who understood, knew of the power of the Internet. The applications were not "there" in a way useful to the average businessperson.

If you wanted to download the latest version of the data incorporated into the graph above, you would have to know that the system that held the data was *ftp.nw.com* and that the file you wanted was in the directory named *zone* and that the file was called *report.doc.* Here is what a typical ftp session looks like:

```
APlatform> ftp ftp.nw.com
Connected to nw.com.
220 nw.com FTP server (Version wu-2.4(1) Fri Jan 17 12:05:30 MST
  1997) ready.
Name (ftp.nw.com:grant): ftp
331 Guest login ok, send your complete e-mail address as password.
Password:
230-**
230-** Please note that this system is NOT catalog.com.
230-**
230-
230 Guest login ok, access restrictions apply.
Remote system type is UNIX.
Using binary mode to transfer files.
ftp> cd zone
250 CWD command successful.
ftp> get report.doc
local: report.doc remote: report.doc
200 PORT command successful.
150 Opening BINARY mode data connection for report.doc (5251
  bytes).
226 Transfer complete.
5251 bytes received in 0.149 secs (34 Kbytes/sec)
ftp>bye
221 Goodbye.
Aplatform>
```

There was also a very large barrier for business use of the Internet: the "Acceptable Use Policy" put forth by the U.S. government agencies that funded the backbone and its maintenance (the National Science Foundation or NSF, and DARPA). This policy stated that the Internet backbone could not be used for commercial purposes. It was built to allow researchers to communicate, not for financial gain, and the government was not willing to give the private sector a free ride. Businesses could communicate with researchers when and if it furthered research, but they could not "sell" over the Internet.

This began to change as the government withdrew funding for maintenance of the backbone. In 1991, the NSF removed the restrictions on commercial traffic on the Internet. The opportunity was there, but the applications were still lagging. The only exceptions to this were e-mail and newsgroups, which some companies did use.

E-mail was reasonably easy to use, and allowed companies to communicate with their customers (especially in universities and research facilities, which dominated the Internet until the early 1990s). Newsgroups enabled people with like interests to carry on a dialogue about a topic, and anyone with a newsreader was able to join in the discussion. These were still primarily used by technically savvy users, but then as now, e-mail was one of the top uses of the Internet.

E-mail and Customer Service

In the late 1980s several computer companies (most notably Sun Microsystems) began to develop e-mail distribution lists to communicate with their customers. They also started to offer customer support over the Internet. This was one of the first "big wins" in the commercial sector: customer service. By the early 1990s most computer hardware vendors offered online interfaces into their support functions, and software vendors have followed that trend. The savings have been tremendous. Instead of a customer having to wait on the telephone for a support representative, he or she could send an e-mail with their problem and get a response.

Costs were cut and customer satisfaction improved. A problem could be forwarded to the correct expert to solve a problem, including all information the customer had provided. There were no telephone costs involved in answering the message, so costs for 800 numbers went down. Telephone tag was eliminated, and a customer could be given pointers to online "patches" that would fix their problem. The Internet now was beginning to get some attention at the technology companies.

The World Wide Web

In 1989 Tim Berners-Lee published a paper titled *Information Management: A Proposal*, which spoke about linked information systems. These systems eventually became what we know of today as the World Wide Web. In early 1991, this development was followed up with the first web browser, a mere shadow of today's browsers, but an important start. The real "killer application" came when NCSA released *Mosaic*, the browser that changed the face of the Internet, and the Rubicon was crossed once more. The rest of that year saw tremendous growth of web servers, primarily at universities and research facilities. 1993 saw the White House go on the web at www.whitehouse.gov.

Growth exploded. It was simple for anyone to create a web server or use a web browser, because they were all free. Because there were no funds required for the Internet-connected company to create a web site, companies could put up a web server by simply writing the web pages. Companies started to use the technology to provide more sophisticated and complex forms of information to their customers than were possible via e-mail. Pictures could be used as well as programs, and interactivity began to grow. Many pioneers saw tremendous opportunity to ride this wave, and a large percentage of the Internet software companies were founded in early 1994.

By 1995 commercial-grade tools for developing web sites began to appear, and the number of web sites took an even sharper rise. From a starting point of virtually 0 in the early 1990s, web site counts went from 18,957 in August of 1995 to 739,688 in February of 1997. By the end of 1996, 98% of the Fortune 500 companies had one or more Internet domains registered, and 86% had one or more web sites. 1996 online sales estimates range between 324 million to 2.3 billion, with forecasts for the year 2000 going as high as 200 billion U.S. dollars.

Figure 1-2

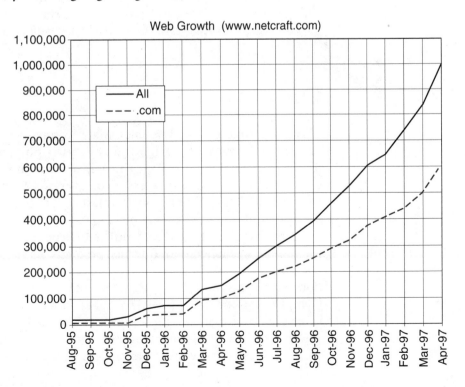

More than Billboards

With the continuing flow of applications and the growth of Internet usage worldwide, companies started doing interesting things with the Internet. Although early web servers were usually just an online version of marketing literature, that began changing. In early 1994, the *Internet Shopping Network* was launched. ISN provided a computer superstore with thousands of products from hundreds of vendors, which could be purchased directly over the Internet. It was so successful that *Home Shopping Network* acquired them in September of that year. In May 1995, Wells Fargo became the first bank to offer account balances and transaction history over the Internet. Since then, hundreds of banks have followed that path. In 1996, 12 banks went on the web each week.

There is a broad spectrum of applications available on the web today. They range from surveys where users register their opinions on topics, to online bill payment systems that banks like Wells Fargo and Bank of America are offering. Stock quotes are available to anyone with a browser. Loan calculators, ATM locators, package tracking, online ordering, travel bookings, database searches, news retrieval, and account management are only a few of the applications now possible. This all works through users filling out forms and the web server passing that information to programs for processing. The program then passes the results back to the user.

Online Sales

The latest surge is in online sales. Many companies are offering to consumers and businesses alike the ability to purchase their products online. Just how big a market this will become is open to debate; forecasts range from Simba/Cowles's prediction of 4.27 billion dollars by the year 2000 to Price Waterhouse's forecast of 175 to 200 billion dollars by the year 2000.

Forrester Research predicts that the Internet economy, which includes the revenues generated via Internet products, services, access, and online sales, will reach 200 billion dollars by the year 2000. Of this figure, 73 billion are for online sales, both retail and business-to-business. Jupiter Communications has forecast 7.3 billion dollars in the year 2000, with three billion of that coming from the travel industry.

Which of these figures is correct? Only time will tell. As more and more businesses and consumers get online, the Internet becomes a more

Figure 1-3

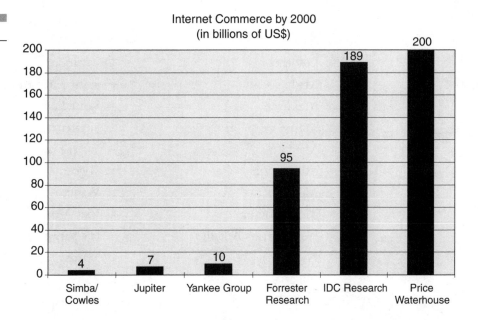

Internet Commerce by 2000
(in billions of US$)

broadly pervasive channel for both communication and sales. As of June 1997, only two of the Fortune 500 companies did not have Internet domains registered, and 95% already have web sites. This is not just a U.S. phenomenon: 94.8% of Fortune's Global 500 have Internet domains registered, and 89% have web sites.

Worldwide Opportunity

The web has provided the application that makes the Internet useful, and Internet growth has expanded the opportunity to a global scale. In 1996, 45 countries and regions joined the Internet. These are:

- Angola
- Aruba
- Benin
- Bosnia and Herzegowina
- Botswana
- Burkina Faso
- Burundi
- Central African Republic

- Congo
- Dominica
- Eritrea
- French Guiana
- French Polynesia
- Guadeloupe
- Guyana
- Honduras

- Isle of Man
- Jersey
- Lesotho
- Madagascar
- Maldives
- Mali
- Mauritius
- Micronesia
- Mongolia
- Mozambique
- Netherlands Antilles
- Niger
- Nigeria
- Norfolk Island
- Papua New Guinea

- Paraguay
- Qatar
- Rwanda
- Saint Kitts and Nevis
- Saint Lucia
- Suriname
- Tanzania
- Togo
- Vanuatu
- Viet Nam
- U.S. Virgin Islands
- Yemen
- Zaire
- Zambia

This brings the number of geographies and countries up to 174. While many of the countries that have recently joined only have a few systems on the Internet, there are sixteen countries with over 100,000 systems directly connected to the Internet. Europe now boasts over four million Internet-connected systems, and the number of such systems in the Far East has more than quintupled since 1995.

This growth means global opportunity. A company on the Internet can now reach most of the world. The only mode of access that is more ubiquitous is the telephone system. Unlike the telephone, however, there is no difference in cost between sending an e-mail to the other side of the globe or sending it down the hall. A web site can be accessed by customers anywhere, around the globe and around the clock, with virtually no additional costs. Yes, there are language barriers, but the cost of translating a site into another language pales in comparison to the cost of opening a branch in another country.

Enter the Intranet

Companies have also discovered that the same technology that allows WWW browsers and servers to connect the world could be used to connect their enterprise and partners. This is having a profound effect on the networks inside corporations, or *intranets*. Zona Research, a division of Intelliquest, pegs the intranet market as twice the size of the Internet market, with over 28 billion dollars being spent annually on intranet applications and services by the year 1999.

Companies are using e-mail and the web to keep their employees informed of what is happening in their organization. Mailing lists keep distant employees current on the latest announcements, price changes, and competitive intelligence. Engineering groups maintain web servers that provide up-to-date status on product developments. Employees can become familiar with a company's new products through web-based training. Marketing groups offer online brochures, and personnel departments allow users to change profile information online. Internal customer support benefits in much the same way as external customer support.

Forrester Research predicts that the growth of intranets will drive 401(k) account viewing online. This makes it easier for employees to keep current on their 401(k), which in turn reduces the costs of customer service for the firm managing the funds. IDC Research heralds the arrival of web-based training on both the Internet and intranets. Using the web, companies can roll-out training globally and track the progress of students around the world. The technology that is being used externally to sell to and service customers can be used internally to improve communications and service of employees. Because the technology is the same, the problems and issues will also be similar, and there is a thorn on this rose: security.

As the functions performed on the Internet and intranets become more sophisticated, the need for assurance of identity and privacy become more pronounced. When the web was used for marketing alone, security was not an issue, because anyone had access to the information and it was freely available. As companies move toward using the Internet as a true business and commerce channel, what was unimportant in 1993 has become of paramount importance today.

2

Security and the Internet

Many users don't trust the security of the Internet. In a 1996 survey by IDC Research, 90% of the users expressed concern over Internet security. Users fear that someone might get their credit card number and charge items to their account if they use their card on the Internet. They fear buying from a web site that is a fake. They fear others discovering their access codes to banking accounts and brokerage accounts, and then transferring funds to the thief's account. Banks and government agencies are concerned about giving confidential information to unauthorized parties. Corporations also worry about giving information to employees who might not be authorized to access that information, or who are trying to snoop on a fellow employee. Organizations worry about their competitors discovering proprietary information that might damage their advantage.

Although consumers tend to lump their concerns together under the general term *security,* there are actually several pieces to the security puzzle. In the context of this book, *security* means keeping something safe. "Something" may be an object, such as a secret, a message, an application, a file, a system, or an interactive communication. "Safe" means protected from unauthorized access, usage, or alteration.

To keep objects safe, the following are necessary:

- Authentication (assurance of identity).
- Authorization (that the party is sanctioned for a particular function).
- Privacy or confidentiality.
- Data integrity (proof that the object has not been altered).
- Nonrepudiation (protection against someone denying they originated a communication or data).

These are the basic requirements for security, which must be provided reliably. The requirements change slightly, depending on what is being secured. The importance of that which is being secured and the potential risk involved in leaving one of these requirements out may force higher levels of security. These are not just requirements for the networked world, but for the physical world as well. These requirements relate directly to the concerns listed above:

Concern	Requirement
Fraud	Authentication
Unauthorized Access	Authorization
Observation/Snooping	Privacy
Message Alteration	Data Integrity
Disavowal	Nonrepudiation

These concerns are not unique to the Internet. Authentication and security of objects is a part of our daily life. Understanding the elements of security and how they work in the physical world can help to explain how these requirements are met in the networked world and where the difficulties lie.

The Physical World vs. the Networked World

There are some very large problems which arise when you move from security in the physical world to security in the networked world of the Internet or intranet. These problems arise because a network is a collection of computers linked together.

Big Problems:

- No one is physically "there."
- Duplication and alteration are easy.
- Tasks can be automated.
- Everyone is virtually everywhere.

The first big problem is that no one is physically "there." Because you are not physically present, many of the forms of security used in day-to-day life cannot be used in cyberspace. This is true of authentication, authorization, privacy, integrity, and nonrepudiation.

There is another aspect of not-there-ness which is the authentication of other parties. Because you do not physically walk into your bank when you bank over the Internet, the problem is twofold: You need to know that the web server you are accessing is really your bank's, and your bank needs to know that you are really their customer and account holder.

The second big problem is that duplication and alteration are easy. If you want a second copy of a document on your computer, you simply use the copy command and create a duplicate of it. Unlike a photocopy, a copy of an electronic file is byte-for-byte identical to the original version of that file. If a 20-dollar bill in the networked world were just a simple file, all you would need to do to get more money is copy the file. It is simple to edit a file and change it. Why not make the 20-dollar bill into a 100-dollar bill? Perhaps a person got an e-mail from his or her boss saying that he or she was fired; what keeps that person from altering it into a sexual harassment and suing the company? In some systems, it might not be possible to tell that anyone had altered the message. Because computer-based information can easily be altered, protection against alteration is critical.

The next big problem is that tasks can be automated. The boon of computing power is the bane of security. It is possible to write programs that automate attempts to break into systems, send electronic mail, copy files, and perform all manner of mischief. Anyone with access to the Internet can copy an excellent program called *crack* to their system. This program compares all the passwords on a computer system to a dictionary, looking for matches. Cracking passwords by hand is hard; task automation makes it orders of magnitude easier.

The final big problem is that everyone in cyberspace is virtually everywhere. Although you are not physically "there" in the networked world, everyone is virtually there, because each system is only a step away. Anyone can attempt to access any system connected to the Internet. A "net presence" is physically in a single location, but is virtually accessible from any other system on the Internet. It is just as easy to access a web server down the hall as it is to access a web server on the other side of the world. That makes the Internet very convenient, but also very dangerous. Everyone lives in a "bad neighborhood" on the Internet. Firewalls (a method of "locking down" systems) can help to reduce this risk, but any system on the Internet or an intranet has some degree of vulnerability. This can also create jurisdictional problems: What if a bank robber in Khazakstan steals money from a bank in Mississippi? Which region's law enforcement agencies should investigate?

There is another aspect to this virtual omnipresence that must be protected against. It is called the *man in the middle* attack. In this attack, an intruder inserts themselves into a stream of communication, modifying and forwarding the communication between two parties after reading it, with both of the legitimate parties thinking they are only communicating with each other. Imagine a situation where Alice and Bob are negotiating a contract via e-mail, with Lee as the man in the middle. Bob sends a message to Alice, stating that he would like to buy 100 tribbles from Alice's company. Lee intercepts the message and changes it to read 100 frisbees, which Bob's company also sells.

Alice sends back a message stating the price of the frisbees, which Lee intercepts, changing frisbees back to tribbles, which is what Bob is expecting to hear about. The price quoted is an excellent price (because tribbles are much more expensive than frisbees), so Bob sends a message saying that he would like to order 100 to be sent to the address listed, along with a P.O. number. Lee intercepts the message and changes the address to his address and the tribbles back to frisbees, and forwards the message to Alice. Alice thanks Bob for the order and gives an expected delivery date. Lee intercepts the message, notes when the frisbees will be delivered, and forwards it to Bob after alteration. When the frisbees arrive, Lee gives them to all his friends and moves to another town. None of this could have taken place if strong authentication and message integrity were employed in Bob and Alice's communication. This is one of the reasons why authentication is so important to Internet security.

Authentication, authorization, privacy, integrity, and nonrepudiation: Most of these requirements are met unconsciously in everyday life. Unfortunately, these big problems make the meeting of security requirements in a networked world more difficult. Before applying these requirements to the Internet or an intranet, let's look at some commonplace ways these requirements are met in the physical world and why the same methods may not apply in the networked world.

Authentication

Authentication is the easiest of the requirements to understand. It is simply "proving" identity. Most authentication in our day-to-day life is casually done, without thought. Everyone unconsciously authenticates people, companies, and locations all the time.

Figure 2-1

Each time you go home, you authenticate your home by comparing it to your memory. If you are visiting a friend's home, you verify that you are in the right location by checking the address given against the street sign and the address number on the house. When you go to the store, you authenticate the owner of that store by the signs out front. When you enter a branch of your bank in a distant location, you authenticate it by its logo and signage.

When you travel abroad, you authenticate a country by the signs that tell you where you are, by the language, by the officials in customs, and through trust in the airline to take you to the indicated destination. Physical authentication can be much more robust than authentication on a network, because you are present and have been authenticating things since you learned to speak and read.

The most popular form of individual authentication is a signature. A signature is used to authenticate an account holder to a bank, to bind a person to room charges in a hotel, and to authenticate the cardholder for credit-card transactions. Most often the signature is used not only to authenticate, but also to authorize. There are centuries of legal regulations that specify what a signature means; these laws can be used in court to enforce contracts. While a signature can be used to authenticate identity, it is also used for authorization.

Visual verification isn't practical over networks because of big problem number one: You are not there. The same is true of a web site you visit on the Internet: It is difficult to be sure that the web server you are visiting truly belongs to the specified company. The cues used in the physical world just aren't there.

Imagine that you want a new television. In the first case, you go to a large store that specializes in televisions. As you enter the store, you see the company logo and banks of television sets (which you have seen them advertise regularly in your local newspaper). You purchase the television and take it home.

In the second case, as you drive home from work, you see a truck parked on the side of the road with a hand-painted sign which says "Brand-Name TVs Cheap." You get a great deal on a state-of-the-art TV. You buy it and take it home.

In the first case, you would have a high degree of confidence that the police were not going to come knocking on your door informing you that you had purchased stolen goods. In the second case, although you might get a great bargain, your confidence would not be as high. The problem with the Internet is that it is difficult to tell the difference between the well-known store and the truck on the side of the road. It is relatively inexpensive to create a web site, and simple to register a domain name. This is great news for small business, but it also makes fraud far simpler in the networked world.

Signatures have a similar problem. It isn't possible today to use your physical signature to authenticate yourself over a network, because you are not physically there to sign a document. A picture of your signature won't help either, because alteration and duplication are possible. The fact that everyone is everywhere means that someone could intercept a document you signed, alter it, and send it on to the recipient. Most of these actions are not something that a naïve user can easily do, but are certainly doable with knowledge and access.

Authorization Authentication

Credentials are used to authenticate a person to unknown parties, but they can also be used as proof of authorization. Individuals have drivers' licenses, which authenticate them as authorized to drive a car. Travelers usually must have a passport to authenticate their residency or citizenship. Some countries also require additional authorization, such as a visa, to enter their borders. When you check in for a flight at a U.S. airport, the airline will ask for a picture ID to authenticate that you are indeed the party listed on the ticket. There are three important assumptions that make credentials work:

Figure 2-2

- There exists a third party which issues the credentials.
- Trust in the ability of that third party to authenticate properly.
- It is difficult to copy, forge, or modify the credentials.

There are laws that protect against fraudulent credentials, and there are sophisticated infrastructures for authenticating unknown parties. As the importance of authentication authorization increases, such as might be needed for a police officer or a doctor, it becomes important to not only know who a person is, but that they are licensed or authorized through additional credentials. These credentials are issued by licensing or accreditation bodies to certify that a person is capable or empowered to perform a particular function. Governments perform this role for enforcement officers and some trades, like construction, and most professions provide the means to verify that an individual or company is indeed licensed to practice their trade.

Credentials also authenticate relationships between two parties. A club membership card states that a person is allowed to use the facilities of the club. An employee ID authenticates that person as having a relationship with a company that allows them access to company property. If a person is fired or fails to pay their membership dues, then their identification is invalidated.

Credentials require infrastructure; there must be locations where the credentials can be procured, people to staff those locations, and policies and procedures which state how the credentials are acquired and how they may be used. For credentials to be useful, they must have credibility. If people do not trust the credentials, the credentials have no value; but where do you go to get your online credentials? How are those credentials tied to you in a way that takes into account the big problems? There will be more on this later, but for now simply remember that, just as the physical world requires infrastructure to authenticate individuals, so will the Internet if it is truly to be trusted.

Privacy and Confidentiality

Privacy (confidentiality) is the ability to ensure that only the intended party or parties have access to something. The most common method of protecting things in the physical world is to use keys and locks. When you buy a car, you are given a key or set of keys that gives you access to the car, starts the engine, opens the doors, and sometimes opens the gas

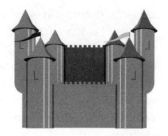

tank. When you buy a house, you are given a set of keys to the entrances. Mailboxes, offices, diaries, safe deposit boxes; many things have keys.

Most keys and locks in the physical world are symmetric: The same key both locks and unlocks something. The more important the item secured, the stronger the lock. Cars, houses, and offices often afford access to multiple parties with identical keys. Where more security is desired, multiple locks are employed so that many people might have access to the office building, but only the employee and the janitor have access to the employee's office. In some critical situations, two parties must both employ their key at the same time to activate a lock.

How much control you have over your keys depends on your control over that which is being locked or secured. That which you ultimately control and involves no other party requires no authorization or permission for change. If you own your house, you can change locks and keys as often as you like because you have authority over that which is being secured. If you rent an apartment, your landlord would probably be quite angry if you changed the lock without providing a key for the owner or manager of the facility. In some locations, changing the lock without permission might be grounds for eviction.

There is a basic assumption with the use of keys: Possession is both authentication and authorization in addition to privacy. Keys do not magically become inoperable in the wrong hands. Your house key in the hands of a thief does not notify the police that a burglar is using it for unauthorized entry. If someone steals your keys they have access to all the things the keys unlock, and your "privacy" has been violated. Unless you change the locks, the thief has access. There is also a very handy warning system that comes with physical keys: If you lose your keys, you generally know it and can take the appropriate action (such as changing your locks). In the networked world, it is possible for someone to take your "keys" without your knowledge by simply making a copy of them. Because of the connectivity of a network, if someone can get access to your keys, they can copy them.

Another method of securing privacy is by concealing objects. Letters are secured in envelopes, curtains provide privacy for a room, and fences provide privacy from neighbors. There are methods of hiding things on the Internet that rely on scrambling the contents of a file or message so that *only someone who knows how the file was scrambled* can retrieve it in a meaningful way.

If the value of the thing being secured is high, its confidentiality can be ensured through monitoring. Cameras in banks and stores are a good example of this. Physically guarding the item being protected also helps to ensure its confidentiality. Many things are secured using multiple forms of protection, to ensure that it truly is secured. A corporate research facility is a good example of something secured with multiple levels of protection; such a facility uses cameras, guards, and multiple sets of locks and keys, with increasing complexity and new levels of protection added for the most critical areas. This is also possible on the Internet; in fact, monitoring is critical to any method of securing systems in a networked world. Monitoring makes sure that the security measures taken have not been suborned.

Data Integrity

There are few examples in the real world that map to data integrity. The most common is the use of seals, especially in the area of imports and exports. The customs officials in one country will inspect a carton of goods to make sure that it contains what is listed on the documentation, then seal it. If the customs officials at the destination see that the seal is still secure, they know that no one has tampered with the cargo in transit.

Seals are also used in retail sales. Many foods have "tamper-evident" packaging so the consumer knows that no one has opened the product. If a consumer purchases a stereo at a store and the packaging has been

Figure 2-4

opened, often he or she will verify that the product has maintained its integrity; this is done by opening the box and inspecting the goods.

In most of the physical world, *data* integrity verification is generally done visually. The absence of signs of tampering are taken to mean that the data has not been changed. When signing a contract, any changes made to the printed page must be initialed by both parties to ensure that they are a part of the agreement and not a sign of an alteration that occurred after signing.

This isn't as easy on the Internet or an intranet because of big problems 2 (duplication is easy) and 4 (everyone is virtually everywhere). Information can be easily altered when stored on a computer, and many people could potentially gain access, making data integrity much more difficult in the networked world. In order to ensure data integrity you need to somehow create a seal that cannot be altered, and that can be used to later verify that the data hasn't been changed.

Another means to verify data integrity is auditing. Companies employ external auditors to ensure that their accounting books correctly state the organization's fiscal position. This helps to maintain the "data integrity" of the reported revenues. Auditing can be a valuable tool to maintaining system and data integrity in the networked world as well.

Trust

Behind all of these aspects of security is the basic assumption of trust: faith or confidence. If a chair looks wobbly, you are unlikely to trust it to hold your weight. Trust in the security of the Internet is much the same. If Internet mechanisms for enabling authentication, authorization, privacy, integrity, and nonrepudiation do not appear sturdy to the users, users will be hesitant to use them. Trust can be lacking for reasons both real and perceived. One of the largest problems of trust on the Internet today is that people simply do not understand it. In spring of 1997, the Social Security Administration was chastised in the press for making data available to customers on the Internet because they felt the methods used to authenticate individuals was lacking, when the methods used were MORE rigorous than are currently used for telephone queries of the same data. This problem of understanding is a critical barrier that must be overcome.

Figure 2-5

The confidence in the ability to authenticate companies and individuals over networks is critical to commerce. If you did not trust that when you walked into your bank, you were truly dealing with authorized agents, banking would take considerably more time than it does today. It is easier to authenticate companies and individuals with whom you have an established relationship or who are introduced to you by someone you trust.

But what about new relationships? Generally, these are authenticated by some third party. You must trust the third party or there is no confidence in the authentication. Trust must also be present for privacy measures: People will not bank with a financial institution that does not employ adequate safeguards to protect their funds from theft. The same is true of data integrity: If a consumer fears that a product might have been altered after manufacture, they will not buy it.

In the networked world, the requirements for trust are not yet well defined or agreed upon. Trust is something that has yet to be firmly established for networked usage. The lack of confidence is part of what is behind the concern that Internet users express as a need for security. In order for the Internet to be used for high-value transactions, trust must be established.

We must not only secure the Internet, but convince consumers and business alike that the security is trustworthy. This will require education, experience, and infrastructure. Users need to understand how Internet security works and the safeguards that protect them. They must be able to try it out, experience it, and become comfortable with it before it will be truly trusted.

CHAPTER 3

Securing the Internet

Authentication, authorization, privacy, integrity, and nonrepudiation: When all of these requirements are met, the Internet can be used with confidence for all business communication. This requires different methods than those we all understand. We've shot down most of the ways in which we achieve security in the physical world as inappropriate or impossible in the networked world. How, then, do we address the problem?

The field of study that addresses most of these requirements has existed for centuries, and the specific technology has existed for decades. It is called *cryptography*. Most people can understand the basic concept of cryptography, which is the scrambling of messages so that only the intended parties can read them.

Cryptography means *hidden writing*. The earliest forms of cryptography made simple substitutions of one letter for another throughout the alphabet. Others would embed the real message within a longer message, so that only every N words had meaning. These are examples of *ciphers*. A cipher is a method of obscuring a message so that unauthorized parties cannot read it. Most ciphers employ some sort of "key" to lock and/or unlock the hidden message, thus increasing the difficulty of unauthorized access. Used this way, cryptography can be used to meet privacy requirements by scrambling messages before we send them and unscrambling them upon receipt. Without the key, the message is completely meaningless, so even if someone manages to intercept it, the privacy of the message is maintained.

Hiding the message is called *encryption* and retrieving the hidden message is called *decryption*. The most common comparison used to explain cryptography is a lock. Lock companies make millions of locks, each with a reasonably unique key to lock it and open it. The stronger the lock, the more intricate the key used to lock and unlock it. Encryption is the locking of the message and decryption is the unlocking of that message. Who can get at the message? Anyone with a key. Because the same key is used to both lock and unlock the message, this type of cryptography is sometimes called "shared secret," because both parties have to know the secret key that unlocks the message. The more formal term for this methodology is *symmetric cryptography*.

Figure 3-1   Shared Secret: Same key used to encrypt and decrypt

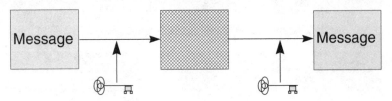

With symmetric cryptography, the sender uses a key to encrypt the message, then sends the encrypted message to the recipient. The recipient uses the same key to decrypt the message. You must have both a cipher and a key to hide the message. When you take the cipher and apply the key to a message, you can either create or unlock the message. Here are some simple examples:

Message	Cipher	Key	Ciphertext
We are safe.	Letter substitution	A=B	Xf bsf tbgf.
We are safe.	Extraneous words	Every 3rd word	What if we know they are really not safe to eat?

There is an implicit assumption here, which is that if you have the key, you are both authorized to read the message and are authenticated as the intended recipient. The multimillion-dollar question is: Is simple possession of a symmetric key sufficient to authenticate an individual or corporation? The answer is a resounding *NO*. The difficult part is authentication: making sure that someone is who they say they are. When you travel abroad, you are authenticated via your passport. The customs official looks at your picture and compares it to your face, and looks at your signature and compares it to the form you filled out. On the Internet, confidence of identity is a much harder problem. Because of the big problems, the simple possession of a key is not a good method of authentication.

To better understand why possession of a key is not sufficient for authentication, let's return to the early ciphers. Why did ciphers change? Because unauthorized parties kept *cracking* or breaking the code used to hide the messages. Governments and wars are responsible for many of the advancements in the art of cryptography. In ancient times, if a leader wanted to communicate with someone at a remote location, they could send messages by couriers. Unfortunately, there was always the possibility of the message falling into the wrong hands. During wars, this could mean the difference between victory and defeat. In politics, it could give an opponent an advantage. The use of cryptography made it much more difficult for unauthorized parties to read the messages. Possession of the keys in earlier days was probably sufficient, because the practice of cryptography was new and there were no computers to abet the thief or snoop.

Before computers, the "cracking" was done with brains and writing materials. Computers and the ability to automate things just made it easier to crack both the cipher and the key. With the rapid advancements in computing power, it has become necessary to develop stronger ciphers with larger and more complex keys. Why increase the size of the key? Keys have been enhanced to increase the difficulty of going through all the possibilities of what the key might be—commonly called a *brute-force attack*—to decipher the message.

Looking at the simple letter substitution example cipher, the "key" was simply which letter equaled A, which means there would only be 25 possibilities, because a key of A=A wouldn't hide the message and the rest of the alphabet followed in order. To find the solution, one could go through all the possible substitutions very quickly with a computer. If the key was a complete list of the whole alphabet, with each letter substituted for any other letter, the correct combination would be much harder to figure out; but this is also easily discovered by analyzing the encrypted text. The trend has been to move from this type of cipher to mathematical equations, where the key is the variable upon which the equation is based. The goal of these equations is to produce output that looks as much like random bits as possible. The larger the key, the harder it is to break the ciphertext using a brute force attack.

Most key lengths today are expressed in *bits*. A bit is the smallest amount of information that can be represented on a computer. A bit is either off or on, representing either 0 or 1. The possible number of keys of a particular key length is 2 to the power of the key length. There are, therefore, 256 possible eight-bit keys, because eight bits is 2^8 or 256. The most common symmetric algorithm is the Digital Encryption Standard or DES, which uses 56-bit keys. The largest exportable key length that the U.S. government allows is 40 bits. Here is a table of some of the common key lengths and the number of feasible keys for each:

Size of Key	Number of Possible Keys
8	256
40	1,099,511,627,776
56	72,057,594,037,927,936
64	18,446,744,073,709,600,000
128	3.40282×10^{38}
256	1.15792×10^{77}
512	1.3408×10^{154}

Breaking a 56-bit key is feasible with extremely expensive hardware, but not with general-purpose computers using software—at least not today. Most experts agree that 128-bit keys are quite safe for the foreseeable future. Note that these figures are for symmetric cryptography, and only for brute-force attacks. There are other ways to break codes (the practice is called *cryptanalysis*), but the algorithms that are in common use today have generally been chosen because they are currently resistant to known methods of cryptanalysis.

With symmetric-key cryptography, if you figure out the key, you can decrypt the message and you can also create new messages using that key. This presents a serious problem: Not only can someone know what you are communicating, but they can change your communication or impersonate an authorized party. There is another problem associated with symmetric systems: How do both parties get the key? Keys for today's symmetric systems are very large; they are typically between 40 and 128 bits, which is more than mere mortals can generally remember. So the keys must be communicated via some electronic form. When dealing with people you know, you could simply copy the key to a floppy disk and give it to them; but what about people you don't know? How do you get keys to them? And do you want to trust them not to divulge that key to someone else?

To solve this problem, researchers Whitfield Diffie and Martin Hellman came up with asymmetric-key cryptography in 1975. With this

Figure 3-2

Authentication:
Shared Secret Vs Public Key

Shared Secret: Same key used to encrypt and decrypt

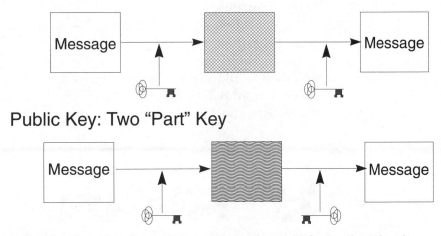

Public Key: Two "Part" Key

Public Key Cryptography is primarily used for authentication

system, everyone who might possibly want to communicate has a pair of keys: a public key and a private key. These keys are mathematically related, but the private key cannot be discovered from the public key. To use the lock analogy, imagine a lock that requires one key to lock it and another key to open it. This is how most asymmetric systems work.

With symmetric cryptography, both parties have the same key. This single key can be used to both encrypt and decrypt messages. Asymmetric cryptography is named because the keys used by the different parties are not the same, so the system is not "symmetric." There is also another name for this type of system: *public key cryptography*. There are several different public key cryptosystems that use different algorithms, which means that the way that the private and public components of the keys are generated differ. There is only one public key cryptosystem that is in wide acceptance today. This is called *RSA*, and it is named for its inventors, Ron Rivest, Adi Shamir, and Leonard Adelman. Other public key systems will be discussed briefly in Part 3, but the focus of this book is RSA.

The name *public key cryptography* is derived from the fact that one of your keys is "public" or distributed widely. This does not compromise your private key, because it cannot be derived from your public key. The public key is given to anyone who wants to communicate with you. Anyone can use your public key to encrypt a message (using a public key algorithm as the cipher) and you can decrypt it using your private key. Now keys are NOT the same; each person has their own pair of keys. The likelihood of someone divulging a key is less, because it could be discovered that it was the key in their possession that was used. Public key cryptography is the first ingredient in the recipe for digital signatures.

Alice and Bob want to establish two-way communication. To accomplish this, each party would give their public key to the other party. Alice would use Bob's public key to encrypt the message going from Alice to Bob. Bob would use his private key to decrypt the message. For the response from Bob to Alice, Bob would use Alice's public key to encrypt the message, and Alice would use her private key to decrypt the message.

Figure 3-3

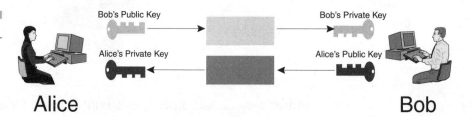

Alice   Bob

Unfortunately, public key cryptography is very expensive computationally, so real Alices and Bobs generally don't use it for general communication. Symmetric systems are much faster. When securing communication, the public key is used to encrypt a shared secret by one of the parties, and symmetric cryptography is used for communication.

Figure 3-4

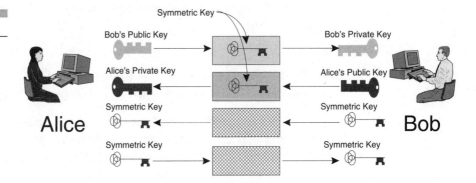

Alice's software generates a symmetric key and uses Bob's public key to encrypt it, then sends it to Bob. Bob then uses Alice's public key to encrypt the same key she just sent, and sends it back. This confirms that it really was Bob that got the key. Now they can use this key to continue communication with the faster symmetric ciphers.

An important characteristic of RSA public key cryptography is that either key can decrypt what its mate encrypted. For securing privacy, this isn't much use. If you used your private key to encrypt data, anyone could read that data by using your public key to decrypt it.

Figure 3-5

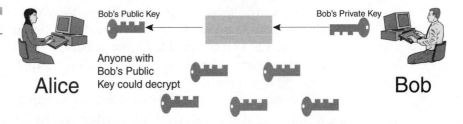

This reciprocity of keys is VERY useful for authentication, however. Because your key pair is unique, if you encrypt something with your private key, then the recipient can be certain that only you could have sent that message. The catch is that they must believe that it really is you who holds the private component of the key. But how does the recipient know that you are really who you say you are AND you were the one who initiated the communication (not an impostor)? This is the point where *certification authorities* enter the scene. As mentioned before, we already use all sorts of certification authorities in the real world for passports, driver's licenses, credit cards, banking accounts, and professional credentials.

There are some basic assumptions you unconsciously make when you sign a document:

■ Your signature binds you to whatever the document states.

■ The document will not be changed after you sign it.

■ Your signature will not be transferred to another document.

There are laws and conventions that make these assumptions valid, but how is this carried into the networked world? We need something that will help us to assure that the message hasn't changed (data integrity) and which also will prevent someone from simply moving our signature to another document we never intended to sign.

This could be accomplished by simply using our private key to encrypt the whole document. As noted before, this would be very slow, because of the computational expense of public key algorithms. Just as people use public key cryptography to exchange a shared secret, then use symmetric ciphers to protect their communication, there are algorithms that will reduce documents to a small, unique "thumbprint" of the data. This type of algorithm is called a *one-way hash* or *message digest*. These algorithms are used to take a document of any size and create a unique digest of it that is always the same length. A message digest cannot be reversed. It is computationally impossible to deduce the message from the digest; therefore, someone must have the original document to create the digest. Because these digests are quite small, it takes much less time to encrypt the digest with a public key algorithm. Message digests are the second ingredient in the recipe for a digital signature.

We still aren't there yet. If we just send the document and the digest together, someone could simply change the message and recreate the digest. We must protect the digest from alteration. To accomplish this, we create the digest and then use our private key to encrypt the digest. The digest protects the document from alteration, and the use of public key cryptography protects the digest from alteration. No one can change it. This digest, encrypted with the sender's private key, is a form of digital signature.

Figure 3-6

How Digital Signatures Work

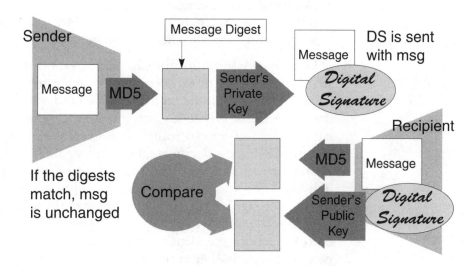

The sender creates a message digest of the document he or she wants to send, and encrypts it using the private key. The message, containing the document and the "signature," is then sent to the recipient. If the sender desires privacy, the message is encrypted. The recipient applies the sender's public key to the digital signature. He or she does this to retrieve the message digest from the digital signature that the sender created prior to sending. Next, the recipient creates a new message digest from the message received and compares that to the one that was inside the digital signature. If the two are the same, then the message was truly sent by the sender and arrived unaltered.

All of these actions are taken by the software used to sign and send or receive and verify. The user might see some indication on the screen that these actions are taking place, but the tasks are all automated. The user simply sees that the document is received and verified.

Under this system one can send a message to anyone and have confidence that it has not been changed. If the user doesn't want anyone to be able to read the message, the user can encrypt both the message and the signature prior to sending. If we believe that the private key used to "sign" the digest truly belongs to the sender, we have:

■ Authentication: We have confidence the sender was the only one who could have sent the message.

- Message integrity: We have confidence that the message arrived unchanged.
- Nonrepudiation: Because key pairs are unique, we can be confident that only the sender could have signed the message digest. The sender cannot deny having sent the message.

Digital signatures do not provide privacy, but that can be easily accomplished with the extra encryption step mentioned above. However, we still don't have all the ingredients. We need some way to be sure that the owner of the private key used to sign the message digest is who they say they are. All we can really tell is that the holder of the key is the one who signed the document. How can we be sure that the key holder is who they say they are? We need a way to bind a particular key to an individual or corporation. The real challenge is ensuring that the private key used to "sign" the digest truly belongs to the sender.

We have the ability to create digital signatures, but we still need someone to vouch for the identity of the sender. Without some way to tie a person or organization to the private key, the digital signature is useless. The solution to this problem is to have someone else certify that the private key belongs to the sender. The binding of identity to a particular key pair is done using a certificate that attests to the owner's identity. This certification must be issued by a certification authority, an organization that verifies identities and issues certificates that bind key pairs to that identity. A certification authority has five primary functions:

- Accepting applications for certificates.
- Verifying the identity of the person or company applying for the certificate.
- Issuing certificates.
- Revoking certificates.
- Providing status information about the certificates that it has issued.

Certification authorities (CA) provide an important component of the infrastructure that makes public key cryptosystems useful in authenticating parties over the Internet and intranets. Sometimes these functions are split between different organizations; for example, a company might manage the verification of identity and then pass confirmation of that identity on to a CA. Revocation lists and directory services can be also done by a third party, acting on behalf of multiple CAs. Once the CA has verified the identity of the applicant, they issue a certificate that lists:

- The owner of the key pair.
- The organization of the owner.
- The owner's public key.
- Expiration information.
- A digital signature, created using the CA's private key, that shows that the certificate has not been changed.

Figure 3-7

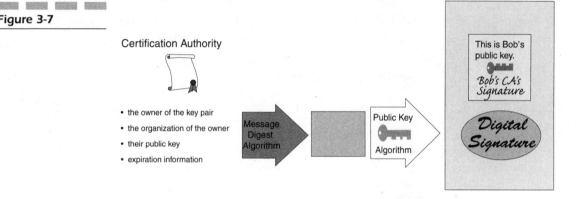

Software on each system stores both the owners' keys and certificates. The public keys of all major CAs are built into the applications that use public key systems, so the software can easily validate the certificate. All that is added to the diagram above is a step that checks the certificates of both parties:

Figure 3-8

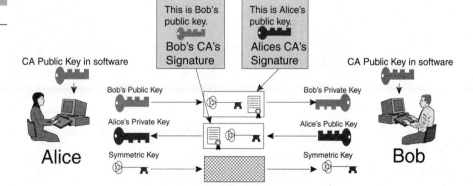

Certification authorities and certificates are the final elements in the recipe for a digital signature. In the previous example, both Alice and Bob have the same CA, but they could have different CAs. As long as the user's software has the public key for a CA, certificates issued by that CA can be verified.

Now we have a completed list of ingredients for a digital signature:

- Public key cryptography, with its paired-key architecture, to provide the methodology and the ciphers.
- Message digests, to reduce the size of the object to be signed.
- Digital signatures, to apply public key cryptography to the message digest in order to protect it from alteration.
- Certification authorities and certificates to bind the keys to a particular individual or company.

Figure 3-9

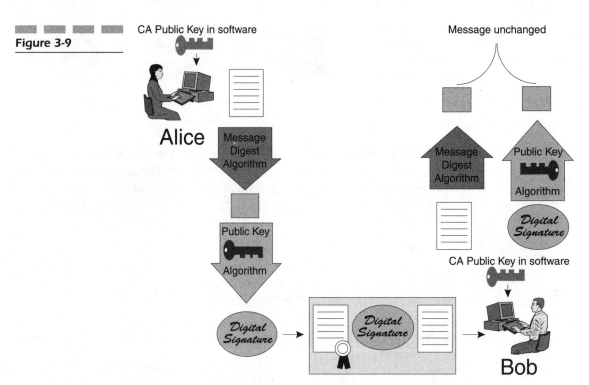

Here are the steps to create and verify a digital signature:

1. Prior to the communication, Alice procures a certificate that verifies her identity and binds it to her public key.

2. Alice creates a message digest of the document she wants to sign, and signs the digest using a public-key cryptographic algorithm and her private key.

3. Alice sends the message and the digital signature to Bob.

4. Bob verifies that the key received is Alice's key using her certificate.

5. Bob verifies that Alice's certificate has not expired or been revoked.

6. Bob decrypts the message digest with Alice's public key.

7. Bob creates a new message digest for the document he received, and compares the new digest with the one that was in the digital signature.

8. If the message digests match, the document received is the same one that was sent.

This seems complicated, but most of these operations aren't even seen by the users. The application that Alice uses to send the signed document does all the work. The only thing that Alice has to do is choose which certificate and key pair she wants to use to sign the document, and where she wants to send it.

People in the future will have different certificates issued by various CAs for the many relationships and roles in their jobs and life. Sometimes the certificates will be used to sign documents. On other occasions, the certificates will be used to authenticate individuals or companies to access private information. Whatever the use, confidence of identity is critical. Confidence requires an infrastructure to issue and verify certificates and cooperation between software vendors and businesses to make it all work.

4

Public Key Infrastructure

The size of a community determines the amount of infrastructure that is necessary to support that community. A small town needs less infrastructure than a city or country because there are less people to support with roads, utilities, schools, social services, and housing. As the size of a community grows, so does the complexity of the infrastructure. In the networked world, the industry is moving toward public-key certification authorities to provide authentication infrastructure. The broad reach of the Internet will require an equally broad-reaching infrastructure to support the use of public key technology over the Internet.

Public key infrastructure is necessary to give meaning to public keys. A public key must be bound to a certificate that vouches for the person's or corporation's identity; otherwise, it is not useful for authentication. Used properly, a digital signature is as robust as a physical signature. A physical signature is reasonably unique, so it can be used to "authenticate" you. On a computer network, you cannot reach through the ether to apply a pen to paper; but if your identity can be verified, you can be issued a unique key pair that can be bound to your identity.

The goal of this infrastructure is to enable anyone to be authenticated online, and for the authenticator to know what a certificate means. The certification authority must verify the identity of the applicant, issue the certificate, and manage the status of that certificate over its lifetime. Anyone must be able to verify the issued certificate and be able to check its current status. The basics are relatively simple, and can be created by simply extending relationships in the physical world into the networked world.

The banking industry is a good example of a global infrastructure that acts as a type of certifying authority. Customers establish relationships with local banks. The relationship starts with opening an account of some type: a loan, a checking account, a savings account, or a business account. The customer is given an account number that identifies them to that bank. When the customer issues instructions to pay another vendor out of an account, the bank executes that instruction. The remote bank doesn't know the customer, but they do know the bank. In a sense, the bank authenticates the customer to the foreign bank. Let's say that the account is a business account, and the company that holds that account wants to buy or sell in another country. Their bank, which has had a relationship with them and knows their credit history, will issue a "letter of credit." This letter of credit promises that the customer listed in the letter of credit is who they say they are and that they are good for the amount listed in the letter of credit.

This example can be extended into the networked world via certificates and digital signatures. The bank issues the account holder a certificate via their certification authority. The account holder sends the request for the letter of credit to their bank, signing the request. Once the details have been worked out, the bank sends a digitally signed letter of credit to the seller's bank, guaranteeing payment upon receipt of goods. The seller's bank can verify the identity of both the bank and the buyer through using their certificates. This is a simple example of how certificates can be used.

Network of Trust

The global nature of the Internet allows people from anywhere to visit a web site. If the site has the capability, that visitor can also conduct business with that company. When dealing with existing trading partners, trust (confidence of identity) is relatively easy to establish. This is not the case with new customers. It is not possible to know everyone that might want to do business with you electronically, but you might be able to rely on trusted third parties to verify the new customer's identity. If you trust the CA and their policies and practices for verifying identities, you can trust a certificate issued by that CA. This is much easier than trying to verify the identity of each new online customer.

Certificates allow a business to trust a new customer's identity, if they are issued by a trusted CA. A network of trust is a group of certification authorities that a business decides to trust for the issuance of certificates. This is a business decision that should be based on the practices of the CA, their methods of identity verification, and their policies for certificate revocation.

Identity Verification

This can be done in a number of ways, depending on how the certificate will be used. A corporation might run a CA for internal use to authenticate employees for access to proprietary information. They might issue the certificate when a new employee is hired. Typically the verification step is separated from the actual certificate issuance, especially if the verification takes place in person.

Equally important are the processes used to verify the identity of a certificate applicant. This form of robustness is usually referred to as the "level of assurance" associated with a certificate. A low-assurance certificate means that the CA has made some effort to verify identity, but that fraud is possible.

A good example of a low-assurance certificate is a certificate that is bound to an e-mail address. These personal certificates are typically issued if the CA can send an e-mail message to the listed address. While this might be sufficient for low-value transactions, a corporation would hardly be willing to accept a multimillion-dollar order on the strength of this certificate. *Server certificates* are an example of a higher-assurance certificate. These certificates originally required that a corporation send a copy of their incorporation papers, and that the application be signed by a corporate officer. The "distinguished name" on a server certificate is the name of the server, typically www.companyname.com. When a user accesses a web site that has a server certificate, they can check the identity listed in the certificate to make sure that the server is indeed owned by the expected company.

The question remains: What does the certificate mean? Applications that are currently being deployed use special-purpose certificates. There is no universal certificate that can be used for all purposes. This means that a user must also manage their many certificates and present the correct one for any given application. Certificates today are very much like the credit cards and identification cards that you find in your wallet. You have different cards and IDs for different purposes. This might change in the future, but today's systems tend toward these special-purpose certificates. The issues that are raised in this chapter will be dealt with in more detail in Part 3.

There are three major components to public key infrastructure:

- Technology: Public key cryptography, digital signatures, certification authority software, and certificates.
- Policies, procedures and practices: Decisions made about how things are done and what is required by a particular CA.
- Operations: The actual systems and staff that run the CA and enforce the policies and procedures.

Technology

CAs come in all sizes and flavors. Some might be commercial CA vendors that provide general-purpose certificates or specialized services to organizations for a particular application. Other CAs will be run by a corporation for internal usage, or for their trading partners. Other CAs will be maintained by banks for issuing certificates for their customer. A certification authority is known by their *root key*. This key is the one that is used to sign certificates. Because all certificates that a CA issues are signed with this key, keeping it safe is paramount.

The technology components include the software that will issue the certificate, load it into an application, respond to a request for the status of a certificate, revoke a certificate, and provide a directory of certificates. There is freely available software that will issue certificates. You can simply download this software over the Internet and set up your own CA; but what applications have your root key? For an application to verify that a user's certificate is valid, they must have a copy of the root key embedded in the application, or a way to get that root key to validate users. If the certificate is to be used by the application, not just validated, there needs to be a software module that knows how to load the certificate into the software. Here is what happens today when a certificate is issued:

Figure 4-1

How A Certificate Is Issued

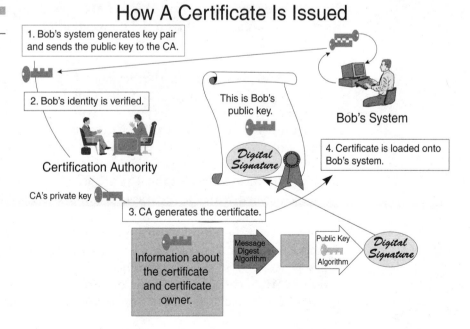

1. Bob's system generates key pair and sends the public key to the CA.

2. Bob's identity is verified.

This is Bob's public key.

Bob's System

Digital Signature

Certification Authority

4. Certificate is loaded onto Bob's system.

CA's private key

3. CA generates the certificate.

Information about the certificate and certificate owner.

Message Digest Algorithm

Public Key

Algorithm

Digital Signature

The lifecycle of a certificate starts with the keys being generated. Bob's system or the CA must generate a key pair that will be used for signing and reading signatures. Usually the key pair is generated either by Bob's system, or by a smart card or a special hardware box that does cryptographic operations that Bob uses with his system. After this has occurred, the applicant's identity is verified. The CA then creates a certificate. The certificate is created by the CA signing a message digest of the certificate information, which includes the public key of the applicant. After the key pair has been generated and the certificate that attests to the ownership of the key pair has been completed, they are loaded into the application that will use the certificate and key. There is no standard method for doing this, so the certification authority must have application modules for loading certificates into all supported applications. Quite often the application for the certificate and the actual loading of the certificate and key pair are separated by a period of time; during this time additional verification can be performed.

Applying for a Certificate

Early business applications that are using certificates and digital signatures are centered around e-mail and web-based applications. The first experience that any users of this technology will experience is the application for a certificate. Figure 4-2 shows an example of the VeriSign Digital ID Center application process for adding a certificate to a Netscape browser.

The user first goes to the VeriSign Digital ID Center, located at http://digitalid.verisign.com, and clicks on *Request an ID* on the task bar. The next screen asks for the type of certificate being requested (Fig. 4-3).

Because this certificate will be used with a Netscape browser, the user clicks on *Netscape.* The next screen allows the user to choose the class of certificate desired and what each type can be used for. For VeriSign, a Class I ID means that minimal verification is done and that the insurance associated with the certificate is limited to 1,000 U.S. dollars. A Class II ID requires more effort to verify the identity of the applicant; VeriSign uses the Equifax consumer credit database to obtain the information used for verification. The key pair is generated via a hardware key generator, and the insurance for this level of certificate is 25,000 U.S. dollars. After choosing the type of certificate (in this case, we chose a Class I certificate), the certificate application is displayed (Figs. 4-4 and 4-

Figure 4-2

Figure 4-3

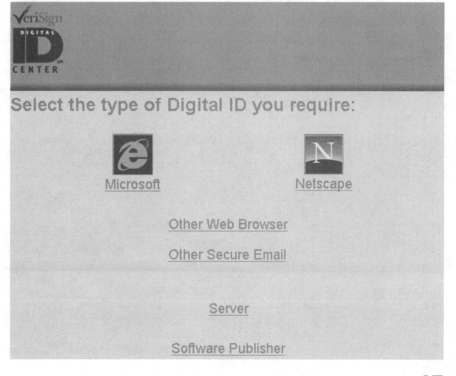

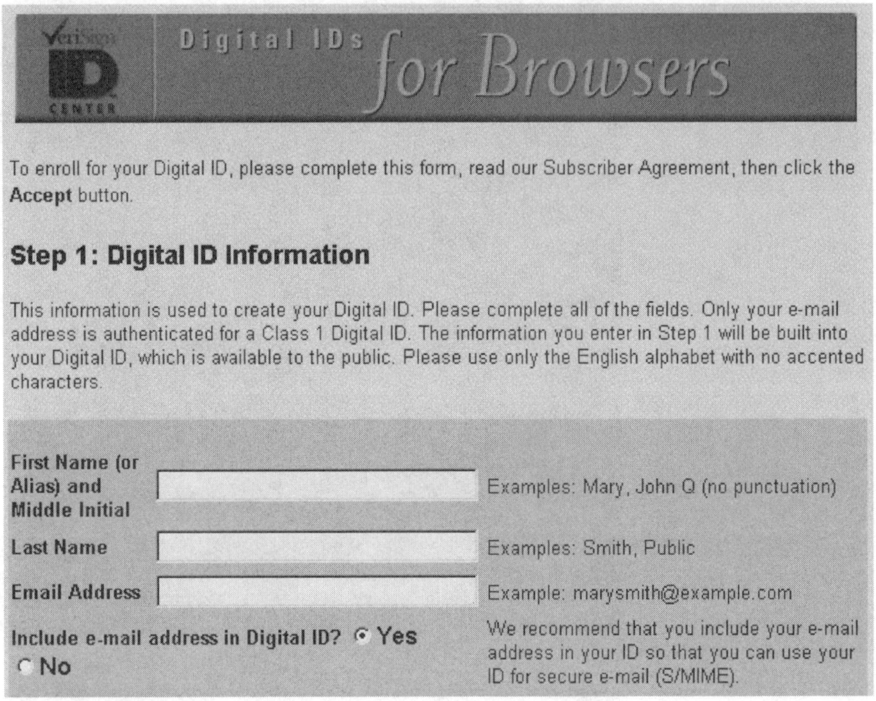

Figure 4-4

To enroll for your Digital ID, please complete this form, read our Subscriber Agreement, then click the **Accept** button.

Step 1: Digital ID Information

This information is used to create your Digital ID. Please complete all of the fields. Only your e-mail address is authenticated for a Class 1 Digital ID. The information you enter in Step 1 will be built into your Digital ID, which is available to the public. Please use only the English alphabet with no accented characters.

First Name (or Alias) and Middle Initial   Examples: Mary, John Q (no punctuation)

Last Name   Examples: Smith, Public

Email Address   Example: marysmith@example.com

Include e-mail address in Digital ID? ⦿ Yes ◯ No   We recommend that you include your e-mail address in your ID so that you can use your ID for secure e-mail (S/MIME).

Figure 4-5

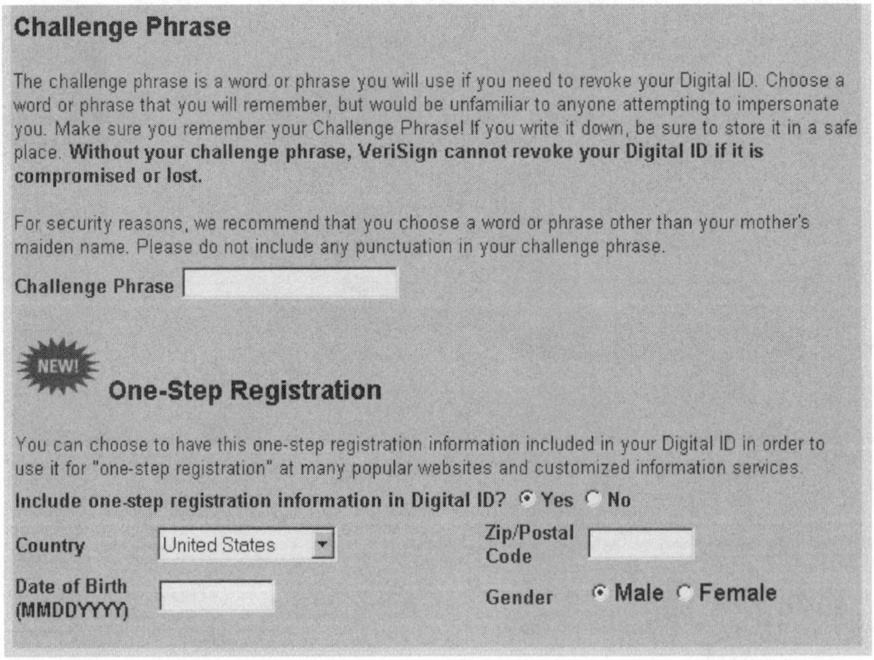

Challenge Phrase

The challenge phrase is a word or phrase you will use if you need to revoke your Digital ID. Choose a word or phrase that you will remember, but would be unfamiliar to anyone attempting to impersonate you. Make sure you remember your Challenge Phrase! If you write it down, be sure to store it in a safe place. **Without your challenge phrase, VeriSign cannot revoke your Digital ID if it is compromised or lost.**

For security reasons, we recommend that you choose a word or phrase other than your mother's maiden name. Please do not include any punctuation in your challenge phrase.

Challenge Phrase

NEW! One-Step Registration

You can choose to have this one-step registration information included in your Digital ID in order to use it for "one-step registration" at many popular websites and customized information services.

Include one-step registration information in Digital ID? ⦿ Yes ◯ No

Country United States

Date of Birth (MMDDYYYY)

Zip/Postal Code

Gender ⦿ Male ◯ Female

Figure 4-6

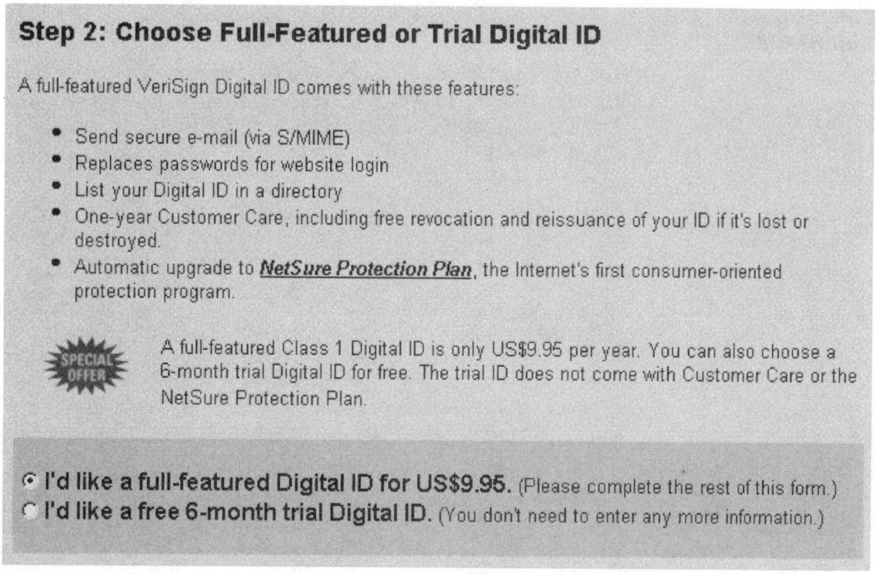

Step 2: Choose Full-Featured or Trial Digital ID

A full-featured VeriSign Digital ID comes with these features:

- Send secure e-mail (via S/MIME)
- Replaces passwords for website login
- List your Digital ID in a directory
- One-year Customer Care, including free revocation and reissuance of your ID if it's lost or destroyed.
- Automatic upgrade to **_NetSure Protection Plan_**, the Internet's first consumer-oriented protection program.

A full-featured Class 1 Digital ID is only US$9.95 per year. You can also choose a 6-month trial Digital ID for free. The trial ID does not come with Customer Care or the NetSure Protection Plan.

○ **I'd like a full-featured Digital ID for US$9.95.** (Please complete the rest of this form.)
○ **I'd like a free 6-month trial Digital ID.** (You don't need to enter any more information.)

Figure 4-7

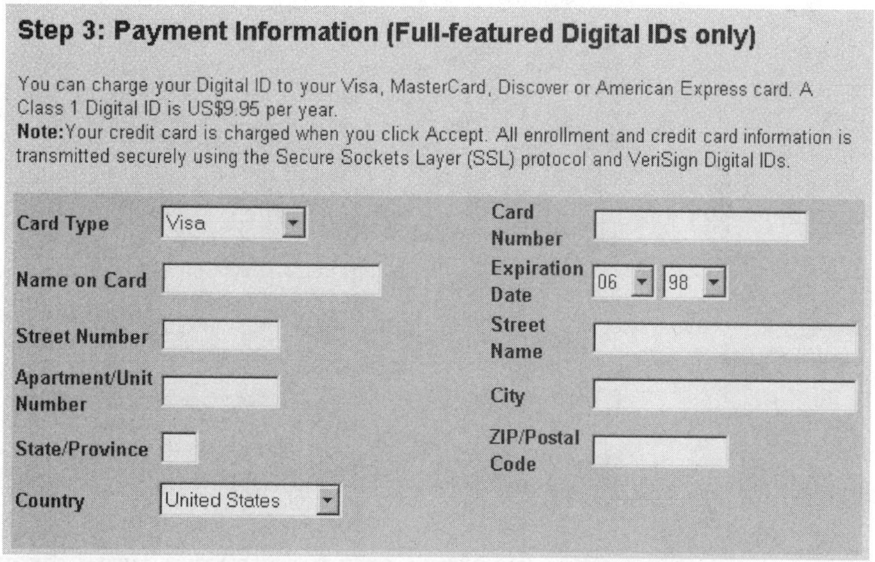

Step 3: Payment Information (Full-featured Digital IDs only)

You can charge your Digital ID to your Visa, MasterCard, Discover or American Express card. A Class 1 Digital ID is US$9.95 per year.
Note: Your credit card is charged when you click Accept. All enrollment and credit card information is transmitted securely using the Secure Sockets Layer (SSL) protocol and VeriSign Digital IDs.

Card Type	Visa ▼		Card Number	
Name on Card			Expiration Date	06 ▼ 98 ▼
Street Number			Street Name	
Apartment/Unit Number			City	
State/Province			ZIP/Postal Code	
Country	United States ▼			

Class I certificate), the certificate application is displayed (Figs. 4-4 and 4-5).

Figure 4-8

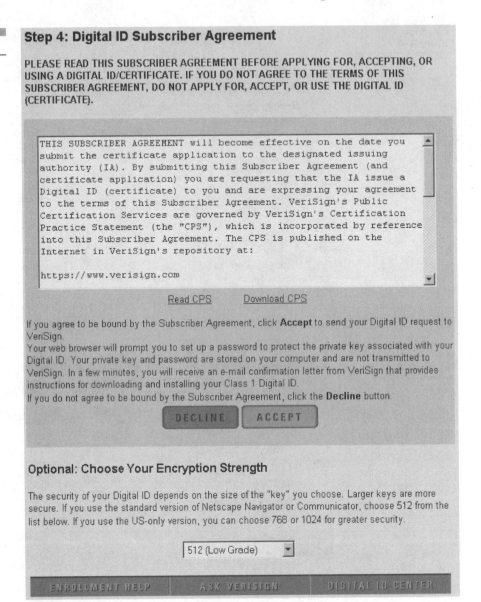

Step 4: Digital ID Subscriber Agreement

PLEASE READ THIS SUBSCRIBER AGREEMENT BEFORE APPLYING FOR, ACCEPTING, OR USING A DIGITAL ID/CERTIFICATE. IF YOU DO NOT AGREE TO THE TERMS OF THIS SUBSCRIBER AGREEMENT, DO NOT APPLY FOR, ACCEPT, OR USE THE DIGITAL ID (CERTIFICATE).

```
THIS SUBSCRIBER AGREEMENT will become effective on the date you
submit the certificate application to the designated issuing
authority (IA). By submitting this Subscriber Agreement (and
certificate application) you are requesting that the IA issue a
Digital ID (certificate) to you and are expressing your agreement
to the terms of this Subscriber Agreement. VeriSign's Public
Certification Services are governed by VeriSign's Certification
Practice Statement (the "CPS"), which is incorporated by reference
into this Subscriber Agreement. The CPS is published on the
Internet in VeriSign's repository at:

https://www.verisign.com
```

Read CPS   Download CPS

If you agree to be bound by the Subscriber Agreement, click **Accept** to send your Digital ID request to VeriSign.
Your web browser will prompt you to set up a password to protect the private key associated with your Digital ID. Your private key and password are stored on your computer and are not transmitted to VeriSign. In a few minutes, you will receive an e-mail confirmation letter from VeriSign that provides instructions for downloading and installing your Class 1 Digital ID.
If you do not agree to be bound by the Subscriber Agreement, click the **Decline** button.

DECLINE   ACCEPT

Optional: Choose Your Encryption Strength

The security of your Digital ID depends on the size of the "key" you choose. Larger keys are more secure. If you use the standard version of Netscape Navigator or Communicator, choose 512 from the list below. If you use the US-only version, you can choose 768 or 1024 for greater security.

512 (Low Grade)

ENROLLMENT HELP   ASK VERISIGN   DIGITAL ID CENTER

Because this is only a Class I certificate, the applicant is not even required to give their real name. The only piece of data that must be real is the e-mail address. The user then enters a challenge phrase, which will be used to make changes to or revoke the certificate. Some web sites will allow users to register for using their digital certificate instead of a username and password. If the applicant wants to use this certificate in that manner, they must fill in this additional information. Note that this information is not checked for accuracy for this type of certificate.In the next step, the user chooses either a free six-month trial certificate or a full-featured certificate. If they choose the full-featured certificate, they must also fill in their payment information.

Because the application is being completed using SSL to protect the privacy of the information, this sensitive data can be safely entered into the form. The next step is the user agreement.

The user must agree to the terms and conditions of the certificate in order for the application to be processed. This certificate also offers three choices of *encryption strength* (this is simply the size of the keys to be generated). Once the application has been completed, the user is instructed to wait for an e-mail message. The e-mail message will include the digital PIN that is needed to retrieve the certificate.

Certificate Management

After a certificate has been created and the owner begins to use it, there are several functions that a CA must support related to that certificate:

- Search: Although the applications usually take care of the exchange of certificates, a person might want to find the certificate that relates to a particular person or organization.

- Revocation: If a certificate is lost, the owner needs to be able to inform their CA that the certificate is no longer valid. This is similar to reporting a lost credit card so that the number can be entered into the system as being no longer valid. Just as a cardholder and the bank that issues a credit card want to know that it is no longer in the hands of the owner, a certificate holder wants to let their CA know that their certificate has been compromised by someone getting access to their private key.

- Suspension: Some CAs offer the ability to suspend a certificate so that, for a period of time, it is not considered valid. One reason for this might be that the owner is going on vacation and does not want their key to be available.

- Status: Some users who receive a certificate might want to check that the certificate is still valid and that it has not been revoked or suspended. This process is often handled through *Certificate*

Revocation Lists (CRLs) that contain information about the certificates from a CA that have not yet expired, but are no longer valid.

Many of these functions are still not well defined, and have yet to be broadly deployed and stressed with high volumes. As the applications that use certificates mature, these functions and the software that implements them will become robust.

While the technology is easy to articulate, the difficult part starts when you try to decide who will run the CA and what the certificates it issues mean. There are vendors that will run the entire CA for a company or organization. They configure the system to the customer's specifications, even to the point of writing an application to do online verification of identity. The other option is for a company to run its own CA. Whichever path is chosen, there are decisions to be made about the certificates. How will the applicant's identity be verified? Are the certificates general-purpose certificates for identity to be used with any application? Is the certificate simply an online employee I.D. that is only to be used for internal purposes? If they were generated for one application, can they be used with another? This brings us to the three Ps: Policies, Procedures, and Practices.

Policies, Procedures, and Practices

The policies, procedures, and practices are critical to a successful implementation. Policies are generally realized in procedures, practices, and software programs that enforce them. A good example of a policy is to require three forms of ID to issue a certificate. This could be realized by the verifier (either a person or a software program) requesting three forms of identification. Another example of a policy might be that applications for a certificate are only accepted from particular systems, such as *.company.com. This would be implemented by rejecting applications from other systems.

Policies relate to identity verification, system security, and operational practices. The first critical question is: How is an identity verified?

Certification authorities provide many ways of verifying identity, but a certificate is only as good as the policies and processes used to verify that identity and protect their keys and systems. The rigor of the verification process should be directly related to the risk of a certificate that is incorrectly issued. The certificate based on 10 proofs of identity including a photo ID prior to issuance is more robust than a certificate application that just asks for an e-mail address and sends a message to confirm it. Unfortunately, there is no way today of determining the degree of effort that went into verification of certificate applicant today. This is one of the reasons that companies use special-purpose CAs for their applications. When they control the CA, they control what the certificate means, including the policies and practices related to the issuance of the certificate.

Many commercial CAs have a *Certification Practice Statement* (CPS) that describes their policies and procedures. This can be useful in helping a company decide if a particular CA is the right one for their company to use, if they choose a service. The reasons for these statements are discussed more fully in Part 3.

Operations

There are three critical requirements for the operation of a certification authority: robustness, availability, and staff trustworthiness. Without these characteristics, a CA should not be trusted. If a company is planning to implement their own CA, they should make sure that they can fulfill these requirements.

Robustness is critical for both the security of the systems that a CA uses and in their processes and procedures for verifying identity. If a CA's private key is compromised, the entire hierarchy of certificates they have issued is also compromised. To avoid this problem, strong security measures must be taken to ensure the security of the systems. Many companies are choosing to outsource their need for certificate issuance because of these requirements.

Availability requirements vary, depending on the purpose of a CA. The first questions a company implementing a CA should consider are who will use the certificates, where are these users located, and what is the nature of the application that uses certificates? A small company with all their offices in one time zone might not need 7-by-24 customer service for their employee-only CA. On the other hand, a company that is providing CA services for customers around the world would need to have around-the-clock customer service to answer questions and help customers with any difficulties they might have in procuring and using their certificates. Even if the customers are broadly dispersed, if the application is just a noncritical information server, it might not require 7-by-24 staffing. Availability and freshness of revocation data is also important.

The other aspect to availability rests with the systems that run the software. Once again, size and importance help to dictate system choices. If being down means a company cannot do business, then highly available, fault-tolerant systems might be required. Another option is multiple-hosted sites, where there are many servers that all share the same database sited in different locations. These are sometimes called *mirror sites* because they mirror the main server. During certain hours of the day, it can be very difficult for a person from Europe or Asia to access a server in the United States. Placing one or more servers in Europe and/or Asia might help improve availability.

The final operational requirement is trusted operators. An operator could potentially generate additional certificates for the purposes of fraud, list critical certificates as revoked, and wreak all manner of havoc and financial loss. Some companies are solving this problem through bonding staff who run their systems. Bonding, combined with good employee screening, can ensure that those operating the systems do not violate the customer's (and employer's) trust.

In summary, a CA provides the public key infrastructure that enables the binding of keys to a particular identity for a particular purpose. During the life of a certificate, this infrastructure helps users to validate certificates and change their status as necessary. To understand how this infrastructure is used, let's look at how companies are using it and their reasons for doing so.

2

Case Studies

This section provides specific examples of how public key systems can be used. It starts with an introductory chapter that explains how companies justify the use of public key, its benefits, and the different applications of public key systems. The examples are then grouped into chapters of related usage. Each chapter starts with a general introduction of the type of application covered in the chapter, followed by actual case studies of companies that are using public key technology in that manner.

The groupings for the chapters are identification/authentication, securing communication, and application integration. Secure Electronic Transactions (SET) protocol is actually an identification/integrity application, but it is given its own chapter because it will be the first broadscale deployment of PKI.

An additional case study was inadvertently left out of the text of this section. It covers the U.S. Government's use of public key certificates. Rather than leave it out of the book entirely, it has been included as Appendix VI.

CHAPTER 5

Uses of Public Key Systems

As discussed in Chapter 2, the general things that public key systems can provide are authentication, authorization, privacy, message integrity, and nonrepudiation; but all of these, except privacy, require additional work in order to function adequately. This work is done through agreements on what the certificates (and their use) mean and what each party promises about safeguarding their keys and other practices. Not all applications use all of these capabilities. Some only use a public key for authentication of one party. Others use it for two-way authentication. Still others use it for message integrity. A few rely on digital signatures for authentication, message integrity, and nonrepudiation. Remember: Most systems today use symmetric cryptographic algorithms for privacy because of the cost, in terms of computational time, of public key cryptography for encryption. Public key cryptography is used primarily for authentication, message integrity, and nonrepudiation—*not* to provide privacy. This is an important distinction that many people miss.

But what are the business reasons behind public key cryptography and its use? What causes a company to choose this over other options? How are they using it, and what have been their results? This chapter is intended to give the reader a sense of the ways that public key cryptography is being deployed on the Internet and intranets.

Justification

We've talked about the technology and the infrastructure, but what is driving companies to choose this technology over other solutions? Where do they see the benefits in its use? There are several reasons for this choice.

The first reason is robustness. Public key systems offer the strongest practical software-based system available today. It can also be implemented in hardware. Public key crypto is relatively easy to implement, and the wait for the "signing" of a key or message digest is bearable. Public key has been around for a while now, and has stood the test of time. Years of attempts to break the RSA algorithms have been unsuccessful. This does not mean that successful attacks could not potentially happen in the future, but it does mean that the system to date has withstood intense scrutiny.

Public key encryption is practical to use because there are several applications that integrate certificates into their operations. All web server authentication is done using public key certificates. All the major web browsers support the technology, and many e-mail packages support it as well. Using a technology that has already been integrated into the major applications means less development time for a company to deploy an application, so application availability is a major benefit.

Remember our discussion about wanting to do business with new companies? The ability to authenticate unknown parties without ever meeting them is one of the most attractive attributes of public key systems. As long as both users trust each other's CA, authentication can take place. The Internet offers a low-cost way to offer services to a broader population. Companies, however, need to have some confidence that the company that is ordering their product really is who they purport to be. Public key encryption enables that strong authentication. This is a tremendous advantage to companies that want to do business with new partners.

Digital signatures are an important part of the justification for using public key cryptography. The ability to sign a message and have confidence that it has not been changed by anyone else in transit is a key benefit of public key systems. The fact that a party who signs a message cannot deny that signing, or nonrepudiability, is also key to the benefits of public key cryptography.

Another reason for usage is acceptance. Because of the application availability, more companies are starting to deploy certificate-based systems. This makes it more likely to find partners who already have some familiarity with the workings of public key systems, making future applications easier to administer. Many countries in North America, Asia, and Europe are looking at public key systems as the basis of establishing trust over the Internet.

Public key systems separate *validation* of a certificate from *authentication*. This makes for a more complex system, but it also means that there is a way to invalidate a set of keys without taking down the entire system or regenerating everyone's keys. This is not the case with pure symmetric systems. If a large number of parties share a secret and just one person compromises that key, each must get a new key in order to continue doing business. With public-key systems, a certificate can be revoked for a single key pair and immediately reissued for a new set of keys without impacting other certificate and key holders.

Finally, legislation is just beginning to be drafted that recognizes digital signatures as a valid tool for codifying and validating agreements between parties. This is happening in many countries, not just the USA. This will provide the legal framework for creating a truly paperless business environment.

The picture is not all rosy. There are some issues that must be dealt with. These will be presented in the next section, after the reader has been exposed to how some companies are using public key cryptography and certificates. Once you have a better understanding of how companies are using the technology, the issues will be easier to grasp.

Public Key Buckets

As with any technology, the possibilities for usage are fairly broad, but early usage will tend to be limited. Although public key systems have been around for a long time, Internet/intranet usage and the types of applications that are being planned and deployed has accelerated the adoption of this technology. The early applications tend to use public key systems primarily for some form of authentication, or to establish symmetric encryption. Usage tends to fall into one of three "buckets":

- Identification of who is accessing something or providing that information.
- Securing communication between certain systems.
- Application integration for authentication and data integrity.

These lines are drawn rather arbitrarily to make it possible to split up these case studies into groups, but each bucket does share characteristics not found in other buckets. When reading the case studies, it is useful to think about:

- What problem is being solved.
- Who is involved in the transaction.
- How visible the use of the certificate and encryption is to the user.

In all instances, some form of identification or authentication is being done, but the problems being solved are slightly different from each other. For example, the bank that wants to authenticate their users will have a slightly different implementation than a distributed system that wants to protect, authenticate, and maintain integrity of system calls across diverse systems. The web server that wants to keep prying eyes away from proprietary information might just use an application that encrypts the username and password, and use public key only to distribute a shared secret that can be used to encrypt communication between the server and browser.

The matter of just who is involved in the transaction that uses public key cryptography also influences the implementation. If the parties involved in the transaction are systems rather than people, the behavior might be very different from that of user-oriented applications. If a user is involved, as much as possible of the technical bits will be hidden from their view. When the parties involved are applications, then the interface must be specified and explicit so that the receiving application knows what to do with the encrypted data.

Closely related to the identities of the parties involved is the issue of how much of the process is visible to the user. In some instances, applications make a conscious choice to involve the user, or allow the user to choose to be involved. A good example of this is the security notification options that most browsers offer. A user can choose to know if they have moved from a secure to an insecure document, or limit the CAs from which they will accept a certificate. Showing more of what is going on might be done to give the user something to look at while the application is doing the processing, or to make the user feel more secure, knowing that strong protections are being applied to their access to sensitive information.

Identification

The most common usage of public key encryption in the future will be identification or authentication. Web servers need to identify users. In the early days of the Internet, the simplest way of doing this was through restricting access to those who had a particular username and password. Some sites use the same username and password for large numbers of people; this is not a wise practice, because the more people who know the "secret" (in this case, the username/password pair), the higher the likelihood of unauthorized parties getting access. The other common form of identification is server authentication. How do you know that www.abc.com is really ABC's web site? By using a server certificate that verifies the identity of the owner, the web site can be authenticated.

This is an example of how authentication might work:

1. The user goes to a web site and clicks on *members only*.
2. The web server requests a certificate.

Figure 5-1

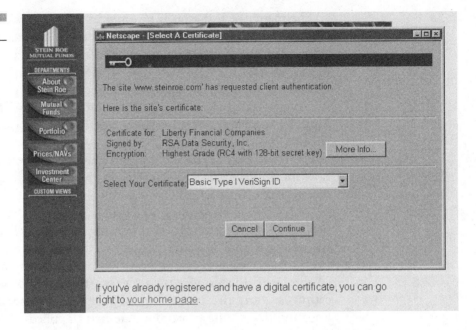

The user's browser then prompts the user for that certificate to provide to the web server.

■ The server then verifies the certificate and grants access.

Securing Communication

The most common use of public key systems today is for the securing of communication via Secure Sockets Layer (SSL), a protocol developed by Netscape Communications. As with most systems, SSL does not use public key cryptography for encryption, but only for the exchanging of a shared-secret key to be used for encrypting the communication. This allows for the authentication of the server, and provides an easy way to establish a shared-secret key for encrypting the data flowing between the browser and web server.

The certificate allows the user to authenticate the web site. When accessing a secure site, the Uniform Resource Locator (URL) is https://www.abc.com instead of simply http://www.abc.com (which is the way to access an unsecured site). The user's browser uses the pub-

Figure 5-2

lic key of the server to send a session key securely to the server. After the session key has been confirmed, a secure session has been established and the server and browser can communicate securely. No one else can eavesdrop on the communication between the browser and server, allowing confidential communication over the Internet.

Application Integration

Another usage of public key encryption that is relatively new is using public key cryptography to authenticate and protect the integrity for remote components of distributed systems. In distributed computing, it is possible to have an application that is spread over many different systems on a network. How does a system know that the system that sent them a request is friend or foe? Public key cryptography can be used to ensure this.

In Figure 5-3, the different systems each have a particular task to perform. Perhaps the task is maintaining the records of a database for local clients. The user asks to see the regional earnings, and her application goes out over the Internet to request the information from the

Figure 5-3

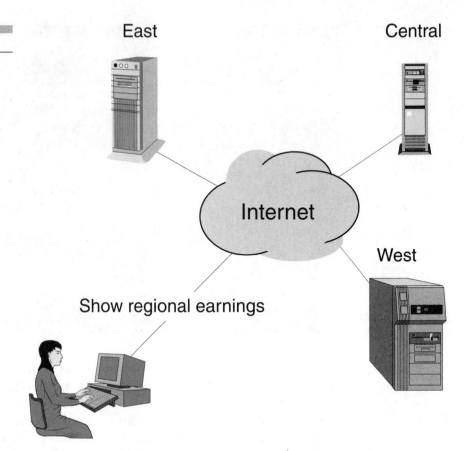

appropriate systems. When the systems have a message to send to other systems, they can authenticate and guarantee message integrity of the request by using public key encryption. There are other ways to do this, but the robustness of public key encryption will lend itself to future applications choosing it to provide this service.

CHAPTER 6

Identification and Authentication

There are two primary forms of identification and authentication: one-way and two-way. In one-way authentication, only one of the parties' identity is authenticated. This is usually the server, and forms the basis for securing communication between the client and server, which will be discussed in the next chapter. Server authentication can also be done without the use of encryption, using a script to present the server's certificate to the user for verification of identity. This is useful in establishing consumer confidence in online stores or government information sites, assuring the user that the server is indeed owned by the purported organization. Although there are a couple examples of this type of usage, the focus of this chapter will be on user authentication and two-way authentication.

The web was designed for a research environment, not business. In a research environment, the need to limit access to areas is rather casual. The goal is not robust security to keep out concerted attempts at penetration, but more of a courtesy fence that is intended to keep honest citizens off the grass. When someone gains access to a restricted area of a web server, their username and password are sent in the clear, without encryption. While this is fine for a courtesy fence, this doesn't provide much protection. Many sites are moving to the use of certificates for identifying who their customers are.

The case studies all hold in common that they are using public key cryptography for authentication. The thing that is different between the organizations is the problems they were trying to solve and the business application they wanted to enable. They all share a common concern as well: Only the "right people" should be able to access the application or data.

GE Research Center

Schenectady, NY
   http://www.crd.ge.com

Background   GE is a diverse company, with 12 distinct businesses based on technology, manufacturing, and services. These businesses make aircraft engines, appliances, electricity distribution, medical systems, plastics, power systems, transportation systems, and lighting. Services include consulting, information services, and financial services. GE employs 239,000 people in over 100 countries. 1996 revenues were $79.18 billion. GE also does work for the federal government.

GE's Corporate Research Center has implemented a public key infrastructure-based project for streamlining "multi-tiered" supply chains, as part of a DARPA initiative in agile manufacturing. As part of this project, the technology is being demonstrated on projects involving the design of aluminum and steel sand-mold castings.

Problem   When a company wants to get a new sand-mold casting it involves a multidisciplinary team of foundries, pattern-makers, and analysis teams. Sometimes there are multiple foundries, and in other instances only one. The parties involved do not have access to all the information; they only can access the information that they need to complete their tasks. For example, a foundry might have proprietary information that they want to share with the analysis team, but not with the pattern-maker nor the end customer.

GE, as well as other manufacturing companies, uses teams of contractors to implement various industrial projects. These teams need a way of sharing information on manufacturing projects (or tenders for manufacturing projects). Contractors are geographically distant from each other and require a common interface for workgroup collaboration. The Internet provides a cost-effective and flexible interface for intra-enterprise collaboration. However, projects are proprietary in nature and might include sensitive military information; security is therefore of paramount importance.

Why Public Key Certificates?   GE's Corporate Research Center is building the integration technology for these supply chains. A design is made up of many different documents, with different members of the team needing access to different portions. This data includes sensitive trade secrets that are being sent over the Internet, which is where public key cryptography comes in. Xcert's Sentry CA forms the core of the communications and collaborative environment.

How the Application Works   GE might have multiple contracts (and several teams of contractors) for each project. GE project managers require access to information from all teams or workgroups; however, contractors should only be aware of the team activities in which they participate.

The application provides a technical working area where everyone involved in the design can get the latest information. All pages are generated out of a database on-the-fly based on permissions, which in turn are determined by the user's authenticated identity, which is provided by the public key certificate. Sentry is being used to provide stringent user authentication and strong security in an intranet/extranet environment. GE's Research Center has used Sentry CA to maintain a corporate certification authority that signs and issues client certificates to trusted users. Certificates are used to authenticate user identity and to control access to centrally maintained content and write permissions.

The CA accepts certificate requests from users. Users are processed according to the established security procedures. Client certificates are then signed by the certification authority and distributed to appropriate users. When a user requests access to a secure file or directory, the secure server will require the presentation of a client certificate signed by the certification authority. If the client certificate is valid, the user is granted access to the secure information.

User attributes are stored in a back end database and mapped to certificates. This enables personalized or dynamic web pages to be presented to each user, and information such as client state can be logged to or retrieved from the user database. Users are able to access secure data from a standard web browser and submit information in a secure, authenticated environment. Access control can be fine-grained or general, depending on the security status of the user. Secure data transport is provided by Stronghold, an SSL server product integrated with Sentry CA.

Issues One of the challenges was merging security attributes with the cert owner. The existing software had awareness of people signing on, but no encryption or strong authentication built in. Bridging software had to be written to communicate between the CA and the application. For example, the application would generate an invitation to a supplier to join a virtual enterprise, but didn't know if that supplier already had a cert for that server. If they didn't, code had to be written to provide an interface to the CA to guide a supplier through the process of getting an appropriate certificate.

Benefits "Without security, we couldn't even begin to think about putting this online," said Bruce Bernstein, a systems engineer at GE Research Center. The benefits of this application are that GE can use the Internet to speed the production process. Public key cryptography makes that use possible by providing strong authentication and secured transactions. This technology is not limited to just sand-molding; it is transferable to other multi-tiered sourcing problems, providing reusability in future projects.

GTE

Irving, TX
http://www.gte.com

Background   GTE, with revenues of more than $21 billion in 1996, is the seventh largest telecommunications company in the world. GTE offers local and wireless service in 29 states and long-distance service in all 50 states in the USA. Internationally, the company serves over 6.5 million customers. In addition to traditional telecommunications, GTE also has business units that focus on government and defense communications systems and equipment, directories and telecommunications-based services, and aircraft-passenger telecommunications.

This case study focuses on the carrier markets, a part of GTE Telephone Operations. This part of the business sells access to the GTE network to other carriers, such as AT&T, MCI, and Sprint. The service records and billing information that this usage generates are voluminous, with hundreds of individual bills and thousands of pages in each bill.

Problem   In the past, GTE had provided access to the billing detail through modems and a dial-up service; but there were several problems with this. The speed of the access was limited to the speed of the modems, making downloading a lengthy process; further, the costs of the infrastructure limited the service to only the largest carriers. To solve this problem, GTE wanted to move the service to the Internet. The objective of the project was to make detail available to the carriers as needed, but to avoid sending paper if possible. It was critical to make sure that only authorized users had access to the information. "If Joe Ordinary could access the information, he could potentially do some damage," commented Karen Cantu, a Section Manager at GTE Telephone Operations.

Why Public Key Certificates?   "One of our objectives make it as simple as possible, but very secure," stated Cantu. The first options that were examined were token cards, such as SecureID and smart cards. The problems with these methods were that they required distributing the devices to all the users, creating a lag for start-up as well as making logging in a more complex process. Public key certificates did not require physical distribution. Their use could be made virtually transparent to the customer. Certificates also provided the strong security the application required.

Figure 6-1

[Billing] [CFA] [Library] [Help Line] [Other GTE Sites]

Welcome to the ACG Information Highway Entrance.

Find out the latest additions/updates to the
ACG family of applications here.

Only authorized users may access the applications of ACG.
To request access to the ACG applications,
please fill out the Access Request form.

This page has been accessed **430** times since **Aug 16, 1997**

Access Customer Gateway
Mail Comments to: acgweb@telops.gte.com

Copyright © 1996, GTE, all rights reserved.
URL: http://www.acgweb.gte.net/homepage.shtml

How the Application Works   To make sure that the certificates are distributed to the correct personnel, the GTE account manager works with the customer to get a list of people who should have access. Each of these people is sent a contact ID, which can then be used to apply for a certificate online. Once the user has their certificate, they are able to use it to access the application.

When the user accesses the web site, their certificate is checked to make sure that they are an authorized user. An additional level of security is added by requiring a username and password. After they have been authenticated, they are shown the page pictured in Figure 6-2. They can now either search a particular bill for an entry, or check the service records for a particular account. A second application allows them to view assignment information for facilities they have ordered from GTE.

Benefits   The use of public key certificates allows GTE to make this service available to many more customers than in the old dial-up environment. It is more cost-effective for GTE and their customers: Support costs are lower, and special modems no longer have to be dedicated to this task on either end. By using the Internet, this also gives their customers control over access speeds, because they can simply upgrade their Internet connection to get higher bandwidth. The use of certificates also gives both GTE and the carriers a high degree of confidence that this sensitive information is not being accessed by unauthorized parties.

Hewlett-Packard

Palo Alto, CA
   http://www.hp.com

Background   Hewlett-Packard Company is the second largest computer manufacturer in the USA, with revenues of $38.4 billion in the year ending in October of 1996. HP designs, manufactures, and services computers and systems for measurement and communications used by companies in industry, business, medicine, science, research, and education. The company sells and services over 24,000 different products, from computers and printers to medical instruments. HP employs over 90,000 people in over 120 countries.

Problem   Hewlett-Packard is investigating the use of digital signatures for solving a business problem that many other large corporations have—how to provide a unique and persistent way to identify each employee. In a company with over 90,000 employees, some of them have the same or similar names. They frequently move from one entity to another within the corporation, and increasing numbers of them are accessing the corporate intranet from their homes or from remote offices and hotel rooms. HP has therefore begun a project to provide each of its employees with a unique digital signature.

Why Public Key Certificates?   Certificates offer the type of robust authentication that HP feels is necessary to protect their corporate data and networks. By using public key certificates, they can identify employees worldwide.

How the Application Works   Once all of its employees have unique digital IDs, many paper-based corporate processes can be handled online. For example, employees can use their digital identity to obtain disbursement vouchers for petty cash, reimbursement of travel expenses without waiting for an expense check, and even direct payroll disbursements. For employees working at home or on the road, a digital ID provides authentication both at the session level and at the IP level for gaining remote access to the corporate intranet. Anyone who knows the employee's public key will be able to find this person in the corporate directory, regardless of how many others share the same first and last name or how many times the person has switched positions within the corporation.

HP plans to make its Human Resources department responsible for issuing and revoking the digital ID, in effect functioning as the CA. Future directions for using public key technology to establish unique identifications for employees might include replacing today's employee badge with a next-generation badge that combines a digital and physical identity. The badge could be a smart card that contains the employee's key pair.

Benefits   The robust nature of public key encryption and the confidence of identity that it provides will enable strong cost-savings over paper processing.

Liberty Financial Companies, Inc.

New York, NY
   http://www.steinroe.com

Background Liberty Financial Companies (NYSE:L) is a diversified asset management organization with more than $47 billion in assets under management. It provides an array of fixed, variable, and indexed annuities and management of private and institutional accounts in addition to 60 mutual funds that meet the investing needs of over 1.4 million investors worldwide. Its subsidiaries include Keyport Life Insurance Company, The Colonial Group, Inc., Stein Roe & Farnham Incorporated, Independent Financial Marketing Group, Newport Pacific Management, and Liberty Asset Management Company.

Problem Liberty Financial realized that they needed to integrate the Internet into its existing business model to provide customers, distributors, and employees with secure, direct access to their accounts, product information, and market data. Liberty Financial also saw the opportunity to take the Internet to the next level—beyond an alternate distribution medium for electronic brochures. Liberty Financial wanted to create web sites that were secure, personalized experiences that allow interaction with their customers on a one-to-one basis.

The application delivers financial services via the Internet via a secure, personalized, and customizable Internet site based on a new architecture named LEAPS (Liberty Environment for Advanced Personalized Services). The sites using LEAPS represent the first announced client use of digital certificates for secure account access and transactions on the Internet. LEAPS enables users to safely conduct business with Liberty Financial's operating companies on the Internet.

Currently, three of Liberty Financial's operating units are taking advantage of the LEAPS architecture. Chicago-based Stein Roe (www.steinroe.com) is offering retail investors access to its mutual fund site, which includes market commentary, fund performance data, account access, and full transaction capabilities including the ability to buy and redeem shares from a linked bank account. Keyport Life (www.keyport.com) will provide its business partners access to its broker dealer distribution system, including client policy information, online forms, and sales materials. Colonial Mutual Funds is currently developing a robust intranet site to provide sales reps fast, easy access to key product and account information.

Why Public Key Certificates? Liberty Financial wanted their customers to feel secure and comfortable that they were at the right site and that no one could snoop on their interactions with the system. Secure session technology (which enables encryption of data as it is transmitted) is not enough to ensure security, because it does not solve the problem of

Figure 6-2

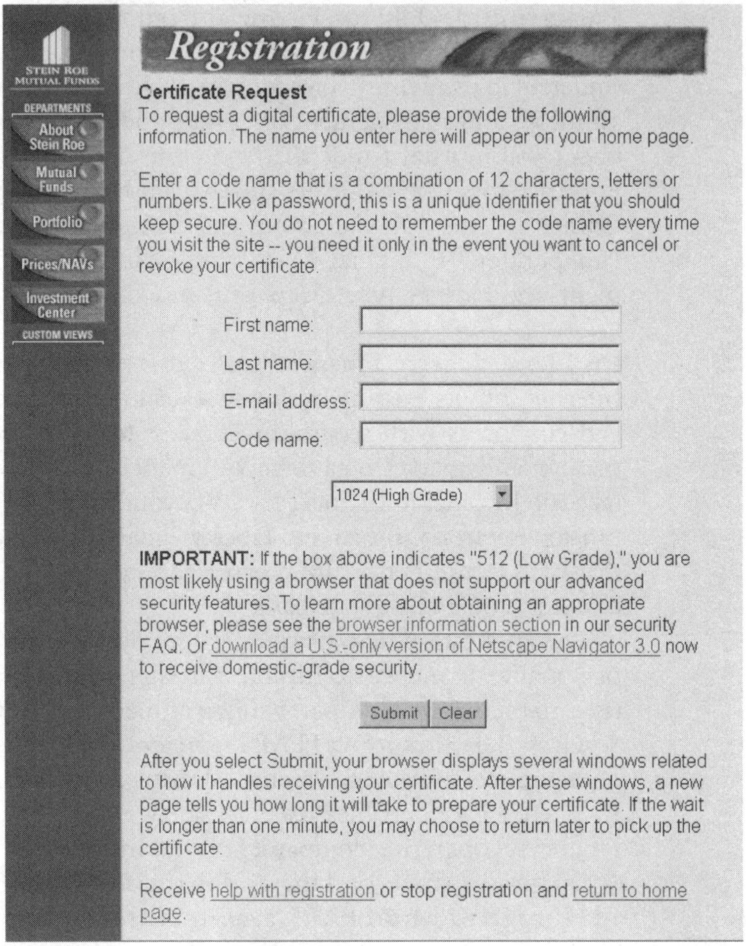
Registration
STEIN ROE MUTUAL FUNDS
DEPARTMENTS
About Stein Roe
Mutual Funds
Portfolio
Prices/NAVs
Investment Center
CUSTOM VIEWS
Certificate Request
To request a digital certificate, please provide the following information. The name you enter here will appear on your home page.
Enter a code name that is a combination of 12 characters, letters or numbers. Like a password, this is a unique identifier that you should keep secure. You do not need to remember the code name every time you visit the site -- you need it only in the event you want to cancel or revoke your certificate.
First name:
Last name:
E-mail address:
Code name:
1024 (High Grade)
IMPORTANT: If the box above indicates "512 (Low Grade)," you are most likely using a browser that does not support our advanced security features. To learn more about obtaining an appropriate browser, please see the browser information section in our security FAQ. Or download a U.S.-only version of Netscape Navigator 3.0 now to receive domestic-grade security.
Submit
Clear
After you select Submit, your browser displays several windows related to how it handles receiving your certificate. After these windows, a new page tells you how long it will take to prepare your certificate. If the wait is longer than one minute, you may choose to return later to pick up the certificate.
Receive help with registration or stop registration and return to home page.

authentication—knowing that the person originating the communication is not an impostor. Liberty believes that the combination of secure sessions and digital certificates makes the web robust enough to make transactions. In addition, digital certificates improve the ease of use for the end user by removing the need for usernames and passwords. Lastly, the strong authentication capabilities enabled by digital certificates are used as a feed into their personalization software to enable each client to have a unique and personalized experience when dealing with Liberty and its operating companies using the Internet.

One of the first decisions that Liberty Financial made was to become its own certificate authority licensing the BBN SafeKeyper Enterprise CMS from BBN Cambridge MA. It was important to Liberty and its operating companies to remain in control over the client relationship, making outsourcing of the registration and certificate management process undesirable. In addition, after researching available offerings, both product and service, Liberty chose BBN because it is a superior technology platform and because of the no-fee-per-certificate/per-user pricing scheme.

How the Application Works *Registration Process:* To ensure that the digital certificate is being given to the correct person, an access number is required. This is acquired via an *out of band* process: calling a Stein Roe account representative at an 800 number for the user's access number. Then, using their access number, they can apply for a Stein Roe digital certificate right on the web by going to the Stein Roe home page and selecting *Request a Certificate.* After review of the Stein Roe user agreement, they are asked to enter their name, account number, and access number on a short form. It takes about a minute to generate your certificate. When it's ready, they are asked to verify the information on the form just completed. The certificate is then downloaded to the user's hard drive. The entire registration process takes less than five minutes to complete.

Using the Certificate: Each time a customer goes to Stein Roe's site, their browser will ask them to choose the Stein Roe certificate they wish to use. This is a one- or two-click procedure, depending on the number of certificates stored in the browser.

To protect customers' ability to make secure transactions on the World Wide Web, Stein Roe requires a Stein Roe digital certificate and written notification that they wish to add this privilege to their account.

Notifying Stein Roe in writing is a simple three-step process:

Figure 6-3

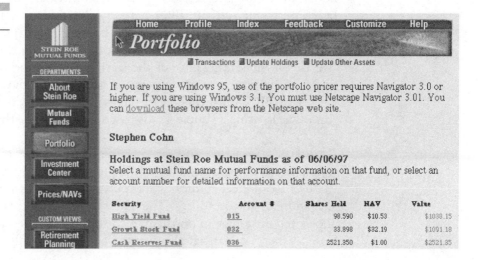

- Download an online transaction privileges form and fill it out.
- Take the completed form to the customer's bank or broker to have the signature authorized—this is known as getting a "signature guarantee."
- Return the completed form and signature guarantee to Stein Roe by mail.

A few days after Stein Roe receives a completed form and signature guarantee, the customer should be able to conduct transactions by simply clicking on the desired action. The first time a customer uses their certificate, the web site prompts for the appropriate Social Security or tax identification number, and asks the user to create a password to be used to confirm each transaction.

Through a combination of the strong authentication and the personalized software, profiles are updated on an ongoing basis and contain all the supplied information and activity history. It is used exclusively by Stein Roe to present material that matches the user's financial needs. Users can view, edit, and delete any part of their profile at any time.

Revoking/Canceling a Certificate   Users can cancel their own certificate by simply calling an 800 number. Stein Roe might choose to revoke a certificate if it has expired, or if the user has violated the terms and conditions of the Stein Roe user agreement.

Issues   The primary issue was one of education. Liberty Financial did not want to use a technology that was so difficult that few users would be comfortable with it. BBN helped Liberty Financial through this process. This issue will be ameliorated by time and experience with more public key cryptography-based applications among the general public. "We are on the leading edge of the learning curve, and have the responsibility of helping our customers use this technology," said Catherine Kniker of BBN. With their help, Liberty Financial was able to overcome this obstacle using a simple forms-based web interface they designed.

Benefits   Security and personalization are the main benefits of public key cryptography. Liberty Financial wanted to create a site where the user would feel comfortable inputting personal information, such as age, address, and holdings. The security of public key cryptography allows the customer to do this with little fear of the site being compromised. Liberty Financial also wanted create a friendly, personalized site that offered so much in terms of both service and ease of use that the customer would be tempted to come back again and again. The site remembers the information the customer has input in past visits, and is therefore able to call up the customer's personal security portfolio—automatically updated to calculate any changes in the value of the securities. Liberty's electronic commerce architecture also allows the user to personalize the site, specifying interface preferences such as the size of the type, the color of the backgrounds, and the shape and number of buttons. The use of certificates for robust authentication makes this personalization possible.

State of Massachusetts

Boston, MA
   http://www.state.ma.us/itd/legal

Background   Similar to any large enterprise, the Commonwealth of Massachusetts performs a high volume of transactions within their organization. They also conduct a large number of transactions between the state and outside parties, including citizens, businesses, and other governments.

The Commonwealth of Massachusetts performs a very large number of consumer-type transactions each year that will be performed more efficiently and at higher service quality levels over the Internet. One category particularly well suited to Internet solutions is licensing, including driver license renewals, professional licenses, recreational licenses (i.e., fishing, hunting, etc.), and so on. Similarly, the state is looking at ways to conduct the permit application process, grant applications, accept submission of bids for public works, and several other transactions over the Internet.

Problem   Several of the transactions that Massachusetts wants to do over the Internet have information security requirements that derive from legal or business needs. In some cases, the law requires that only certain people or entities be permitted to access information or conduct a transaction. In other cases, though no strict legal rule requires authentication, prudent business practice demands the ability to prevent unauthorized access or to hold a party to the substance of a network transaction. In addition to authentication requirements (either for access control or for nonrepudiation), some transactions might also require that the data remains private while in transit over the network.

Why Public Key Certificates? "We have discovered that it is not sufficient to declare that these transactions must be 'secure.' Rather, it is more useful to determine what security might be required for a given transaction," commented Dan Greenwood, Deputy General Counsel of the Information Technology Division of the Commonwealth of Massachusetts. "As noted, some transactions might require confidentiality, nonrepudiation, access control, or some combination (or perhaps none) of the above. There are a number of technologies that can provide parts of these information security requirements. At present, the Commonwealth is exploring uses of public key cryptography to achieve these security features."

The Commonwealth recognizes that public key cryptosystems, if implemented in a sound manner, have the potential to provide a high degree of confidence in the information security of network transactions and other network traffic. However, this should be viewed as one among many technical and practical methods of securing networks. The Commonwealth chose a pilot project to gain more experience with public key systems and ascertain whether and how we might seek greater use of such systems.

How the Application Works The Commonwealth of Massachusetts is currently using public key systems in two important online transactions with outside parties. First, the Registry of Motor Vehicles uses an SSL version 2 implementation of public key cryptography that is built into web browsers and many web servers. This implementation allows point-to-point encryption of data between a browser and a server. "We specifically chose transactions at the RMV that only required confidentiality and not authentication of the end user, because SSL version 2 provides no such authentication," noted Greenwood. The transactions currently available at the Commonwealth's RMV web site include vehicle registration renewal, payment of citations, and the ability to order a vanity license plate. They are accepting credit cards to process these fee-based transactions, and believe that the information should be confidential; *that* SSL version 2 can provide. A back-end database is updated with information from a web form, and the transactions are processed automatically. "In the Commonwealth of Massachusetts, we believe the citizen would rather be online than in line. This online RMV program has met with wide approval by the public, and has created interest by other states," commented Greenwood.

Figure 6-4

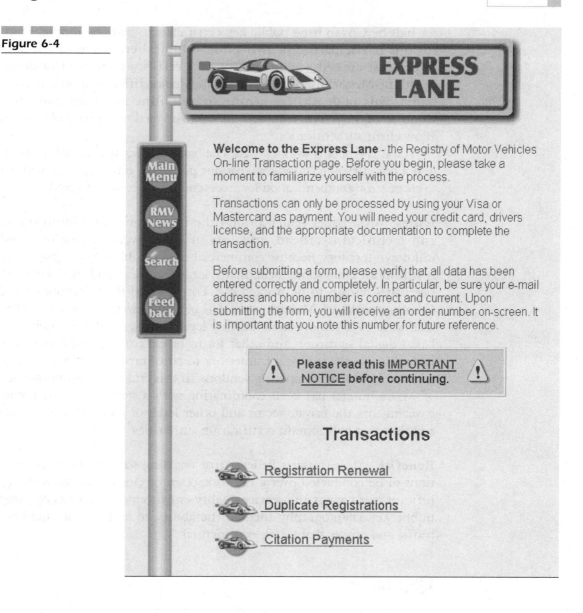

The second public key—based project was designed to attempt to create authentication using an X.509v3 public key certificate. They will use this authentication to achieve access control to a particular application on their private network to be accessed over the Internet. The application will enable banks and other financial institutions to file forms with the Massachusetts Division of Banks. The current filing process for these forms is paper- and fax-based and requires data entry. To choose a certification authority, Massachusetts conducted a request for bids by CAs to issue public key certificates to banks and other institutions participating in this pilot. GTE Cybertrust won the bid. Cybertrust created a pilot project root certificate for the Commonwealth of Massachusetts that is used to issue certificates to pilot participants. This pilot was beginning to go online in spring and early summer of 1997. The transactions use SSL version 3 protocols, which allow client authentication.

"The RMV pilot is working well. The banking pilot will go online shortly, but our current tests indicate that our public key certificates are working to create strong authentication for access control," Greenwood stated.

Issues Most issues center around the high degrees of administrative and technical overhead, and lots of unanswered questions and unknown territory. Because commercial use of public key cryptography is still in an embryonic form, many legal, technical, and business practice issues remain to be worked out. For instance, the Governor of the Commonwealth of Massachusetts will be filing electronic signature legislation soon to remove some existing legal obstacles to use of public key based digital signatures and other forms of electronic signatures. Other issues include the lack of a framework to cross-certify or accredit certificate authorities by competing vendors. To this end, the Commonwealth of Massachusetts has been coordinating with a number of other state governments, the private sector, and other levels of government to create a project that will accredit certification authorities.

Benefits Massachusetts believes that enabling some of these transactions to be conducted over a network, open or closed, can result in significant cost savings and service quality enhancement. Benefits of using public key cryptography include the ability to authenticate network traffic and render that traffic confidential.

QSpace

Oakland, CA
   http://www.qspace.com

Background QSpace, Inc. was founded in September 1995 by I.O.A. Eze and Arash Saffarnia. Having decided that they wanted to develop some type of web-based business, they spent six months investigating the possibilities, secured seed-round financing, and incorporated the company in August 1996. Online financial services were chosen as the most likely candidate. Initially, the business was intended to be a sideline, but as they talked to more partners and prospective clients, the interest they found led them to develop it into a full-time enterprise.

Problem Credit report information is highly confidential. Strong authentication was needed to ensure that only the authorized individual got the information. Issuing reports to the proper individual was the most important and crucial part of the business. They needed to have strong authentication to combat this potential problem. To solve this problem, QSpace looked at two options: smart cards and Digital IDs (or certificates).

Why Public Key Certificates? The problems with smart cards were a lack of their support on home systems, and the expense and difficulty of deploying a smart card to each user. "By using Digital IDs or certificates, we have incorporated the most straightforward and safest way to authenticate a user online," stated I.O.A. Eze, President of QSpace. When looking for an authentication mechanism 20 months ago, VeriSign was

Figure 6-5

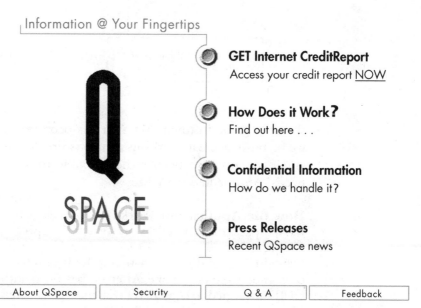

Information @ Your Fingertips

GET Internet CreditReport
Access your credit report <u>NOW</u>

How Does it Work?
Find out here . . .

Confidential Information
How do we handle it?

Press Releases
Recent QSpace news

| About QSpace | Security | Q & A | Feedback |

Figure 6-6

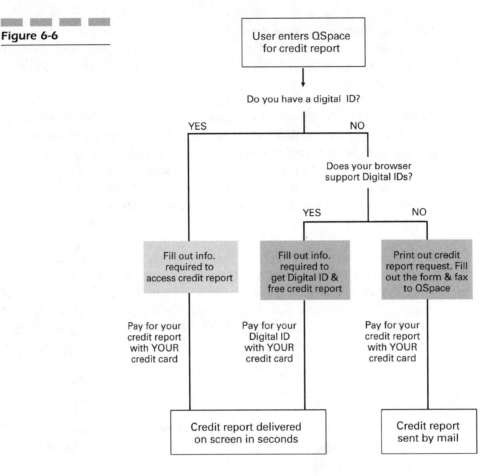

the only game in town. "VeriSign has been very easy to deal with, and we've built a great working relationship. Stratton [CEO of VeriSign] and his team have been rather flexible in accommodating with our needs," commented I.O.A. Eze.

How the Application Works   A user goes to the QSpace web site at www.qspace.com, and clicks on the credit report of interest and fills out a request form. The user is then authenticated using his VeriSign Class II Digital ID. If he does not have one, he is pointed to the QSpace/VeriSign co-branded site to get one. After he has been authenticated by his Digital ID or issued a Digital ID (via the QSpace/VeriSign co-branded site), his credit report is displayed on his browser and his credit card charged. The displayed credit report is provided with an electronic guide to explain the elements of a credit report, and to decipher sometimes cryptic credit codes.

Benefits   Getting credit reports individually from each of the major credit bureaus can be time-consuming as well as exhausting. This online service offers convenient, one-stop shopping for credit reports. Without certificates, authentication would be too expensive for this service to be viable. By using VeriSign's Class II Digital IDs, the cost to QSpace for verification is substantially reduced, and the user can use this general certificate (or Digital ID) for other applications at other web sites.

USWeb

Santa Clara, CA
  http://www.usweb.com

Background   USWeb is a national, single source for professional services helping clients be more successful by implementing web-based business solutions. With more than 60 offices, they provide a single source for Internet and intranet services. The organization offers end-to-end solutions, including needs analysis, architecture planning, Internet and intranet web consulting, design, development, access, hosting, site marketing, and education services. USWeb Corporation is headquartered in Santa Clara, California.

Problem   USWeb has offices throughout the USA, and needed to be able to authenticate their employees in order to give them access to the corporate intranet. It was critical that external parties, especially competitors, not be able to access proprietary corporate information. They needed something stronger than username/password access, because this can be broken using standard programs available over the Internet.

Why Public Key Certificates?   "The ability to use digital certificates (X.509) for user authentication is built into Microsoft IIS, making deployment much easier than trying to integrate security middleware," commented Daniel Todd of USWeb. "We use public key cryptography to provide user/server authentication and privacy. We use standard SSL

V3 as included in MS IIS to do this." The robust nature of public key cryptography, coupled with its integration into their web server of choice, made public key certificates a logical choice.

How the Application Works   USWeb is working with a private-label certification service. USWeb manages the issuance and revocation of certificates using a remote registration authority. USWeb uses a custom tool to sign approved Certificate Signing Requests (CSRs) and Revocation Requests. These approved requests are then sent to the certification authority, signed with USWeb's key, and returned to the applicant. This relieves USWeb of the maintenance tasks of creating and maintaining audit logs and physical security of the CA's private key. "We find great value in the ability to outsource our CA operations even on a small scale," commented Todd. After an employee has received their certificate, they have access to the corporate intranet.

Issues   USWeb's biggest issue is the ability to make certificates transportable and/or allow for multiple certificates to be associated with a single identity, because employees might need to access the corporate intranet from multiple locations. "The inability to use multiple browsers or do field demonstrations of our intranet is our main obstacle today," reported Todd.

Benefits   The ability to use the Internet securely has allowed USWeb to extend their intranet without the cost of a private network. Public key cryptography made this possible. "We really like the simple, inexpensive solution of a private-label CA service. It enables us to outsource the CA operations and focus on our business and only control the portion we need to control: who gets certificates," said Todd.

CHAPTER **7**

Securing
Communication

The first use of RSA public key cryptography on the web was for securing communication, and it is still the most prevalent usage today. This securing of communication is done using SSL. Although authentication plays a role in the establishment of the secure channel, the primary benefit is the privacy. As has been repeatedly stated, public key encryption is rarely used for privacy, but often used to *establish* privacy. Here is how it works:

Figure 7-1

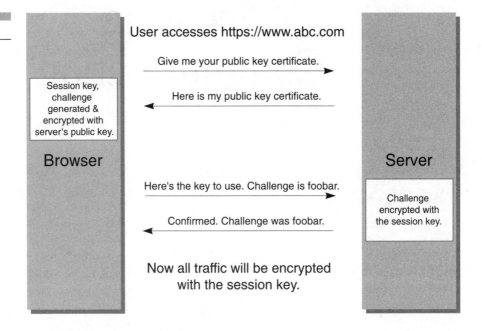

When establishing an SSL connection, the client application (the web browser) sends a request to the web server for its public key certificate. When the certificate is returned, the browser software then generates a shared-secret key (to be used with symmetric cryptography to provide privacy), plus a clear text challenge. The browser encrypts the key and challenge with the server's public key, and sends it to the server. The server then decrypts the shared secret/challenge with its private key. Because only the server has its private key, no one else can decrypt that message. The server then encrypts the challenge with the session key and sends it to the browser. Now both parties can communicate privately, without network eavesdroppers.

These case studies all include some authentication, but are in this chapter because the privacy (which is secured using public key cryptography) is one of the key factors in allowing them to use the Internet.

Many companies are moving from value-added networks (VANs) or private networks for a network infrastructure to the Internet. The biggest reason for this is cost savings and availability. Companies don't have to maintain banks of modems for customers or employees to use for connection, and they don't have to lease another private line to expand their internal network.

Both Diamond Shamrock and Mellon Bank are moving traffic that traditionally operated over a VAN to the Internet. For PrimeHost and Wells Fargo, the secured connection is used to protect credit card information.

Ultramar Diamond Shamrock

San Antonio, TX
   http://www.diasham.com

Background   Ultramar Diamond Shamrock was formed in December 1996 following a merger of Diamond Shamrock, Inc. and Ultramar Corporation. The company has a network of 4,400 locations in 10 Southwestern states and Eastern Canada under the Diamond Shamrock, Corner Stores, and Stop N Go brands, plus 350 locations in California and 1,330 locations under the Ultramar and Sergaz brands in Eastern Canada. The company also operates a number of additional related businesses, including petrochemical processing, anhydrous ammonia, and natural gas liquids storage, marketing, distribution, and is one of the largest retail home heating oil companies in North America, selling the product to over 175,000 households in Eastern Canada and New England.

San Antonio-based gasoline and convenience store retailer Diamond Shamrock has continued its pioneering efforts in electronic commerce by participating in a pilot program to send financial EDI transactions over the Internet to its banking partner.

Problem   Diamond Shamrock wanted to send financial EDI transactions over the Internet to its banking partner (Chase Manhattan Bank) instead of using a VAN, but there was a problem. The costs of using a VAN are high. The Internet, while much cheaper, is not secure. The risks of these transactions being exposed to hackers or competitors was high, so they needed strong technology. Both trading partners are using a combination of two public and two private keys, and each is using the Templar,

an encryption and authentication software package from Premenos of
Concord, CA, for secure financial transactions over the Internet.

Why Public Key Certificates? Diamond Shamrock needed transactions that were not only secured, but authenticated, unaltered, and nonrepudiable. Only public key cryptography could provide this. The ability
to digitally sign the messages, creating a tamper-proof, validated message
was critical to the project's success.

How the Application Works In a phased implementation, Shamrock began paying about 25% of its 300 trading partners, mainly utility
and freight-handling companies, over the Internet. In November 1996,
Shamrock started using Templar to send EDI transactions via the VAN
IBM Advantis and also to conduct the same transactions via the Internet. In either case, Diamond Shamrock initiates a payment instruction
and sends the message from its business application to the Premenos
EDI translator. The translator formats the data into an EDI 820 payment addressed to the appropriate automated clearinghouse. From the
translator, the 820 moves to Templar for encryption, and then is sent to
Chase.

   Chase receives the 820 into Templar, and the message is decrypted,
authenticated, and nonrepudiated. Chase then sends Shamrock an acknowledgment for audit purposes. It is not necessary for Shamrock's suppliers to
have a presence on the Internet, because the portion of the transaction
that involves the payee proceeds through traditional banking channels.

   When Shamrock "goes live" it will continue to send the 820s via the
Internet and discontinue use of the VAN for these transactions. In con-
trast to the batch-processed files transmitted via VANs, EDI files sent via
the Internet reach their destination in near real-time. "The speed is very
impressive. Sometimes I know the message has arrived just seconds after
I sent it," commented Gerlinde Pyron, Diamond Shamrock's manager of
electronic commerce.

Benefits "Eventually we plan to use the Internet for paying all our
high-volume bills such as phone bills," says Pyron. Other petroleum
companies are also among Shamrock's trading partners. Pyron has had
several inquiries from electronic commerce managers at other petro-
chemical companies who are interested in setting up secure EDI transactions for their wholesale fuel exchanges. "When they are ready to trade
this way, we will be, too. Costs for transmitting via the Internet are
almost nil, and it's secure," she says.

Mellon Bank

Pittsburgh, PA
 http://www.mellon.com

Background   Mellon Bank was founded in 1869 and today is a major financial services company in the USA. It is headquartered in Pittsburgh, Pennsylvania, and has assets of approximately $43 billion and approximately $1.3 trillion in assets under management or administration. Mellon has two core businesses: investment services and banking services. Investment services focuses on providing trust and investment products and private asset management for consumers, plus master trust, global custody, foreign exchange, securities lending, cash management, and investment management for corporations and institutions. Mellon also has a mutual fund business known as The Dreyfus Corporation. Banking services provides financial services to consumers, small business and private banking customers in the mid-Atlantic region, and credit card and mortgage services nationwide. They also provide products in corporate/institutional banking, international banking, middle market banking, asset-based lending, leasing, real estate finance, capital markets/venture capital, and insurance premium finance for corporations and institutions.

Problem   Mellon Bank is investigating use of the Internet as a faster and more cost-effective means of transmitting sensitive payment information to its international customers. At least ten of its international customers are interested in participating in a trial that would involve using a T1 line and Templar public key-based encryption and authentication software from Premenos of Concord, CA, for secure transmission of payment messages in automated clearinghouse (ACH) format.

For Mellon, international customers are first priority for Internet-based business-to-business EDI services, because VAN and ACH charges for international transmissions are prohibitively expensive (especially for long messages).

The problem is that this is very sensitive data. The banks involved must have confidence that the information cannot be viewed by unauthorized parties, and that the information is going to the right party.

Why Public Key Certificates?   The use of public key certificates for authentication and key exchange provides a robust framework for this data exchange.

Benefits   Mauro DeFelice, Mellon's manager of security and technology for Mellon Global Cash Management, estimates that Mellon could realize a savings of 90% by installing T1 lines and using secure software instead of a VAN. VAN service charges for international EDI can run Mellon over $500,000 a year. Aside from the software licensing charges and one-time costs of installing multiple firewalls for its servers located in Pittsburgh and Philadelphia, the only expense of Internet EDI is about $7,000 for setting up a T1 line that can also be used for non-EDI data transfer.

The time savings for using the Internet are as compelling as the cost savings, especially because international connect time is more expensive than domestic time. For example, a 40-megabyte bisynchronous file transfer would take 16 to 18 hours to transmit via a 9,600 BPS modem, and furthermore, transmissions of this length cannot be completed in a single dial-up. On the Internet, a 40 megabyte transmission recently took 27 minutes, and was accomplished without breaking the message into smaller portions and thereby introducing a greater possibility of errors. While the Internet makes these savings possible, it could not safely be used without robust authentication and privacy that public key encryption—combined with symmetric cryptography—provides.

PrimeHost

Vienna, VA
  http://www.primehost.com

Background   America Online is the largest online service provider in the USA, with over eight million subscribers. AOL is a publicly traded company with annual revenues of $1.1 billion in the year that ended in June 1996. America Online's PrimeHost is dedicated to bringing small businesses to the web, offering web hosting options geared toward companies interested in marketing themselves or selling their products. The services offered range from traditional web sites to a complete storefront package, including CyberCash transactions.

Problem   Many of PrimeHost's storefront merchants needed to be able to secure their interactions with customers to ensure a worry-free shopping experience. They did not want the risks inherent in using the Internet with interactions in the clear. Merchants also wanted to be able to prove to their customers that they were who they claimed to be, so as to improve the confidence of the shoppers.

Why Public Key Certificates? "Digital signatures afford merchants two key services," explained Phillip Zakas, Director of Technology Strategy for PrimeHost. "Their customers are assured that they are dealing with a merchant who is interested in secure transactions to protect their customers and they can assure their customers that their web site is the authentic site for their company." The combined ability to authenticate and secure transactions made public key the solution of choice.

How the Application Works PrimeHost's storefront package allows merchants to sell products via the web. Merchants can create virtual storefronts with multiple stores, departments, and categories, each populated with hundreds of products. The storefront allows a merchant's customers to browse the stores, add items to a shopping cart, and pay for their purchases with major credit cards. Today, transactions are completed through CyberCash, giving the merchants real-time credit card authorization and payment while providing their customers the ability to close sales without having to call or e-mail their order to a merchant.

Each merchant has their own VeriSign Class III Digital ID (public key certificate). When a PrimeHost merchant decides they want a certificate, they simply inform PrimeHost. PrimeHost generates the keys for the merchant, takes the required information from their merchant database, and sends it to VeriSign. VeriSign then calls the merchant to procure the additional information required for a Class III certificate. Once the verification of identity is complete, VeriSign sends the certificate PINs to PrimeHost, who then downloads the certificates and installs them on the merchant's system. PrimeHost and VeriSign are working together to further streamline this process, to make it as painless as possible for the merchant.

A customer who wishes to pay for items in a shopping cart begins by entering shipping and payment instructions on a form. This information is sent via SSL to the merchant's storefront. From there, the credit card information is securely routed to an encrypted CyberCash gateway for authorization and payment.

Benefits "Clearly, the advantage is that customers can feel safe shopping with a PrimeHost merchant, while the merchant can feel secure that their reputation will not be damaged by having customer information stolen," says Zakas. "In effect, we have created an environment safe for web shoppers." This safe environment was made possible by the use of public key cryptography, used in both the web server and CyberCash.

Wells Fargo

San Francisco, CA
  http://www.wellsfargo.com

Background   Wells Fargo Bank is the eighth largest bank in the USA, with close to 2,000 branches in eleven western states. Wells Fargo offers consumer and business services, including credit cards and credit card processing. Wells Fargo has been an innovator in the area of electronic commerce, with both consumer and business solutions. This case study is from Merchant Card Services (MCS), which delivers payment options for merchants both in the physical world and over the Internet. Wells Fargo MCS is at the forefront in offering Internet-based payment solutions for virtual merchants.

Problem   Merchants with WF merchant accounts have been asking for a branded Wells Fargo Internet payment processing. Merchants felt that a service branded by Wells Fargo, a well-known bank in the western USA, would improve buyer confidence in the service. To meet this need, Wells Fargo Merchant Card Services wanted to offer credit card processing over the Internet, but wanted stronger authentication than offered by using SSL alone. The project will be implemented in two stages. In the first stage, merchants are authenticated via public key certificates of SET. Stage 2 will involve implementing the consumer to merchant authentication portion of SET.

Why Public Key Certificates?   "Public key systems allow you to exchange encrypted data with a large number of businesses without all of the key synchronization issues inherent to a private key system," stated Tim Knowlton, Internet Product Manager of Merchant Card Services at Wells Fargo. They felt that the operational overhead of symmetric systems was too great for the Internet environment. Their deployment is using SET, the future standard for credit card transactions. One of the unique qualities of this deployment is the staged deployment mentioned above.

How the Application Works   Merchant Card Services issues digital certificates to merchants using the Wells Fargo Branded VeriFone vPOS payment product. Wells Fargo acts as the Registration Authority (RA), and GTE CyberTrust is the CA. Merchants request and retrieve their certificates from a Wells Fargo branded area on the GTE Cybertrust web site.
  Merchants request a merchant account using vPOS. When the merchant is approved, they are provided with the information they use to request

Figure 7-2

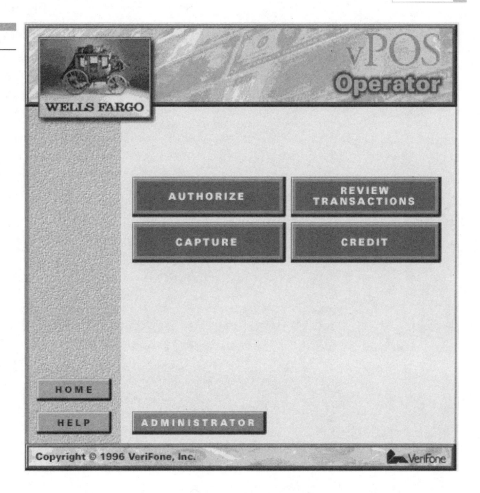

their certificates. The merchant then installs the vPOS software, and logs on to the GTE Cybertrust site to request their certificates. Wells Fargo validates the certificate requests and approves them. GTE creates the certificates, and sends the merchant an e-mail indicating that their certificates are ready for pickup. Merchant logs on to the GTE Cybertrust web site and downloads their certificates. After the process is complete, the merchant can process online credit card purchases using the VeriFone vPOS application. "The process has been very smooth," commented Knowlton.

Benefits   The strong authentication of public key provides Wells Fargo with confidence that only authenticated merchants are using their payment gateway. The use of SET as the framework for the application provides a standard protocol.

CHAPTER 8

Application Integration

Application integration is the way of the future. As more and more companies connect to the Internet, there will be a growth of distributed applications that use the Internet or intranet to communicate with servers in remote locations. With public key cryptography, it is possible to put a "trusted" system or component in an untrusted environment like the Internet.

A good example of this is an ATM machine. ATMs are very secure, and represent a trusted extension of the financial networks. They securely store cash that may only be withdrawn by authenticated individuals. The personal identification number (PIN) is heavily protected, being encrypted by hardware and sent through the network to the appropriate bank. If that bank verifies the accuracy of the PIN, the user may withdraw cash and perform other operations. This is all possible because the systems are secure and cannot be easily accessed by unauthorized parties. Public key cryptography can provide a similar sort of protection to remote "branches" of applications.

These case studies give a few examples of how applications might work in the future. CyberCash offers a service for collecting different forms of payment over the Internet. Open Market sells electronic commerce management software. NetDox offers a service for e-mail, and E-Stamp sells a PC solution which enables U.S. digital postage to be purchased and loaded over the Internet. Each uses public key cryptography for slightly different purposes, but they all rely on it to enable trust of remote components of distributed systems.

CyberCash

Vienna, VA
   http://www.cybercash.com

Background   CyberCash, Inc. was founded in August 1994 by Bill Melton (one of the founders of both VeriFone and Transaction Network Systems), Dan Lynch (founder of InterOp), Steve Crocker, Magdalena Yesil, and Bruce Wilson. The company focuses on providing secure, real-time financial transaction services over the Internet. Their current products support credit card transactions and micropayment, with support for electronic checks slated for a future release. Their system is called the CyberCash Secure Internet Payment System. It secures transactions between buyers and merchants, as well as between merchants and their banks. The eventual goal is peer-to-peer payment that allows anyone to pay anyone else using the Internet. CyberCash was the first company to develop an Internet commerce offering that uses public key cryptography and also gain permission for export of their technology worldwide.

Problem CyberCash wanted to build a robust payment system that enabled anyone anywhere in the world to easily pay for goods and services over the Internet. The problem with Internet transactions is that they aren't secure, and SSL is not exportable with the larger key sizes. To deploy a system that banks would be willing to endorse meant solving the security problem in a robust, yet exportable manner. There was another problem that SSL didn't address: merchant fraud. A large portion of credit card fraud is not from stolen cards, but from fraudulent merchants. To solve this problem, the customer's credit card number had to be shielded from the merchant.

Why Public Key Certificates? "We wanted a system the banks would trust, and public key cryptography enabled us to build such a system. No other technology enabled us to secure the transaction and authenticate all parties involved in a cost-effective manner," stated Steve Crocker, Chief Technology Officer at CyberCash. By using public key certificates, all parties involved in a transaction are authenticated and the transaction is secured. Because the system uses cryptography to secure a financial transaction only, CyberCash was able to get permission from the U.S. government to export the technology worldwide.

How the Application Works Once a buyer has selected an item for purchase, he or she clicks on a *buy* button. This activates the Cyber-Cash wallet. The buyer chooses how he or she will pay for the goods, and then clicks on *okay*. The transaction is then encrypted and sent to the merchant's CashRegister, which assigns a transaction number and forwards the transaction on to a CyberCash Payment gateway. The transaction is processed and the authorization code is sent back to the merchant. If the buyer does not have a CyberCash wallet, they are redirected to the CyberCash site to download a wallet.

Benefits The use of public key cryptography enables CyberCash to hide the credit card information from the merchant and authenticate all parties involved in the transaction. With the latest release of CyberCash, even transactions that do not use a wallet have the credit card number secured on the merchant's system by encrypting the number with the payment gateway's public key, adding further protection for stored credit card numbers.

E-Stamp

Palo Alto, CA
  http://www.estamp.com

Background   E-Stamp's main business is to create the electronic commerce platform for postal services worldwide. E-Stamp Corporation was founded in 1994 and is a privately held company. Its vision is to create a series of branded products and services to unite the physical and electronic communication needs of the worldwide information economy. The company has been working with the United States Postal Service (USPS) for several years on developing a PC postage solution that prints digital stamps. Digital stamps, represented by a bar code, can be printed onto a mailpiece using a PC and printer, and are functionally equivalent to traditional postage stamps. See the product section (Chapter 15) for more information on the company.

Problem   "We were trying to create a PC-based solution that would enable anyone with a PC and printer to quickly purchase postage—without having to go to the post office—and apply it to their outgoing mail in a time-saving automated way," stated Milton Howard of E-Stamp. The USPS wanted to define a system that would reduce fraudulent use of existing postage-meter technology. As a result, the USPS has put forth a new specification for a digital stamp that includes bar-coded information such as the identity of the sender of the mailpiece, a unique serial number for every stamp produced, and either an RSA or DSS digital signature.

Why Public Key Certificates?   "We chose RSA 1,024-bit public key crypto because it was one of the approved options given by the United States Postal Service for producing a secure digital stamp, and the most widely accepted standard for conducting transactions over the Internet," said Milton Howard.

How Does the Application Work?   Our application, "E-Stamp SoHo," is a software and hardware solution that enables users to purchase digital postage quickly and easily via E-Stamp's Internet Post Office web site, using a variety of secure payment options. Once purchased, the postage is secured and stored in an electronic vault attached to a PC. Users print USPS-approved digital stamps—which show proof of payment for delivery of mail—on envelopes, labels (for packages), and letters all in one quick and easy step. In this case, the computer not only queues a printing request, it also debits an account set up in the electronic vault (the E-Stamp Postal Security Device, or PSD) attached to the PC.

Figure 8-1

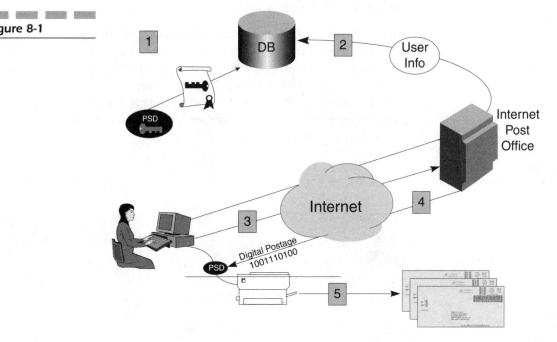

1. Before shipping to the customer, the E-Stamp Postal Security Device generates a 1,024-bit RSA public/private key pair. The private key remains secretly stored in the PSD, and E-Stamp keeps a copy of the PSD serial number and its public key in a customer database.

2. The user installs the E-Stamp SoHo software and attaches the PSD to the printer port—between the computer and printer. The user must then "personalize" the PSD, which simply means that the user enters their identification information (name, address, phone, etc.) into a local form, and then that information along with the PSD serial number (encrypted and digitally signed by the PSD private key stored in the PSD) is sent over the Internet to E-Stamp's Internet Post Office server and stored in a customer database.

3. Using E-Stamp SoHo, the user purchases postage over the Internet at the Internet Post Office using a credit card, electronic funds transfer, or check. The request for postage is digitally signed and encrypted by the E-Stamp PSD.

4. The Internet Post Office server responds with the dollar amount of the postage purchased—digitally signed and encrypted using the Internet Post Office private key—and downloaded into the PSD attached to the PC. The Internet Post Office public key is shipped with E-Stamp SoHo.

The user can then "spend" the postage by printing the recipient address and digital stamps on envelopes, labels (for packages), and letters all in one step. In this case, the computer not only queues a printing request, it also debits the postage balance stored in the PSD. Each digital stamp dispensed by the PSD is a bar code that includes the sender of the mailpiece, a unique serial number for every stamp produced, and a 1,024-bit RSA digital signature.

Figure 8-2

Issues   The main issue is distributing the PSD public keys to the USPS' distribution centers around the U.S., where the digital stamps will be scanned and authenticated. The current method is to simply include the PSD certificate as part of the bar-coded information in the digital stamp, but this makes the size of the stamp larger than desired.

Benefits   Postage purchases can be made securely over the Internet thanks to public key cryptography. The digital stamps cannot be photocopied and used multiple times because of the protections built into the stamp's bar code. Communication between the computer and PSD is secure, so that the amount of postage stored in the PSD cannot be increased unless it is legitimately purchased; public key authentication is used when loading a postage value increment.

NetDox

Deerfield, IL
   http://www.netdox.com

Background NetDox, Inc. is a new business venture founded by Deloitte & Touche LLP and the Thurston Group, Inc. in April 1996. Its charter is to provide the first commercial-quality means of delivering sensitive and high-value documents over the Internet. Initial capital was provided to NetDox by Deloitte & Touche and the Thurston Group. Deloitte & Touche provides accounting, auditing, tax, and management consulting services through over 16,000 people in offices in more than 100 U.S. cities. The Thurston Group is a private merchant bank based in Chicago, specializing in start-ups such as American Communications Services Inc. and Avery Telecommunications.

The NetDox service provides a general-purpose Internet messaging solution that offers secure, global, end-to-end document delivery with comprehensive verification and authentication services provided by a commercially trusted third party. As a third-party online document delivery service, NetDox will provide a trustworthy electronic means of transmitting documents requiring protection of privacy and message integrity, authentication of sender and receiver identity, and the accessibility of tracking data. Secure Multipurpose Internet Mail Extension (S/MIME) -based messages will go through a central hub that will authenticate, record, and "digitally notarize" every message sent, without compromising the privacy of those messages, using a pay-per-use system similar to existing overnight delivery services.

Problem Businesses are reluctant to use Internet e-mail for transmitting sensitive data, due to legitimate concerns about privacy of messages sent and authenticity of messages received. E-mail, while quick, cheap, and easy, lacks the security and auditability provided by traditional message delivery services. To send an important message, such as a contract or legal document, the message must be safe from tampering and eavesdropping, and the transmission must be verifiable so that sending and receipt—and often content—can be proven in the event of dispute. There are numerous business documents that require absolute confidentiality and reliability of receipt: contracts, letters of credit, insurance claims, motions, invoices, and any number of confidential business or legal documents. For security purposes, costly and inefficient ground delivery is used when electronic transmission would be not only cheaper and faster, but potentially more reliable and secure.

Why Public Key Certificates? Public key certificates have a couple of important attributes: They provide a basis for privacy and authentication, and they are virtually universally available. These attributes were the reasons that NetDox chose to use public key certs to enable their solution. That the S/MIME standard (which also uses public key cryptography) is beginning to be widely adopted was another reason for this choice.

How the Application Works NetDox will offer an interoperable, secure messaging service for business communications overlaid on the S/MIME, an open standard for public-key encryption developed by RSA Data Security, Inc. NetDox will also act as a clearinghouse for digital certificates, or digital IDs. The NetDox user composes his or her message using the NetDox application (or, in the future, a standard S/MIME mailer that supports NetDox). When the message is completed, the user clicks on the *send* key.

Figure 8-3

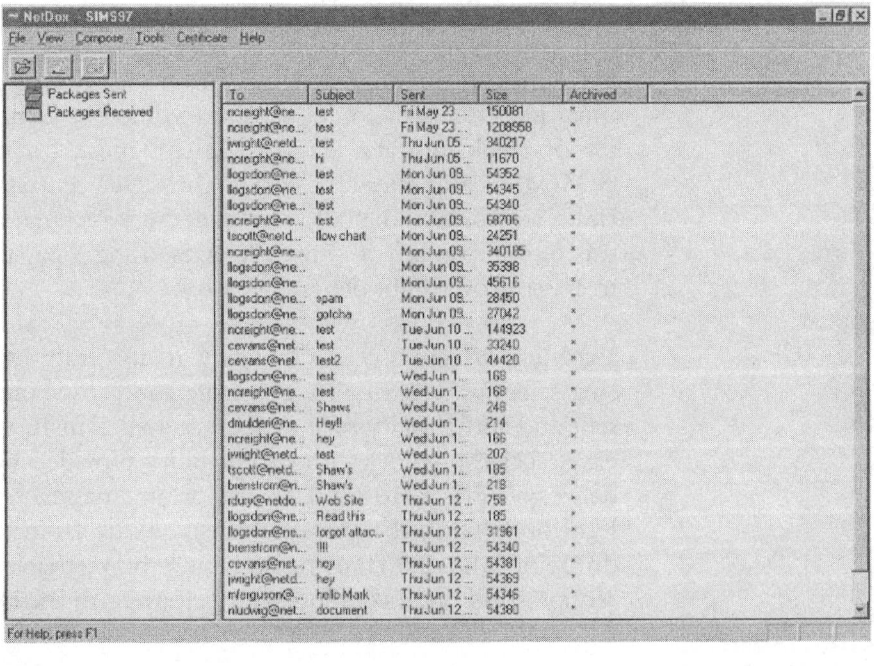

Figure 8-4

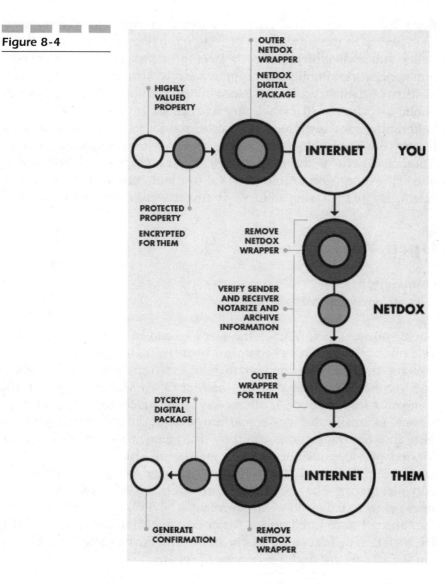

NetDox messages will not travel directly from sender to receiver. Rather, each message will route first to a NetDox hub, which will forward the message to the recipient and record comprehensive data about the transmission. Thus, NetDox will be able to provide complete post-delivery verification of message status as well as content. By using digital hashing to record the unique identity or "fingerprint" of each message, attestations can be made regarding message content without compromising the confidentiality of the message.

Benefits   NetDox will alleviate customer concerns about the commercial viability of the Internet by providing the necessary trust, confidentiality, and auditability currently lacking in messaging products over public networks. Public key cryptography is what makes this possible. Holders of digital certificates issued by different certificate authorities, public or private, will be able to exchange secure documents without holding the root keys from each certificate authority on their desktop, thereby enabling ubiquitous, secure, and easy-to-use message delivery. Another benefit of the use of public key cryptography is the robustness. This robustness enables NetDox to stand behind their service by financially guaranteeing all messages that pass through their hub.

Open Market, Inc.

Cambridge, MA
   http://www.openmarket.com

Background   Open Market, Inc. was founded in April of 1994 to provide transaction services to companies wanting to sell goods and services over the Internet. The company develops software that enables companies to conduct business over the Internet. Open Market Transact is the company's lead product. It allows service providers to offer commerce services to smaller businesses and provides the infrastructure for complete Internet transactions and their management for larger companies. Services provided include payment processing, shipping and handling, tax, transaction records, and self-serve customer service for both buyers and merchants. The company went public in May of 1996. Major investors include Greylock Management, The Tribune Company, Time, Inc., and Advance Publications. Major customers include AT&T, C/NET, UUNET, British Telecomm, Telstra, Bank One, First Union Bank, Disney Online, Bloomberg, and the Tribune Company.

Problem   Transact is a distributed commerce infrastructure that manages transactions for multiple merchant sites. In order to secure transactions, Open Market uses a mechanism they call *digital offers*. Digital offers are specialized Uniform Resource Locators (URLs) that a merchant constructs to pass to Transact what they are offering for sale, its price, and other information such as tax code, shipping weight, etc. These specialized URLs are protected from tampering by a message authentication code (MAC) that uses a shared-secret key, unique to each merchant.

Merchants can be located anywhere in the world. Using Transact, merchants can change information about their store, retrieve order records, change order status, and add stores. The challenge was to provide a strong method of authentication for merchants and a robust way to distribute the shared-secret keys between the Transact system and the merchants it serves. Open Market chose to use certificates to authenticate all sensitive Transact accounts. These include the Transact system manager, keymasters (people who generate the shared secrets and upload them to Transact), and the merchants. Transact also uses certificates to allow the different systems that are a part of Transact to communicate securely.

Why Public Key Certificates? Open Market chose public key certificates because they were the most robust form of authentication available. Public key certificates and keys are used for two things: signing the set of MAC keys (from the keymaster), and distributing the public key of Transact for encrypting the set of MAC keys. Physical devices were considered for usage, but the distribution of these devices to hundreds or thousands of merchants was logistically difficult and costly, both in terms of funds and the time for configuration management. Public key certificates offered an accepted method for authentication, with lighter requirements than physical devices such as smart cards and challenge-response tokens, and provided a secure and easy way to distribute keys.

How the Application Works When a Transact system is installed, the organization managing the system must procure public key certificates for each of the servers that comprise the system, plus certificates for the system manager and other support functions. These are loaded into the system and must be presented to enable log on to the administrative functions. When a new merchant registers for services, he or she must also have a certificate to authenticate their identity.

A special use of certificates is the uploading of shared-secret keys from the merchant's system to Transact. The merchant's keymaster generates the keys for the appropriate stores and logs into Transact. A special form is used to allow the keymaster to cut and paste the keys into a form that is then securely transmitted to the Transact system and loaded into the database. Using these keys, the merchant can now create digital offers for products and services that are for sale, and Transact can validate those offers using the shared-secret keys.

Benefits The benefits of using public key certificates lies in the time savings for key distribution. If there was no way to do strong authentication, keys would have to be distributed through regular paper mail or on a floppy. For commerce service providers with a large number of merchants, this could severely affect costs. This method also allows for quick turnaround of security events. If shared-secret keys have been compromised, the keymaster can upload a new file and those keys become active immediately, replacing the compromised set. Without public key encryption, this would be a costly procedure in time and money.

United States Postal Service

Washington, D.C.
   http://www.usps.gov

Background The United States Postal Service has a long history of innovation in national infrastructure. During early colonial days, mail was delivered haphazardly by friends and merchants as they traveled between the colonies. In 1775, the Continental Congress appointed Benjamin Franklin the first Postmaster General of a new Post Office Department, designed to bring organization and efficiency to mail delivery. Regular intercolony service was accomplished over roads developed as *post roads.* Over time, these roads grew into a network that served far more than postal purposes, eventually becoming the basis of the interstate highway system.

Likewise, the needs of mail delivery have caused the postal service to be out in front of other infrastructure needs, as they were early users and developers of waterway and railroad routes, and even initiated the first scheduled commercial air service.

In 1971, when the Postal Reorganization Act created the U.S. Postal Service as a self-supporting postal corporation wholly owned by the federal government, its mission was spelled out:

The Postal Service shall have as its basic function the obligation to provide postal services to bind the Nation together through the personal, educational, literary, and business correspondence of the people.

As the correspondence of the people expands to electronic channels, the USPS sees its mission as expanding to ensure enablement through these channels as well.

Problem As companies and individuals have turned to electronic channels for correspondence and commerce, concerns of security, integrity, and other features that have come to be able to be taken for granted in the hard-copy mail world have surfaced. The Postal Service is developing electronic commerce services to translate these features and assurances to these new media. In order to do so in a secure messaging environment prior to implementation of a full-blown certificate system, public key infrastructure is being used as a security system in communications that pass through the USPS postmarking system. In this system, public key cryptography provides document security without overly encumbering senders or receivers.

Why Public Key Certificates? The architecture being used by the USPS postmarking service requires security on a two-legged communication, with a check on document integrity happening in the middle. In order to accomplish this without multiple key pairs or exchanges of information or passwords, public key cryptography is being used around the USPS' public/private key pair.

How the Application Works The Electronic Postmark offers customers an official time and date stamp applied to transmitted electronic files. It also provides assurance of document integrity through application, and revalidation of unique cryptographic descriptions of documents that accompany them between the sender and the postmarker, and between the postmarker and the recipient. If a file fails a validation test, a message of possible file corruption or tampering is returned. Near-future features and enhancements to be added to this system mirror many hard-copy mail options, such as return receipt and registered mail.

The electronic postmark might be used in conjunction with most existing commercial e-mail packages or browsers that are used for electronic document transfer. Electronic Document Archiving provides postmarked off-site storage of electronic files and documents in a

Figure 8-5

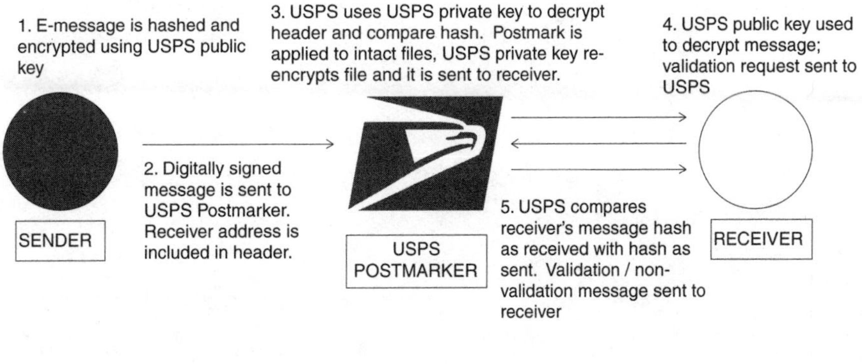

1. E-message is hashed and encrypted using USPS public key

2. Digitally signed message is sent to USPS Postmarker. Receiver address is included in header.

SENDER

3. USPS uses USPS private key to decrypt header and compare hash. Postmark is applied to intact files, USPS private key re-encrypts file and it is sent to receiver.

USPS POSTMARKER

4. USPS public key used to decrypt message; validation request sent to USPS

5. USPS compares receiver's message hash as received with hash as sent. Validation / non-validation message sent to receiver

RECEIVER

USPS-maintained facility for future access and retrieval. A little further in the future, USPS will provide a certificate-issuing and management system, providing assurance of identity as well as security in electronic document exchange.

Benefits The benefits to the USPS of public key cryptography are robustness, availability, and reach. Because of the robustness of public key cryptography, USPS can have confidence that the applications deployed are virtually tamper-proof. This confidence means broader deployment and greater availability to businesses and consumers alike. With strong authentication, the USPS can "be" just about everywhere, providing valuable services to the populace.

CHAPTER 9

Secure Electronic Transaction Protocol

Business Situation

Credit cards are a rapidly growing method of payment. There are over one billion credit cards in the world today. There are three types of cards: those issued by banks (such as Visa, MasterCard, Europay, and JCB), those issued by other companies for broad-scale use (such as American Express, Discover, and Bravo), and private-label credit cards (such as a Sears or Macy's card). In 1996, hundreds of millions of dollars in credit card transactions were completed over the Internet. This number is slated to grow into the billions by the year 2000.

The earliest practice of companies accepting credit cards over the Internet, in payment for goods and services, was to simply collect the credit card number and cardholder information on a form, with no encryption at all. Needless to say, this was not secure. Proponents stated that there was so much traffic going across the Internet that it was not worthwhile to try and capture messages to find credit card numbers. In the United States, buyers didn't need to worry too much, because regulations state that the cardholder is only liable for the first $50.00 of transactions if his or her credit card is lost or stolen. The merchants or the banks must absorb the loss for transactions on cards reported lost or stolen. Outside the USA, there is no such protection for cardholders, making the incentive to have transactions secured not just a bank concern, but also a consumer concern.

The user browses a catalog and finds what he or she wants to buy. In this example, what is being sold is flowers. The user finds the flowers he or she wants, and then clicks on the *buy* button. He or she is then prompted for credit card information, including his or her name, address, card number, card type, and expiration date. When he or she clicks on the *submit* button, the information is sent to the server and the processing is either done via human modem (a human being taking the information from the form and manually entering it onto a credit card slip or running it through a point-of-sale device) or by a program that does credit card authorization. All this information was transmitted in the clear. Think of it as sending a postcard with your credit card information in the mail, and you are close to the level of security provided. Actually, a postcard is more secure, because there are laws that apply to reading someone else's mail, but there are no laws that relate specifically to this type of transaction.

This was quickly replaced by the use of a security protocol built into browsers. This protocol is called Secure Sockets Layer, or SSL. It requires that the server have a certificate, but not the user. With SSL, the transaction is protected from snooping by using symmetric cryptography.

Figure 9-1

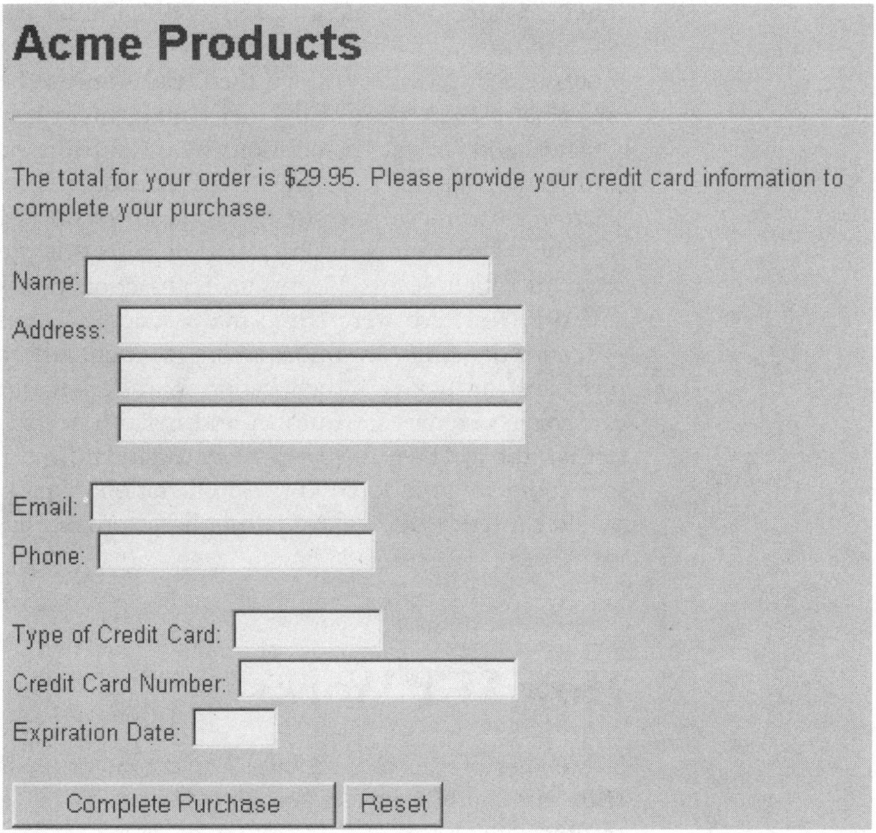

Acme Products

The total for your order is $29.95. Please provide your credit card information to complete your purchase.

Name:

Address:

Email:

Phone:

Type of Credit Card:

Credit Card Number:

Expiration Date:

[Complete Purchase] [Reset]

In this scenario, exactly the same flow of events take place. The big difference is that the information is encrypted. Encryption is done by the user's browser taking the public key of the server and using it to encrypt a key that the browser has generated. This key is sent to the server and, once it has been verified, the information that was entered on the form is sent over the Internet encrypted.

However, there was still a problem: Only "weak" cryptography is allowed to be exported by the U.S. government. Because almost all of the browsers in use today are created in the USA, this created a problem: Was encryption using a 40-bit key sufficient? The banks and card associations did not think so.

There are several things that SSL does not provide. It provides no way to authenticate the buyer as being the authorized holder of the credit card, for example. So, transactions that occur using SSL are authentication by possession, which we have already shown to be a bad idea. There is also no way to authenticate the merchant. Merchant fraud is a large component of the total figure for credit card fraud. There was also no way to authenticate that the processor was a valid credit card processor. SSL provides privacy, then, and some authentication of the web server, but no guarantee of the merchant or his or her banking relationship.

Banks and the card associations were rightfully concerned about credit card fraud over the Internet. Banks wanted to encourage the growth of electronic commerce because it is good for business, but they wanted it to be robust and secure. In order to deal with this problem, they created a standard called Secure Electronic Transaction protocol, more commonly called SET. There were three main security goals in the creation of SET: confidentiality of information, payment information integrity, and merchant/cardholder authentication. With SET it is possible to protect the cardholder's credit card number and make sure that only authorized parties can use it. The idea was to create a standardized protocol that all products could support, to avoid the proliferation of proprietary solutions that would slow deployment and complicate processing for both banks and merchants.

How SET Works

SET is one of the most robust implementations of an application that fully uses public key cryptography and its infrastructure to secure transactions. Because it is a "first of breed," it is worthwhile to take a detailed look at just how it works. Figure 9-2 provides a simpler view: The buyer sends a payment request to a merchant, who forwards it to the payment gateway (or their authorized processor). The gateway processes the request and sends back the status. The numbers next to the arrows match the text that follows.

1. This flow does take place until the buyer has found what he or she wants to purchase and is ready to pay for it.

2. Cardholder software sends an initiate request to the merchant.

3. Merchant software receives the initiate request.

4. Merchant software generates a response and digitally signs it by generating a message digest of the response and encrypting it with the merchant's private signature key.

5. Merchant software sends the response along with the merchant and payment gateway certs to the cardholder.

Figure 9-2

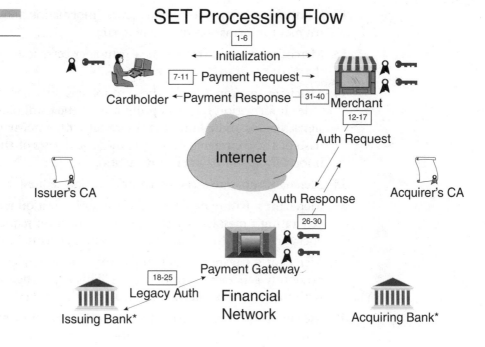

SET Processing Flow

'or their authorized processor

   6. Cardholder software receives the initiate response and verifies certificates by traversing the trust chain to the root key.

   7. Cardholder software verifies the merchant's signature by decrypting it with the merchant public signature key and comparing the result to a newly generated hash of the response.

   8. Cardholder software creates order information using information from the shopping phase.

   9. The cardholder completes the payment instructions.

   10. Cardholder software generates a dual signature by hashing a concatenation of the message digests of the order information and the payment information, and encrypting the resulting dual hash with the cardholder's private signature key.

   11. Cardholder software encrypts the payment information with a randomly generated symmetric key. This key, along with the cardholder's account information, is then encrypted with the payment gateway public key-exchange key.

12. Cardholder software transmits order information and encrypted payment information to the merchant.

13. Merchant software verifies the cardholder certificate by traversing the trust chain to the root key.

14. Merchant software verifies the cardholder's dual signature on the order information by decrypting it with the cardholder public signature key and comparing the result with a newly generated hash of the concatenation of the message digests of the order information and payment information.

15. Merchant software creates an authorization request.

16. Merchant software digitally signs the authorization request by generating a message digest of the authorization request and encrypting it with the merchant private signature key.

17. Merchant software encrypts the authorization request with a randomly generated symmetric key. This key is then encrypted with the payment gateway public key-exchange key.

18. Merchant software transmits the encrypted authorization request and encrypted payment information from the cardholder purchase request to the payment gateway.

19. The gateway verifies the merchant certificates by traversing the trust chain to the root key.

20. The gateway decrypts the symmetric key with the gateway private key-exchange key, then decrypts the authorization request using the symmetric key.

21. The gateway verifies the merchant digital signature by decrypting it with the merchant public signature key and comparing the result with a newly generated hash of the authorization request.

22. The gateway verifies the cardholder's certificate by traversing the trust chain to the root key.

23. The gateway decrypts the symmetric key and cardholder account information with the gateway private key-exchange key, then decrypts the payment information using the symmetric key.

24. The gateway verifies the cardholder's dual signature on the payment information by decrypting it with the cardholder public signature key, and comparing the result with a newly generated hash of the concatenation of the message digests of the order information and the payment information.

25. The gateway ensures consistency between the merchant's authorization request and the cardholder's payment information.

26. The gateway sends an authorization request through a financial network to the cardholder's financial institution.

27. The gateway creates an authorization response message and digitally signs it by generating a message digest of the authorization response and encrypting it with the gateway private signature key.

28. The gateway encrypts an authorization request response with a new randomly generated symmetric key. This key is then encrypted with the merchant's public key-exchange key.

29. The gateway creates a capture token.

30. The gateway encrypts the capture token with a new randomly generated symmetric key. This key and the cardholder account information is then encrypted with the gateway public key-exchange key.

31. The gateway transmits an encrypted authorization response to the merchant.

32. Merchant software verifies the gateway certificate by traversing the trust chain to the root key.

33. Merchant software decrypts the symmetric key with the merchant private key-exchange key, then decrypts the authorization response using the symmetric key.

34. Merchant software verifies the gateway digital signature by decrypting it with the gateway public signature key, and comparing the result with a newly generated hash of the authorization response.

35. The merchant stores the encrypted capture token and envelope for later capture processing.

36. Merchant software creates a purchase response, including the merchant signature certificate, and digitally signs it by generating a message digest of the purchase response and encrypting it with the merchant private signature key.

37. Merchant software transmits a purchase response to the cardholder.

38. If the transaction was authorized, the merchant fulfills the order to the cardholder.

39. Cardholder software verifies the merchant signature certificate by traversing the trust chain to the root key.

40. Cardholder software verifies the merchant signature by decrypting it with the merchant public signature key and comparing the result with a newly generated hash of the purchase response.

41. The cardholder software stores a purchase response.

Benefits This highly robust flow of the transaction makes SET very secure. If a merchant is dropped by a merchant bank, then the transaction will not succeed. If someone tries to alter the transaction in transit, it will not succeed because of the digital signature protecting the payment and order information. Only the payment gateway can read the payment information, because it is encrypted with the gateway's key. And, if a credit card holder loses a credit card or has his or her system compromised, the certificate can be revoked, thus preventing fraud.

SET has been undergoing protocol refinement over the past year, and applications with support SET are now being tested. Pilots are under way in countries around the world, and broadscale deployment is expected in late 1997 or early 1998. This will be the first broadscale, international, multicompany, multi-tiered implementation of public key cryptography.

PART 3

Issues

Although public key encryption offers great potential to meet the requirements for doing commerce over the Internet and intranets, there are numerous business and legal issues that need to be addressed in order for public key encryption usage to succeed. Those issues will be the focus of this section. After giving the "big picture" of the issues, each will be discussed in more detail. Where possible, examples of ways to address the issues will be covered.

The issues are grouped into technical issues, business and operational issues, and legal issues. Technical issues focus on challenges related to the technology and implementation choices. Business issues cover topics that deal with business models, requirements, operational concerns, and risk analysis. Legal issues deal with responsibilities, agreements, legislation, and issues of responsibilities and redress.

Because this book is for businesspeople, the explanations of all the issues are from that viewpoint. Many of the issues appear in multiple sections, because they affect multiple disciplines within a company. The technical choices, for example, have a budgetary implication: The technical staff might insist on cryptographic hardware from end to end, but there might not be enough money to deploy such a solution. Buying a product to be managed in-house might be the preferred choice of the businesspeople and technical staff, but the legal counsel might disagree due to liability issues. For the technical staff and legal staff, additional guidance should be sought from experts and publications targeted for that audience.

If public key is trusted to provide authentication, then all the issues that relate to real-world authentication also relate to online authentication, plus the challenges presented in the "big problems" of the networked world discussed in Chapter 2, apply to public key usage. Some of the issues are interrelated: Legislation could affect the technical choices available to an international business. The laws in different countries can influence the policies that a company implements, or the decision about implementing the technology in-house or outsourcing it. The technical options might influence the business choices. The most important thing for a company considering the use of public key infrastructure is to understand the options and develop a set of requirements that meets their needs, can be implemented within budget, and that address the legal issues.

In some instances, how the issues should be addressed is closely related to how the technology will be used in a specific business situation, and the legislation in a particular geography. Different business needs may change infrastructure requirements, and business models may influence which solutions are viable.

CHAPTER 10

Technical Issues

Technical issues involve the technology and its usage. They range from simple decisions (such as the size of the key being used) to complex issues (like key escrow). There are many technical details that address issues that will not be discussed in this book. The only ones that are covered here are major ones that a manager or businessperson needs to understand because of their impact to costs, security, legal, or business concerns. These issues fall into three categories:

- How the technology is implemented.
- What is implemented.
- How it is managed.

The resolution of these issues is usually driven by business, legal, and budgetary reasons. The *how* of implementation includes three issues: hardware vs. software, interoperability, and in-house vs. outsourcing of the implementation. What is implemented relates to the algorithm used to implement public key encryption, its use in applications, standards, and the size and splitting of the keys used. Key escrow, security policies, registration authority functionality, directory services, and revocation lists are the issues of public key system management.

Hardware vs. Software

One of the choices that companies must make is whether to use specialized hardware in their implementation. Several companies manufacture hardware to generate and store private keys and perform the encryption/signing, instead of using software running on general-purpose systems. Hardware can be used by the server, the user, or both. Why use hardware?

The more obstacles that are put in the way of a thief, the more difficult it is for the thief to get access to the keys. Just as a company protects things with multiple locks, adding additional levels of protection or perimeters that an intruder must overcome increases the safety of the thing being protected. With public key cryptography, the keys are the most important thing to protect, because if someone can get access to a company's or user's private key, they can impersonate that company or user. The use of hardware increases the difficulty of getting access to the key.

Software-based solutions use the computing power of a general-purpose system for storing the keys and doing the encryption. If the keys are stored on a hard disk on a generally accessible system, it is possible to copy the keys to another system. The problem with storage of the keys on a general-purpose system's disk is duplication. Although applications generally encrypt the keys, if a thief copies all pertinent files to another system, they can use that system to impersonate the original system. Copying the keys and applications is easier than breaking into special-purpose hardware storing the keys. Some hardware solutions also do encryption; the private key never leaves the hardware box. Here are the different types of hardware that are available for public key cryptography.

Figure 10-1

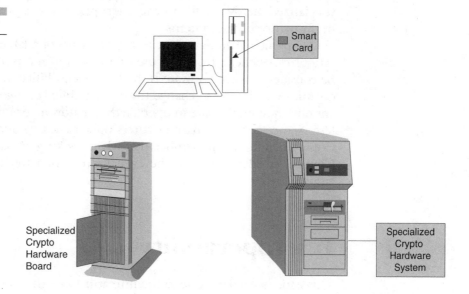

Hardware for public key cryptography comes in three different forms: specialized systems, boards or cards that can be used in a general-purpose system, and smart cards. Smart cards can be used to store keys and sometimes to perform the actual encryption and signing. They can be used on either the client or server end. Separate hardware systems offer the highest level of security because they provide an additional perimeter that a thief must penetrate to get access to the keys. A board on a general-purpose system lacks this additional barrier, because that system must be accessible for general system administration.

Of the hardware systems, the highest security is provided by the separate crypto hardware system. These systems have multiple safeguards that prevent the removal of the private keys, and sensors that prevent moving the system. The next highest level is provided by the hardware board or card that plugs into a PCI or PCMCIA slot on a PC. Smart cards also provide additional protection for the key, because it cannot be removed from the card and cannot be accessed without a personal identification number (PIN).

Security is usually the driving force behind the use of hardware for key storage and encryption. The decision to use a hardware solution for the users, the server, or both is mainly a security concern, but for high-volume applications it can also be chosen for performance reasons. Because of the computational intensity of public key algorithms, companies planning high-volume applications might choose to employ specialized hardware to do the encryption and signing to boost the performance of the systems.

Companies with high security requirements or a large volume of transactions can benefit from the use of hardware. One problem that should be considered with hardware is the lack of flexibility in algorithms. If an organization decides to change from one public key algorithm to a different one, they might have to upgrade their hardware or purchase a new system. Some hardware manufacturers offer easy upgrades; others do not. Companies should remember this when looking at hardware solutions. Changes of algorithm can be even more expensive if the application employs smart cards.

Interoperability

This issue is partially due to the immaturity of the market, but for companies deploying systems today, this can be a problem: Certificates from different CA vendors might not work together. So, if several trading partners want to use e-mail secured with S/MIME, they might be forced to choose a single CA. This problem will disappear as the market matures, but companies deploying in the short term should make sure that all the necessary brands are supported by the applications they intend to deploy, and include a deadline for interoperability with a chosen list of vendors.

In-House vs. Outsourcing

The technical aspect of whether a company hosts its own CA or uses an outsourced service concerns operational capacity:

■ Does the organization have a 7-by-24 service staff?

■ Does the expertise for security policy creation and management exist in-house?

■ Do internal operations have the staff qualified and capable of running a CA?

■ Is the company better equipped, due to strategic advantage or core competence, to provide this service than an outsourcer?

If the answers to all these questions are no, then an organization needs to weigh the costs of adding this staff against the costs of outsourcing. This issue will be discussed in much greater depth in Chapter 12.

Algorithms

Most systems in use on the Internet and intranets today use RSA public key cryptography, but there are many different public key algorithms. What happens if a company starts with one algorithm, and decides at a later date to change to a different public key cryptosystem? As with key escrow, all parties and all software involved in the transaction must be able to deal with this change. First of all, the certificates must be re-issued with a different set of keys. Why? Because different cryptosystems use different algorithms. These different algorithms each compute their key pairs in a manner unique to that algorithm.

Figure 10-2

This step is not as bad as it sounds, because the hard work of verifying an applicant's identity has already been accomplished. All that will be necessary is for the user to be authenticated using their existing key pair. Once this has been done, a new key pair can be computed and a new certificate using that key pair can be issued. Figure 10-2 gives an example of how this might take place. The user goes to the CA's site and requests a replacement certificate. The CA's system verifies the applicant's identity using their certificate. The CA's system checks this information against their database, then issues a new certificate with the new key pair.

There are three alternative algorithms that are in use today: Pretty Good Privacy (PGP), the Digital Signature Algorithm (DSA), and elliptic curve. PGP is widely used for e-mail, but is not covered in this book because it does not use the notion of certification authorities to bind identity to a key pair. Because this book focuses on the use of certificate-based public key cryptography, PGP has not been covered. For more information about PGP, see http://www.pgp.com. DSA is not covered in this book because it is primarily used by the U.S. government, and does not have broad application support.

The only certificate-based alternative to RSA public key that has much general usage is a system called *elliptic curve*. This system is getting a lot of attention because it provides what appears to be very strong protection with much smaller keys. It also takes much less computing power to "sign" a document using elliptic curve. Another benefit to elliptic curve is that it is easier to put into silicon, so that smart cards that include elliptic curve tend to be less expensive to manufacture than those that use RSA public key. The debates about the use of elliptic curve are inconclusive. One side states that elliptic curve has not be subjected to the rigorous attempts at cryptanalysis (trying to break it) as RSA, and therefore it should not be used. The other side says that it has indeed been tested and is much better than RSA. One side states that although elliptic curve is cheaper for signing, it is more expensive for verifying a signature, a more common operation than signing. The other side states that elliptic curve is not more expensive for signature verification. There are currently two sources of elliptic curve: RSA, which is included in Chapter 15 and Certicom. Additional information about Ceritcom can be found on their web site at http://www.certicom.com.

The debate rages on. Any company considering the use of any public key algorithm should make sure that the applications they want to use support it. Another way to help decide on the cryptosystem to use is to look at others in the industry doing similar tasks, to determine that system they are using. The features, such as key escrow, outsourced service, revocation list management, and smart card/hardware support, can help to determine which system is best for a particular company. If the question is still unclear, an organization should consider hiring an independent (not associated with either RSA or Certicom, the primary elliptic curve vendor) crypto expert to help the company decide.

Public Key Cryptography in Applications

Today's implementations of public key cryptography are tightly integrated into the applications that use them. This integration has the benefit of working seamlessly with the application, but it has the disadvantage of limiting the use of public key encryption to the functions the application can perform. The two critical lacks in applications today are the ability to share keys and certificates between applications, and the additional desired functions that the current batch of applications don't perform.

Today's applications tie the key pair and certificate tightly to the application. This means that if a user wants to use the same certificate with another application, they cannot do so, because there is no standard way to extract the key pair from the application. There is a proposed standard for dealing with this issue: Public Key Cryptography Standard 12, more commonly known as PKCS-12. This standard provides a way for users to move certificates, keys, and passwords not only between applications, but between systems as well. Most vendors have committed to support of this standard, but companies should be careful to understand the time frame for support of this standard, because it will differ from vendor to vendor. Today, if a user gets a certificate for their browser, they will not be able to use that certificate for another application from a different vendor. They will also be unable to use that same certificate at the office and at home. Companies considering broad deployment of public key systems should keep this in mind when writing requirements for the applications they plan to deploy, and when evaluating applications for purchase.

Another unfortunate implementation issue is the support of different certificate authorities. Most current applications *hardwire* the CAs that their application supports. A company might find an excellent choice of CA solutions, only to find that the applications that they plan to use don't support that CA. Some applications allow the addition of root keys to support, but many do not. Organizations should be careful to verify that their desired applications or support or that the application is capable of loading additional root keys. This is an issue for browsers, servers, and e-mail products.

Standards

There are several standards that relate to public key cryptography. Where possible, the use of standards can be very useful in allowing interoperability between applications from different vendors. The "cardinal" standard is the X509 standard from the International Organization for Standards (ISO) and the International Electrotechnical Commission (IEC), which includes the specification for certificate format. RSA has a series of Public Key Certificate Standards (PKCS) that are also useful. The Internet Engineering Task Force (IETF) is currently drafting public key infrastructure standards that can be found at http://www.ietf.org/html.charters/pkix-charter.html.

In addition to standards that relate to certificates, there are several that incorporate the use of public key cryptography. These include SSL (web), S/MIME (e-mail), and SET (credit card transactions). When dealing with SSL, it is important to note the version that is supported. Version 2 of SSL does not support client authentication; version 3 does. Most applications support the appropriate standards, but it should be noted that this doesn't necessarily guarantee interoperability. Companies should be careful to not only specify the standards that they require, but specifically call out the interoperability requirements, such as the CAs whose certificates must work with an application and demonstrable proof that they do.

Key Size and Key Splitting

As discussed in Part 1, the size of the keys used can increase the difficulty of breaking the key. While it is virtually impossible with current technology to break a 512-bit RSA key, most domestic applications use at least 1,024-bit keys. Unfortunately, 1,024 keys are not easily exportable. The type of application and whether the keys can be used for only signing or also for encryption might influence exportability.

Companies planning international usage should check with legal counsel to make sure that the larger key size is exportable.

Another aspect of the key is who holds it and how it is held. One interesting possibility is to split the key into multiple parts, so that two or more parties must present their segment of the key to sign a message or document. Some systems are quite sophisticated in their ability to allow multiple splits, and to allow for a "quorum" of key holders (so that six people might hold a key fragment, but only four are required to complete a signing, for example). These systems allow for the serial application of the keys, so that all the parts of the private key are never in the same place. For high-risk/high-value transactions, companies might want to consider using this technology.

Key Recovery/Escrow

Key recovery is the ability to recover a lost or unavailable key for the purposes of recovering data that has been encrypted. Key escrow is the storing of keys for later recovery. The party that escrows the keys could be an internal organization or an external, trusted third party. There are three elements to key recovery and key escrow: technical issues, legal issues, and operational issues. The legal issues will drive the decision whether a business needs to worry about certain aspects of key escrow and recovery. The business issues will also help determine a company's decisions about implementing key escrow and/or key recovery. The technical issues involve how to implement it.

There are several different ways to enable data recovery. The methods themselves are beyond the purview of this book, but the issue of whether to enable data recovery is not. The business and legal aspects will be discussed later, but the technical aspect is one of functionality. If an organization decides to enable data recovery using escrowed keys or some other mechanism, every party in the transaction is impacted.

Users' browsers or other applications that use the keys must know how to escrow the keys or some other means to enable the recovery of the data that was encrypted. Servers must know how to do this as well. If the public key/private key pair is to be escrowed, then the certification authority must be involved as well. With most key recovery/escrow systems, there is some sort of storage of keys. If this is the case, then there might also be an escrow agent. This might be an internal group or system, or a trusted third party.

Figure 10-3

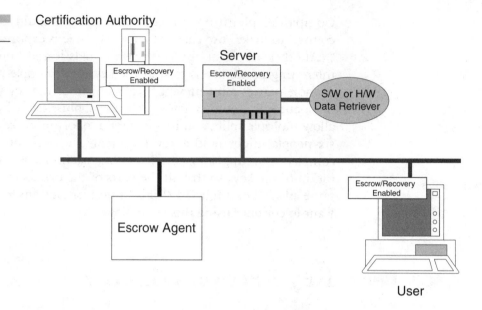

Some systems are now looking at providing two sets of key pairs (one for signing, and one for encryption of shared secrets) to avoid the escrowing of the signing keys. Not only must all these parties know how to enable data recovery, but there must also be a system that knows how to recover the data. This system must have very strong safeguards, because it has the ability to "break" any encryption done by all parties involved.

Security Policies and Procedures

The security of the systems that a CA uses is critical, as discussed in Part 1. If a company plans to act as its own certification authority, it will need to use the same degree of rigor in developing the policies and procedures that govern management of the CA systems as it did in developing the initial encryption system. Poor practices can turn a robust technology into a very insecure system. The single point of failure for a public key infrastructure is the CA's private key. With access to that key, a cyberthief can generate certificates that can bind any identity chosen to a particular key pair. Strong measures must be used to prevent this from happening.

One of the most critical problems, at least in the USA, is internal fraud. Not only must a company protect the CA's private keys from external infiltrators, but also from employees. Some of these policies are decided based on business objectives, but there is a technical element to this: audit logs. Not only must a company have good security policies and procedures, but the following of those policies and procedures must be logged in some manner. Most CA products offer this feature for their product, but what about the additional policies that a company puts in place, such as a telephone call to certificate applicants? If the product used does not offer the ability to customize logged events, then an application for doing so must be developed.

Security events are like fires, and dealing with them is very similar to fighting fires. The first goal should be to prevent their occurrence; but if that should fail, security events must be detected and, when detected, contained. Once an event has been contained, there must be a way to recover from it. Prevent, detect, contain, recover: These terms should be watchwords when developing security policies and procedures.

Registration Authority Functionality

Some CA products have the concept of a *registration authority* (RA). This was mentioned in the Wells Fargo and the USWeb case studies. A registration authority allows a company who wants to outsource their CA services to keep control of the identity verification step of the certification process. Companies that are planning to outsource their CA needs should look closely at the functionality provided by their CA's registration authority, to make sure that it meets their needs.

Directory Services

How do you find a public key certificate? This is a very good question with no good answer today. There are a number of proposed standards for dealing with this issue, but there is no master directory of certificates today. VeriSign and others maintain a searchable directory of all the certificates they issue, but what if the certificate was issued by another CA? How do you find it? This is not a large problem when dealing with the web, because browsers and servers take care of this issue by including certificate presentation in the protocols. It IS an issue if you want to mail a request for quote to a vendor for whom you have no certificate, and who doesn't know you. Companies should closely examine their requirements in this area to determine how much of a problem this might be for them. The first of these solutions can be found in the Net-Dox service, which was discussed in Chapter 8. NetDox provides the service of certificate directory services, as well as making evaluations of the strength of different CA's certificates. Unfortunately, this is one of the few solutions available today. Products and services will appear in this area, but they are not widely present today.

Revocation Lists

The thorniest technical issue is key escrow/key recovery, but a close second is *certificate revocation lists*, often called CRLs. Readers on the high side of 40 might remember the early days of credit cards, when the numbers of lost credit cards that should not be accepted were published in a newsprint booklet. A clerk accepting a customer's credit card at a store would try to match the credit card number on the buyer's card against the thousands of numbers listed in the booklet. If the number was not there, then the credit card had not been revoked, lost, or stolen. Today this process is far more transparent, with all the lookup being done automatically.

Unfortunately, most applications today do not support automated checking of CRLs. What this means is that CRL checking must be added to applications that require valid certs. This is actually one of the reasons that many companies are issuing their own certificates: They know if they have revoked their own certification, so they don't have to deal with finding the revocation list for someone else's CA. As with directory services, these will be appearing over the next one to two years, so the problem is a transient one.

11

Legal Issues

The largest legal issue is the lack of uniform statutes and regulations on the use of digital signatures. This lack has a number of implications. Because there is little to no specific legal framework, all parties involved in the use of digital signatures must agree to what they mean, what constitutes proper usage, where the responsibilities lie, what the liabilities are, and the consequences for failure to meet the stated responsibilities. For a more detailed overview of this issue, see Appendix III. The crux of the matter is aptly stated in that appendix:

> A digital signature is a technical concept. The legal significance of a digital signature will depend on whether it constitutes a signature under the applicable law. Under current law, the legal effect of a digital signature would be determined by looking at the circumstances surrounding a transaction, including whether the party applying the digital signature intended to be legally bound. Although it is possible that a digital signature would be found to be a legally binding signature under either current common law or statute, the result is very uncertain.

Because law does not exist to codify the use of certificates and digital signatures, all the responsibilities, liabilities, and consequences must be dealt with through agreements signed by the participating parties. The general legal issues that must be dealt with include:

- What are the legal consequences if a user loses sole control of their private key? Is there a difference between the loss due to negligence vs. the loss due to theft or abuse of trust by an employee?

- What are the responsibilities of a certification authority (CA) when verifying the identity of certificate applicants?

- What is a CA's responsibility with regards to digital signature verification?

- What is a CA's liability for erroneously issuing a certificate to a fraudulent party, or making an error in the issuance of a certificate?

- Can a CA limit its liability to its certificate holders?

- What are the legal consequences if a CA goes out of business? What happens to the certificates that CA issued?

- Who can act as a CA? What are the requirements to do so?

- What technology might or must be used to create digital signatures and certificates?

■ What happens if someone discovers a way to break the algorithms used to create digital signatures? What are the implications?

■ What is the legal status of certificates issued in other jurisdictions? What if public key cryptography is illegal in the sender or recipient's country?

Digital Signature Legislation

Many states and countries around the world are beginning to formulate legislation to deal with clarifying these items. Because this area is changing so rapidly, a printed book cannot provide an accurate list of the status of these initiatives. This summary should be viewed as a snapshot in time and more recent data should be sought through online resources. An excellent site that summarizes the status of digital signature legislation can be found at http://www.mbc.com/ds_sum.html.

A recent copy of that web page is included as Appendix IV, for those without Internet access. This chapter's summary of legislation has been extracted from that appendix.

All states in the USA, except Alabama, Alaska, Arkansas, Idaho, Missouri, New Jersey, Ohio, Pennsylvania, South Carolina, South Dakota, West Virginia, and Wisconsin have already passed legislation, have bills in progress, or are contemplating legislation concerning the use of digital signatures. Some states are taking a minimalist view and simply equating a digital signature to a handwritten signature. Others are dealing with the complete list of questions above.

The picture at the federal level in the USA is much less clear. The unpopular Electronic Data Security Act of 1997, which focuses on key escrow, includes provision for the Department of Commerce to register certification authorities and key escrow agents. The Food and Drug Administration issued regulations in March 1997 that outline the criteria for electronic submission of data to the FDA. These criteria equate a digital signature to a handwritten signature.

Outside the USA, there are several initiatives under way. The United Nations Commission on International Trade Law (UNCITRAL) began drafting a model digital signature legislation in February of 1997. The European Union has issued a request for proposal for a study on the legal aspects of digital signatures. This report should be available in 1998. The Organisation for Economic Co-operation and Development (OECD) has established a series of guidelines for countries creating legislation concerning privacy and authentication, which includes digital signatures. Canada, Denmark, France, Germany, Italy, Japan, Malaysia, and the U.K. are in various stages of drafting and enacting digital signature legislation.

Certificate Holder Responsibility

If a user loses control of his or her private key, then the party that gains control can impersonate the owner electronically. What is the owner's liability in this instance? There are two basic liability models for determining the answer to this question: fault-based liability (credit card) and activity-based liability (checks). Two pertinent models are credit cards and checks. The statutes for credit cards are based on the nature of the credit card activity, and assume that the bank is better able to bear the liability than the cardholder. In the USA, a cardholder is only liable for up to $50 of charges if his or her credit card is reported lost or stolen. There is no stated responsibility of the cardholder with regards to the protection of their credit card.

Checks have a slightly different model that adds fault as a relevant factor to establishing liability on the part of the check writer. Usually, the bank bears the liability for accepting a forged check. This situation changes if the account holder does not exercise reasonable care in avoiding the possibility of forgery or alteration. If the account holder is negligent, then he or she is liable for the loss.

Most legislation on digital signatures is taking a fault-based approach, where the owner is responsible for the protection of his or her private key. Failure to protect the key would cause the key's owner to be liable for the losses that occurred due to fraudulent usage. This responsibility should be clearly stated in agreements between a CA and its certificate holders.

If a certification authority's keys are compromised, the situation is much more serious, because all certificates they have issued are also compromised. If a thief can get access to the CA's private key, he or she can issue certificates that bind any public key to the identity of their choice. This is equivalent to someone stealing the stock and machines that generate passports: The thief could generate passports for anyone, stating that the bearer was a citizen or permanent resident of that country. Most CAs use hardware systems for the issuance of high-assurance certificates, making theft virtually impossible.

CA Responsibilities and Liabilities

As discussed in Part 1, certification authorities are responsible for:

- Receiving certification requests.
- Verifying the identities of applicants.
- Issuing certificates.
- Revoking certificates.
- Providing information about certificates it has issued.

If a CA fails to meet these responsibilities, it might be liable under either contract or tort law, although it would depend on the circumstances of the failure. One of the most difficult issues is the CA's liability to third parties involved in transactions with the certificate holder. These third parties have no relationship with the CA, but rely on the accuracy of the certificate for conducting business. Until there is legislation to provide a legal framework, agreements between CAs and certificate holders should clearly state the liabilities and responsibilities of the CA to both the certificate holder and those who rely on the accuracy of the certificate. Even with clear attestations, this situation will likely be murky for many years to come; companies that are trusting third-party certificates should be duly diligent in establishing the basis for that trust. See Appendix III, Section VIII for more details on this issue.

CA Requirements

Most jurisdictions that are considering digital signature legislation include the provision for the licensing or accreditation of companies that plan to become certification authorities. One critical question here is whether this licensing or accreditation applies only to CAs that offer publicly available certificates, or if this would also apply to corporations managing private CAs for their employees, customers, or partners. The licensing or accreditation of CAs is strongly needed, but until it occurs, organizations should specifically state their requirements for participating CAs if indeed they allow multiple CAs to work with their application. The Certification Practice Statements referenced on page 138 can act as a guide to the requirements that must be met for usage of a particular CA's certificates.

Technology Implications and Requirements

As mentioned earlier, there are a number of different public key cryptosystems. The technology that is required to be used should be clearly stated in the agreements between parties. The standards mentioned in Chapter 10 might be useful in these specifications, because they are broadly recognized. This should include any technological requirements for key storage as well. For example, a bank that plans to use public key cryptography for high-value interbank transfers might want to stipulate that all private keys must be stored on a hardware device, to increase security. Key size, escrow requirements, and certificate assurance levels are also candidates for stipulation in agreements.

International Issues

The biggest international issue for companies based in the USA is that of export: It is illegal to export strong cryptography without government approval. Until recently, it was illegal to ship applications with keys larger than 40 bits outside the USA, except for banks. This situation has been dramatically relaxed in the past year, with a number of changes in policy. The most significant changes are:

- Complete transfer of the jurisdiction for cryptography exports from the Department of State to the Department of Commerce.

- Ability to export cryptography that uses up to 56-bit keys, after a one-time review, if the company promises to deploy key recovery features within the next two years.

- Introduction of the Promotion of Commerce On-Line in the Digital Era (Pro-CODE) Act of 1997, introduced on Feb. 27, 1997 by Senator Conrad Burns (R-MT).

- Introduction of the Security and Freedom Through Encryption (S.A.F.E.) Act of 1997, introduced Feb. 12, 1997 by Representative Bob Goodlatte (R-VA).

- The Department of Commerce issued a press release saying they would allow the export of the strongest available data encryption products to support global electronic commerce—specifically for financial transactions.

The Pro-CODE and S.A.F.E. bills have both been seriously compromised by recent amendments. These amendments mandate key escrow and reverse the benefits of the original bills. The battles are not yet over, but this raises serious questions about the exportability of commercially viable cryptography.

Strong authentication has always been exportable. The U.S. government allows people to prove identity and protect integrity, but it doesn't allow strong privacy; that can only be had from the use of larger keys. The issue is that RSA public key cryptography can also be used for encryption, even though most programs don't use this capability. The encryption export bills focus on the privacy aspect of cryptography, but where does this leave public key cryptography? The answer is uncertain. Even if the bills pass, there is still the question of whether RSA will be included in that allowance. Because most programs don't use it for encryption (except for a symmetric key), it might be exportable. The trend is toward more relaxed regulation, but only time will answer this question.

The exportability of strong encryption is very important for companies who want to communicate with international partners. Unless they are able to get permission to import the applications (most of which are currently produced in the USA), usage will not be possible outside the United States. So, does this mean that companies outside the USA won't be able to get strong cryptography? Absolutely not. Only that they can't get it from U.S. firms. Sun Microsystems, in a bold move, has announced that they will be using cryptography produced in Russia with its products, handily by-passing the U.S. regulations. RSA has established relationships with NTT to use their chips for the international market. The Department of Commerce seems to be willing to allow the export of applications to preapproved lists of companies as well. All this points to a positive outcome, but the cautious business would do well to seek legal counsel on this matter before planning a global deployment.

The other international issue is the legality of algorithm usage in certain countries. The president's national security advisory commissioned an interagency report titled *A Study of the International Market for Computer Software with Encryption,* which includes information on export controls. It can be found at http://www.epic.org/crypto/export_controls/commerce_study_summary.txt.

In brief, France, Russia, and Israel control the type of cryptography that can be imported and/or exported. The other issue is the legal enforceability of cross-border certificates and signatures. Many of the laws proposed or enacted include provisions for this, but companies should check with legal counsel for countries without these provisions. Only Germany and Malaysia have passed legislation on digital signatures, although many other countries are considering passage.

Certification Practice Statements

Many certification authorities are dealing with these issues by establishing Certification Practice Statements (CPSs). These statements are referred to in agreements, and clearly state the responsibilities to which a CA commits, as well as the responsibilities of certificate holders. A Certification Practice Statement not only protects a CA, it also informs the public about the policies of that CA. This can be useful to an organization in determining whether to trust a particular CA's certificates and in comparing the policies of CAs.

These statements articulate the policies of a CA and how those policies are implemented. A certificate policy is a set of rules that a CA employs in the issuance, management, and revocation of certificates. A CPS commonly includes these policies, plus operating procedures, authentication issuance requirements for different levels or classes of certificates, the operating environment, standards, supported applications, formatting information, security practices (including personnel, system, network, and procedural controls), operational procedures for revocation, certificate alteration, disaster recovery, audit, key recovery, confidentiality of certificate holder information, liability and obligations of the CA, liability and obligations of the certificate holder, CRL and directory services offered, administrative policies, and any cross-certification with other CAs.

The list above might seem daunting, but there is help in developing a CPS. The Internet Engineering Task Force has a draft document titled *Internet Public Key Infrastructure Part IV: Certificate Policy and Certification Practices Framework*.

This document can be very useful in developing a CPS. It can be found from the PKIX working group home page at http://www.ietf.org/html.charters/pkix-charter.html.

Another useful document that explains what needs to be in a CPS can be found on Entrust's web site at http://www.entrust.com/downloads/cps.pdf.

One of the few CPSs available for public review is VeriSign's CPS. This document can be found at http://www.verisign.com/repository/CPS.

In addition, the American Bar Association's Digital Signatures Guidelines has useful information about this and other legal matters. These guidelines can be purchased from the ABA at http://www. abanet.org/scitech/home.html.

This page also contains a free digital signature tutorial that readers might find useful.

Relying Parties

For publicly available certificates, there is an additional issue that must be dealt with: What happens if a third party with no relationship with a CA relies on a certificate's authenticity, only to find that the certificate was invalid? Who is liable? Because this is an issue primarily for CAs that issue publicly available certs, which might be used in multiple applications, this is not discussed here; but it is an issue that any company planning to issue publicly available certificates must address.

Agreements

Who needs to use agreements to codify these items? That depends on the risk involved. For the music store that is selling a customer a CD-ROM, there probably isn't a need for an online agreement, but the higher the value of the transaction and the greater the damage that can be done if the transaction is compromised, the more likely an agreement is needed. There are three very different relationships that make up potential parties to transactions:

- Trading partners.
- Established customers.
- Unknown entities.

Trading partners are the easiest to deal with, because most trading partners already have trading partner agreements. In this instance, all that is necessary is to add an addendum to existing agreements and to incorporate that addendum into the base agreement for signing with future partners. An example of this type of addendum can be found in Appendix II.

Established customers often have some type of agreement that codifies their relationship. The form of the agreement will be determined by the type of certificates that are being used by the intended application. If the certificates are issued for the express purpose of identifying the relationship, then the agreement should include language about the right of revocation, should the relationship terminate or the customer fail to meet his or her responsibilities. If the certificate used is a publicly available certificate, then this section is not necessary.

For unknown entities, there will still be the problem of the legality of a digital signature to bind a party to a contract or agreement. Where the risk is high or repeat business is expected, it might be prudent to provide an online agreement that must be printed, signed, and mailed to the vendor, so that digital signatures can be used in the future.

CHAPTER **12**

Business Issues

There are several decision points related to the use of public key cryptosystems that are business-oriented. These issues relate to business models, costs, and risks involved in public key cryptography usage. One of the things that makes the use of public key infrastructure so difficult for some organizations is the need for business, legal, and technical staff to work closely together and agree on an optimal solution for a corporation. The solution viewed by technical people as optimal might not be compatible with the optimal business solution. The legal staff might put requirements on the system that neither the technical nor business people want. To come to a resolution that meets the business needs, provides legal safeguards, and is supportable by the technical staff, all parties must understand the issues that only they can resolve and work together to arrive at a viable solution. This chapter first examines the pure business issues (business models, risks, and costs), then goes on to highlight where each of the issues discussed in the earlier chapters influence the business decisions.

Business Models and Risks

The term *business model* has many different contextual meanings. For some people, it is the strategy that a company employs to make money. For example, a company might have a product business model, where it sells products. A part of this model might be the distribution channels in use. Another business model is the service model, where the company provides services to its customers. The service business model might be direct, where the company provides services directly to the customer, or indirect, where the company provides the services on behalf of other companies, and the revenues flow from transaction fees or a percentage of the transaction. Another view of business models is one of relationship: What are the relationships between the transacting parties? Relationships and purposes between the transacting parties are issues in the use of public key cryptography. The term *relationship* in this context refers to whether the transacting parties are known to each other and whether they have established agreements or contracts that govern those relationships. The chart on the next page highlights some of the possible types of relationships:

Type	Known	Agreements	Control
Casual or walk-in	No	No	No[*]
Customer	Yes	Might be	Provider can revoke
Employee	Yes	Yes	Provider can revoke
Partner	Yes	Yes	Equal

[*] There might be some requirements that the customer must meet, such as having a valid credit card or proving identity, but the provider does not have the ability to revoke, because revocation implies relationship.

Casual or walk-in transactions are the simplest, because no relationship is involved. A good example of this type of relationship is the QSpace case study. QSpace requires that the potential buyer prove his or her identity and ability to pay, but the certificate that is used to prove that identity is controlled by VeriSign, not QSpace. The PrimeHost case study is also an example of this type of relationship, and the Wells Fargo buyers fall into this category.

A customer transaction is defined as one that involves a user with some type of relationship with a provider. The merchants in the Wells Fargo case study are customers, as well as those of Diamond Shamrock and Mellon Bank. There are signed agreements between these parties, but the provider does have the option of revoking a certificate if a customer fails to meet his or her responsibilities.

An employee transaction is between an employer and his or her employees. This situation gives the most control to the provider, because the designation of the employee is defined by the employer, and the employer has complete control over the issuance and revocation of certificates. Just as an employee would lose his or her employee badge and card keys, he or she would also lose his or her certificate if he or she left the company. The USWeb case study is a good example of this type of transaction.

The primary difference between a partner and a customer transaction is equality of control. A partner can be either an EDI trading partner, a supplier, or someone with whom a company is working jointly to develop a product or service. In this instance, the provider might not have control over the issuance and revocation of the certificate, because it might be used with other parties. Size can often change this: Very large companies might actually issue certificates for the express purpose of establishing secure, authenticated communication with their suppliers. In this instance, the provider would have control over issuance and revocation, but this is an exception to the standard usage. A good example of this type of usage is the NetDox case study. NetDox offers a service to companies, but the companies communicating do not have control over the certificates used in the transaction.

The relationships between the transacting parties are useful pointers to the type of certificate that a company should use. A good exercise for a business considering the use of public key cryptography is to draw out the transaction flow and identify all parties involved, what happens at each step, and what the risks are for each of the steps. For each of these charts, be sure to include an initialization step; this step is the setting up of the relationship between the parties (if applicable), as well as the service steps, where customers make inquiries about status of transactions. The steps should include what happens in the background as well as the visible steps.

Some transactions include a relationship; others are "walk-in" transactions. A buyer purchasing a book from an online bookstore is a good example of a transaction that does not require the establishment of a relationship. Visiting a web site they found through a search engine is a good example of the casual relationship.

Figure 12-1

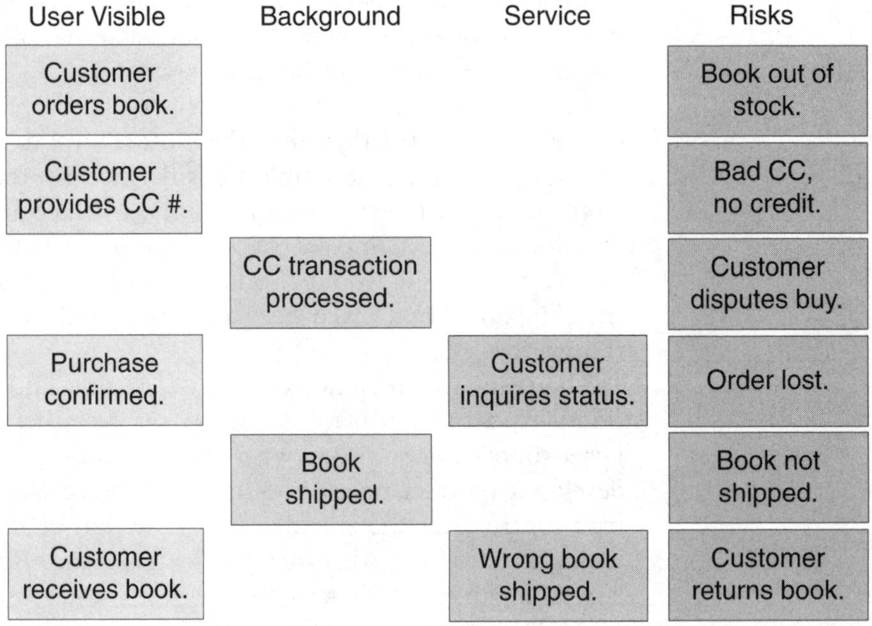

User Visible	Background	Service	Risks
Customer orders book.			Book out of stock.
Customer provides CC #.			Bad CC, no credit.
	CC transaction processed.		Customer disputes buy.
Purchase confirmed.		Customer inquires status.	Order lost.
	Book shipped.		Book not shipped.
Customer receives book.		Wrong book shipped.	Customer returns book.

As you can see in Figure 12-1, the risks are low. This is not the case with high-value or high-risk transactions. The higher the risk, the more critical the policies and procedures. For each diagram, a list should be made of the actions that can be taken to avoid the risk listed, and what can be done to deal with the risk, if the worst case should happen. Each risk-management list should include what can be done to prevent the risk being realized, detect its occurrence, contain it, and recover from it. Figure 12-2 is an example of that chart, using the example from Figure 12-1.

Figure 12-2

Risks	Prevent	Detect	Contain/Recover
Book out of stock.	List only books in stock.	On-Line inventory query.	Book out of stock.
Bad CC, no credit.	Check list of problem buyers.	On-Line authorization.	Donít ship book. Note buyer.
Customer disputes buy.	Send e-mail confirming buy.		Note buyer.
Order lost.	Quality assurance.	Automated order audit.	Give free shipping.
Book not shipped.	Quality assurance.	Automated ship audit.	Give free shipping.
Customer returns book.	Send e-mail confirming buy.		

Although many of these are not security events or security-related risks, their simplicity makes it easier to understand the way that the charts might work. A few trends emerge from this chart: Keeping a list of problem buyers could be useful, and QA can help avoid procedural problems. The next step is to evaluate the severity of the risk. If the risk is low, then the costs of implementing the prevention/detection mechanisms might not be worthwhile. These charts should not be static; they should be re-evaluated on a regular basis. Perhaps initially the bookstore owner might not think that customers ordering books, then denying the order, is a high risk, but examining audit records shows that it has become a significant source of loss. It might then be worthwhile to implement a repeat offender database to help ameliorate the risk. Appendix V shows the transactions and risks involved in home banking log-on to give a more detailed analysis of how this might work with a more complex situation. These charts can also be useful in developing a requirements document.

Hardware vs. Software

The business evaluation of hardware vs. software is driven by risk and costs. As the costs of hardware continue to decline, the cost element will decrease in importance. Hardware can substantially reduce the risk of internal fraud and prevent key compromise. For any company considering a medium- to high-risk usage of PKI, hardware on the server side should be strongly considered. The costs of implementing a hardware solution on the client side might still be too high, but most organizations deploying large-scale certification infrastructures can afford either a box or board solution for their servers.

Interoperability and Cross-Certification

Interoperability is mainly a matter of testing, but there is a business aspect to interoperability: cross-certification. Cross-certification allows different CAs to "trust" each other's certificates because they have confidence in each other's policies and procedures. This could become common among banks and other organizations with similar risk models. Unfortunately, today there is no standard for evaluating a CA's practices. Legislation or industry cooperation might change this, but today there is no easy way to determine if practices are similar. NetDox intends to provide an evaluation of the different classes of certificate and an evaluation of the strength of that certificate, but until CA evaluation becomes regularized, it must be done on a case-by-case basis.

In-House vs. Outsourcing

This issue is shared between technical and business concerns. The reason for the multiplication of certificates is related to logistics and risk. There is no standard for what a certificate means, and the degree of care that goes into verifying identity is markedly different between the various certificates issued. Some certificates simply promise that no one has asked for a certificate for that e-mail address, and that you have access to that e-mail account. Others go to great lengths to authenticate the applicant, even to the point of requiring physical presence for authentication, so that a passport or driver's license picture can be compared to the applicant. The logistics of in-person verification are much more difficult than an online application, but the risk will be lower, because the verification is more rigorous. Companies must decide if they want to manage certification services in-house or outsource it to a service provider.

There is a series of questions that can be used to help make the decision on how to handle this issue. The primary questions when deciding whether to host certificates in-house or outsource it to a third party are:

1. How much verification is necessary? Is the need to identify a person or corporation, or a relationship between my company and the certificate holder?

2. Do I need control over the issuance and revocation of the certificate?

3. Does my company want to manage the process and the implementation internally?

Figure 12-3 shows the decision points and their relationship to the available offerings:

Figure 12-3

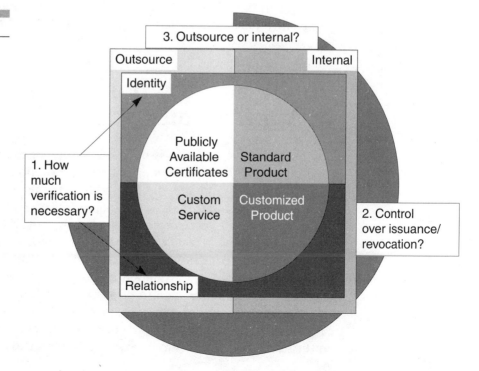

Questions one and three can help to determine which offering works for your company. Question two clarifies the matter further, if you don't know the answer to question three. The critical question is the first one: Whether the information used to verify a user is generic, identity-based information, or relationship/account-specific. If it is identity only, then either a publicly available cert or a standard product should meet a company's needs. If a company wants to outsource, then it can go with either a publicly available identity certificate or a custom service.

When possible, the use of a publicly available certificate is the least expensive option, because there will be no cost for infrastructure. With a generic public cert, the cost of the infrastructure is generally amortized over all the public certificates that are issued by that CA. If a publicly available cert is used, the company using that cert has no control over the issuance or the revocation of the certificate. This means that the certificate cannot be used to verify a relationship between an organization and the certificate holder, because control of the certificate lies with the CA and the cert holder. The organization must use other information to validate an account or relationship with the certificate holder. If a company needs control of the certificate, it must "own" its issuance. Many companies are going in this direction, which means that businesses and individuals will have many different certificates for different roles and relationships.

Public Key Cryptography in Applications

The business aspect of this issue is simply one of availability. Does the application that the organization plans to use support the use of public key cryptography and support the public key operations needed, such as CRL checking and certificate directory services? If it is not possible to use an off-the-shelf product for the support of public key cryptography, internal development costs can increase the funds necessary for implementation. Most companies today are using the functionality available in all popular browsers as the most common user interface for Internet solutions. All companies have to do work to integrate the use of public key cryptography with the business problem they want to solve, but the costs increase substantially if the development must be done not only on the server side, which is to be expected, but on the client side as well.

Key Recovery/Escrow

Most corporations have archiving needs for their data, including encrypted data. The ability to recover the data means that the keys used to encrypt it must be available to the archive restoration application. This requirement does not include ephemeral encryption, which is used interactively but not stored. It should be noted that data that uses SSL for privacy is not generally stored encrypted on the disk of the server or on the user's system, if they save the data to disk. Key escrow or recovery is rarely necessary from a business standpoint for this type of transaction. Where key escrow is especially useful is for data that is stored encrypted. This might be a requirement for a company's business application, but it will rarely relate to communication; usually it will only relate to storage. Organizations should examine the costs associated with key escrow and weigh those costs against its benefits. A more thorny issue is one of audit: How do you prove that a digital signature is valid without at least the signer's certificate and public key? What about expired keys? Companies planning public key deployments that include the storage of encrypted data should keep these questions in mind.

Security Policies and Procedures

The business ramifications of inadequate security policies and procedures are severe. If the CA system is not adequately protected, the entire certificate hierarchy is compromised. If this were to happen, not only would a company lose its users' confidence, but it would also have the difficult operational task of reissuing certificates with a new root key. To avoid this problem, companies should be very careful in the formulation of their policies and procedures related to their secured systems that provide data to users, and especially so with their CA systems.

In addition to the technical details of the policies and procedures, organizations should consider the use of bonding and insurance to mitigate the potential losses from compromised keys. Strong employee screening should be done to avoid problems of internal fraud and close records kept of all activities related to the secured systems. Where possible, automated logging and regular review of those logs should be done by a well-trusted employee. The consequences of violating the policies and procedures should be clearly stated in either the company's general employee agreement, or in a special agreement developed for the employees managing the CA system and services.

Certificate Holder Responsibility

Companies deploying systems that use public key encryption should make a strong effort to educate their users on the importance of key hygiene. This can help to ameliorate the risks from compromised keys, not only making the system more secure, but reducing the costs associated with revocation and reissuance of certificates due to lost keys. This can be done through online tutorials, booklets, or actual training classes if the risk is high. Users do not understand the possible ways that their systems could be compromised, nor do they grasp the ramifications of lost keys. As more systems are deployed, this issue will become less critical, but until there is a general understanding of these issues among the general populace, companies should make sure that their users know how to protect their private keys.

13

Developing Requirements

Several of the companies interviewed for the product section commented that companies rarely know what they need for infrastructure. An organization needs to decide just what it needs before starting to shop for a solution. Unfortunately, the complexity and large number of potential components and usage make this requirements document more complex than a standard requirements document. There are three aspects to the requirements that a company must develop to assist with the choice of solutions: technology, business, and operational (legal and policy). Generally, the business and operational aspects should drive the selection from available technology and solutions, not the other way around. Many companies ignore this step and approach companies with ill-formed plans to "do something" to solve the problem of authentication.

Product or Service?

One of the first things that a company needs to decide is whether to go with a product or service. The diagram and questions in the section *In-House vs. Outsourcing* in the previous chapter can help in making this decision. The requirements for a company that is outsourcing might be very different from those of a company that is planning to manage its own CA services. For example, the organization that is outsourcing need only list the requirements for availability, practices, and identity verification. If the project is done in-house, the staff that will manage the system, the types of hardware and software, the training, and development of specialized registration requirements must all be planned.

Understanding Requirements

To understand the requirements for the product or service, a company must first understand the transaction flow and all its component parts, as discussed in the previous chapter. After understanding the flow, including the background and service components, the risks must be articulated. Figure 13-1 is a simple example of a transaction flow for a company that is maintaining its own CA for access to confidential company data.

Figure 13-1

User Visible	Background	Service	Risks
Request certificate.	CA logs request.	Questions about applying.	CA down.
Identity verified.	Compares info to db.	Questions/ problems.	Fraudulent applicant.
Certificate issued	Cert generated and logged.	Questions about install.	User's key compromised.
Certificate used for access.	Cert status checked.	Questions about usage.	User's key compromised.
Certificate expires.	Cert expired.	Questions about renewal.	User not notified.
Certificate renewed.	Cert re-issued.	Questions about process.	Fraudulent renewer.

In Figure 13-1 there is only one component listed for each step, but your flow might be much more complex. When you create these charts, each box should then be explained in detail, including the requirements and the process required for each. For example, the identity verification for your organization might include multiple steps, such as in-person verification, telephone calls, or confirmation messages. If a registration authority (RA) is used, additional steps need to be inserted in the chart for the CA/RA handshakes for requesting actions to be taken.

The type of application will be intimately related to the requirements, and a completely separate chart should be done for the actual application that uses the certs, stepping through each function that a user can perform and the risks associated with each. After these two charts have been completed, the risk-management chart should be created (see Figure 13-2).

Figure 13-2 shows the things that can be done to mitigate risk. Once again, it is very simplistic, but it can help to identify characteristics that your company requires for certification. As each characteristic is noted, it should be listed under the appropriate functional component. The primary functional components match the tasks of a CA and the operational characteristics. These include:

Figure 13-2

Risks	Prevent	Detect	Contain/Recover
CA down.	Fault-tolerant or distributed.	Monitor systems.	Hot spare.
Fraudulent applicant.	Applicant screening.	Multi-step confirmations.	Hold on ?able applicants.
User's key compromised.	Smart cards.	Velocity/ host usage.	Revoke or suspend.
User's key compromised.	Education about security.	Velocity/ usage logs.	Revoke and re-issue.
User not notified.	Automatic notification.	Auto search of cert db.	Issue new cert.
Fraudulent renewer.	Re-verify identity.	Check of log for hosts.	Hold on ?able applicants.

- Certificate application requests: What are the different ways that people will need to be able to apply for certificates? E-mail? Web? In person?

- Identity verification: This should include requirements for registration authority services, if required.

- Certificate issuance: This includes what algorithms are supported, the ability to do algorithm migration, requirements for key splitting, what application integration (loading of the certificate into a browser or e-mail package) mechanisms are supported, support for multiple certificate hierarchies, rule-based determination of certificate characteristics or attributes, and what provisions are included for key and certificate generation/storage mechanisms, such as hardware systems/boards and smart-card support.

- Revocation and renewal: What are the mechanisms needed for automatic notification of certificate expiration, revocation, and processes for renewal?

- Interfaces: If there is a need to write applications that extract data or interface to different parts of the system, there need to be application programming interfaces.

- Standards support: What standards need to be supported?

For the company planning to operate its own service, the platforms that the products support are also important.

The way that certificates are managed is an important part of the usability and accountability of the system. These characteristics generally deal with the way certificates and/or their statuses are handled after issuance. Certificate management characteristics should include:

- Key escrow/recovery: What does your company need?

- Archiving: What are the requirements for archiving? Many organizations are regulated by governments that have archiving requirements.

- Logging: What information needs to be logged about requests and actions taken for a particular applicant or certificate?

- Directory services: What mechanisms are needed for looking up certificates? Does this need to be limited to a particular group?

- Certificate Revocation Lists (CRLs): How often do revocation lists need to be generated? What mechanisms are needed for using them? What applications need to support a particular product or service's revocation list mechanisms?

- Exportability: Does your company have international requirements? Does the company have an exportable version of the product, if needed? What assistance can it provide in getting export approval, if export is required?

Operational characteristics dictate the day-to-day running of the CA, and its links into the rest of the organization. If you are using a service, these become questions that the CA needs to answer. If you are hosting the CA internally, they become items that the product must provide or allow to be added. Operational considerations should include:

- Availability: What is needed with regards to availability? Does the CA need to be able to continue running during maintenance? What is acceptable downtime for the services provided?

- Performance and capacity: Does a product or service provide the performance required by your application? Can it handle the number of certificates that need to be issued?

- Security policies and procedures: What are your requirements for policies and procedures? If it is a service, can the service provider meet them? If it is for a product, does the product allow for or enable those policies and procedures? Good examples of these are auditing requirements and the use of security tokens or smart cards for administrative access.

- Insurance and bonding: Is liability insurance available for CAs using a product or service? If the company provides a service, are operators bonded?

- Auditing and monitoring: For the product, what tools are available to assist with this task? If the company provides a service, what auditing and monitoring is provided? What QA functions are needed to support practices?

- Reporting and alarms: What reports on activity does the product or service provide? Do those reports meet the needs of the organization? Are there any mechanisms for alerting staff to problems, such as beeping a system manager or security officer if needed?

- Customer service: Does the product have an interface for customer service? What customer service does the service provider offer? This area can be critical to a deployment success, and requirements should be clearly stated.

- Product service and support: What commitments does your company need for product problems? This is very important for mission-critical applications that rely on a CA product. If using a service with a registration authority, be sure to specify these needs as well.

- Training and documentation: This will be especially important for early deployments. If a vendor or provider already has training and documentation that will meet the needs of your organization, this will save the time and expense of developing it.

- Cross-certification and interoperability: What other CAs might be used in this environment, and what are the requirements for interoperability between certificates issued from different CAs?

Futures

Public key infrastructure is in its infancy and, like any small child, it can outgrow its clothes very quickly. When evaluating products and services, make sure that the vendor's planned futures match your anticipated needs. If possible, get any critical item in writing, so that you do not find yourself in the situation of needing something next quarter that your vendor plans to do next year.

Budget

When evaluating products vs. services and the costs associated with both, don't just look at the cost of the CA product or service. There are ancillary costs that should be included in the equation. These include staff training, additional hours or staff for support functions, security policy and procedure development, and the costs of drafting agreements and a CPS.

You can spend as much or little as you want for CA products and services, but be careful of being penny-wise and pound-foolish. A common failing in this area is for a company to decide that they can't afford server crypto hardware. Companies that are deploying systems themselves should strongly consider the use of hardware on their CA system, at least for storing the CA's root key. Crypto hardware has come down in price as the market expands, and should continue to do so.

Pricing

There are three different pricing models for both products and services:

- Per certificate pricing: A base charge for the service or product, and a fixed fee (which might go down with increased volume) per certificate.
- Tiered pricing: Layered pricing based on the number of certificates to be issued, sometimes with the top tier being unlimited.
- Flat pricing: A single cost, regardless of the number of certificates to be issued.

A product that might seem quite inexpensive can become quite costly when the potential number of certificates is included in the costs. Product service costs usually follow the model used for product pricing as a percentage of the cost of the product. Be sure to include expected volumes in your requirements, and get firm quotes for the initial and annual costs.

Requirements Document Contents

The actual format of the requirements document is less important than its content. Some companies already have standard requirements document formats that can easily be adapted to stating the requirements for CA products and services. What is important is to make sure to include the transaction flows and risk assessment diagrams and the text that describes each segment. Knowing how a company intends to use the certificates, and the degrees of risk, can help product and service companies suggest the optimal solution. The functional, management, and operational requirements that were developed from these charts should also be listed. If possible, these requirements should be presented in both prose and a concise tabular format.

Evaluation

Once a company has developed a requirements document, they should develop a plan for evaluation. This should include demonstrations, references, and actual tests of required interoperability. Don't forget to include in the evaluation the applications that must use these certificates. There are some problems that exist with certain applications and certificates from different CAs. Be sure that any evaluation includes a testing phase, where you can assure yourself that the application works with the CA product or service of choice. References can be very helpful in determining how well a vendor works with its customers. Be sure to get references from both new customers and early customers, because there might be differences in experience as an organization matures.

Vendor Review

The companies that offer products which utilize public key technology are very diverse and sometimes not well known. This section attempts to provide the reader with a snapshot of the existing vendors. It is certain that vendors have been missed. There will be a web site associated with this book that will have a more complete list. Check http://www.mcgraw-hill.com to find this book's web site and a more complete list. Readers may also refer to the online resources listed in Appendix IV for additional lists.

Products listed are only public key-based products. Many of the companies listed offer products other than public key-enabled products, but those products are not listed in this book. In addition to the detailed section on CA vendors, lists are provided for many application vendors that support public key. Where there are a very large number of products that are reasonably similar (such as web servers, web browsers, and S/MIME e-mail applications), only the company's name, address, telephone, and web site are listed. To avoid appearance of preference or favoritism, all companies are listed in alphabetical order.

CHAPTER 14

CA Products and Services

The first set of products are infrastructure applications, which are products and services that enable the binding of a certificate to a key pair, or help to manage certificates. These can come in the form of both products (which a company can purchase) and services (either customized or general purpose). There are three ways for a company to establish the infrastructure necessary to incorporate public key cryptography into its applications. It can:

- Use publicly available certificates in its applications.
- Buy a product that allows it to issue and manage certificates.
- Contract with a firm to run such a service for it.

Using publicly available certificates means that a company need only point to the site where a customer can get a cert and have the application recognize those certificates. Use of a software or hardware product to create and manage certificates means that the organization is responsible for the entire process. Services mean that someone else provides certification and certificate management as an outsourced service. As discussed in the previous section, there are advantages and disadvantages to each of these approaches.

The companies listed in this chapter offer products and services that allow an organization to use one of these three approaches to solve the problem of certification. Many of the companies listed in this chapter provide solutions to more than one of the above-listed approaches. When a company is looking for a vendor, it should develop the requirements document listed in the previous section prior to shopping for the product, and use this list to determine which approach best fits its needs.

Atalla Corporation

2304 Zanker Road
  San Jose, CA 95131
  (408) 435-5715 (phone)
  (408) 435-1116 (fax)
  http://www.atalla.com

Company Background Atalla Corporation is a leader in providing security technology using dedicated, specialized hardware. Founded in 1972 and acquired by Tandem Computers in 1987, Atalla brings more than 25 years of experience to the area of electronic commerce security. Atalla pioneered the concept of an end-to-end security architecture for the banking industry, and today is the leading provider of hardware security for financial institutions. In fact, an estimated 70 percent of all banking ATM transactions in the USA are routed through specialized Atalla hardware security modules. Today, Atalla's new Internet Security Processor products bring the same level of transparent, online transaction security to the Internet that previously had only been available through private payment networks such as the ATM, POS, and EFT networks.

Products   Atalla provides a full range of Internet Security Processor (ISP) products for electronic commerce applications. These products are available in a PCI expansion card form factor, and use specialized semiconductor technology and parallel processing techniques to accelerate RSA public key operations and protect private keys.

Atalla PayMaster/PCI ISP:* This product provides all the strong encryption technology required for SET payment processing. It offloads SET cryptographic tasks from the processor and functions as a security coprocessor for merchant or payment gateway applications. It manages keys using secure, high-performance hardware, and supports key lengths up to 2,048 bits. The Atalla PayMaster/PCI ISP provides RSA and DES acceleration, and complies with FIPS 140-1 Level 3 requirements. It is available for export. List price is $4,995 USD.

Atalla SignMaster ISP: This product creates and verifies digital signatures, generates key pairs and digital certificates, and provides hashing of messages for certificate authority applications. It brings the most advanced security features and fastest processing speed to CA applications. It physically and logically isolates cryptographic functions from the server system application, ensuring the integrity of data, keys, and algorithms. It is available as a stand-alone system that provides a full range of physical security features and is FIPS 140-1 Level 3 compliant. It is available for export. The list price is $12,500 USD. The Atalla SignMaster ISP is also available as a PCI expansion card. It is priced at $5,000 USD.

Atalla WebSafe2/PCI ISP: This product adds a dedicated hardware encryption engine to an NT 4.0- or UNIX-based server, and provides speedy, secure key management, encryption/decryption, and certificate management (using DES, RSA, and DSS) in a very cost-effective manner. The Atalla WebSafe2 manages and protects cryptographic keys using specialized hardware, and supports key lengths of up to 2,048 bits for public key operations and from 40 to 128 for symmetric-key operations. It is also FIPS 140-1 Level 3 compliant. It is designed to handle high-volume encryption processing, PEM, and EDI applications. The list price for the

Atalla WebSafe2/PCI product is $5,000 USD. The Atalla WebSafe2 product is also available as a PC chassis-based product that attaches via Ethernet to any open system platform. It is priced at $12,500 USD.

Key Differentiators   Atalla designs its own security processor chips for data encryption known as the NetArmor chip. These chips are fabricated by VLSI Technology, Inc. and integrate a complete data-encryption solution on a single chip ready for design-in on computer and set-top motherboards, PCI expansion cards, and PCMCIA cards. AtallaUs PCI products are rated at more than 50 RSA operations per second using a 1,024-bit key, and offload the burden of public key processing from the host processor. They also store and manage private keys in keys in FIPS 140-1 Level 3 (tamper-resistant) compliant hardware.

Futures   Atalla is focused on high-performance cryptography, and designs its own semiconductor technology for security applications. Smart-card technology, high-performance high-volume encryption processing using 4,096-bit key lengths, and the ability to securely load proprietary and new standard algorithms into its semiconductor technology are areas of expertise and product futures.

List of Major Partners/Customers   More than 1,250 financial institutions use Atalla technology today to secure financial transactions. Here are a few customers that use Atalla products: ANZ Bank, Bank of America, Citicorp, Banc One Corp., Bank of Boston, Chase Bank, First Interstate Bank, First National, Bank of Chicago, First Union Bank, Home Savings, K-mart, MasterCard, NationsBank, Safeway, Star Systems, and Wells Fargo Bank.

BBN Corporation

150 Cambridge Park Drive
   Cambridge, MA 02140
   (800) 295-7897
   (617) 873-4086
   http://www.bbn.com
   E-mail: netsec@bbn.com

Company Background   BBN Corporation (NYSE:BBN), headquartered in Cambridge, MA, is a leading provider of internetworking services for businesses and organizations. BBN provides companies of all sizes with reliable Internet access services, remote access services, network security, web site development and hosting, international connectivity, and electronic commerce and systems integration services to use the Internet effectively for business. BBN's revenue for the nine-month period ended March 31, 1997 was $254 million. See BBN's web site at http://www.bbn.com for more information.

BBN's Systems & Technologies business unit supports BBN's leadership role in internetworking by developing advanced networking technologies and related Internet and intranetworking applications. These applications include public key infrastructure (PKI) products.

Products BBN offers a family of security products and services to support organizations creating Internet- and intranet-based business solutions that integrate digital certificate and digital signature capabilities. The BBN certificate management systems are targeted to those organizations (commercial and government) to which high assurance of the certificate authority is important.

BBN Enterprise CMS: This is a comprehensive, high assurance, scalable, distributed RSA- and DSA-based certificate management system. System components include SafeKeyper Registar (the primary interface to all client applications for certificate requests), SafeKeyper Adjuster (a customizable, automated rule engine that reviews and modifies certificate requests according to a specific rule set), and SafeKeyper Signer (see below). BBN Enterprise CMS addresses the needs of those organizations that plan to issue and manage large numbers of certificates (100,000 or more). Price: $249,900 with yearly maintenance fees. This is a one-time license fee with no per-certificate or per-user fees. BBN also offers a Pilot version of this system to enable organizations to conduct a trial. The price and configuration of the pilot system varies depending on the specific pilot requirements.

BBN Compact CMS: This product is designed for organizations requiring user-token support and centralized, local control over the certificate issuance and management process. It combines the stand-alone design of the BBN NSA CAW with the flexibility to support a wide range of user PCMCIA tokens, certificate formats, and digital signature algorithms. The Compact CMS is targeted to meet the needs of both the government and commercial marketplace where the environment requires: centralized certificate management, issuance and management of certificates in low volumes, and token initialization and management with interoperability with RSA-algorithm—based certificate hierarchies. Price: $25,000, directly from BBN.

BBN NSA Certificate Authority Workstation (CAW): This product was developed for use by the U.S. Department of Defense MISSI program. The CAW is a stand-alone Compartmented Mode Workstation (CMW)—based system capable of the entire range of user registration and certificate management activities, including Fortezza PCMCIA cryptographic card initialization, DSA and KEA key pair generation, CA hierarchy management, X.500 directory system management, and operating system audit support. The CAW is a centralized X.509 certificate, key-generation, and token-initialization system, designed for higher assurance but lower throughput environments than the Enterprise CMS. The primary market for this system is government programs like the Defense Message System. Price: $16,400. It is available through the Air Force DMS contract, NSA IDIQ, or direct from BBN.

BBN SafeKeyper Signer: This security device supports high-assurance digital signature applications that require verification of the author's signature and data integrity. The Signer unit generates and stores cryptographic keys, protecting them from disclosure, misuse, or loss. These keys, particularly the private component of a public key pair, can be used to sign digital documents, thereby guaranteeing both the source of material and its integrity. The SafeKeyper Signer is an integral component of the SafeKeyper Enterprise CMS, protecting the private keys of the certificate authority. It provides certificate signing and managing functionality for secure e-mail, web browsers and servers, and certificate support for IP security protocols. In addition, the appropriate application software can be integrated with the Signer to offer digital signature and authentication capabilities such as software license distribution/usage control, electronic funds transfer, network and host sign-on authorization, and the detection of tampering with, or forgery of, computer-based information. Price: $9,900. A number of maintenance/support options are also offered.

BBN offers a range of professional services to support organizations as they integrate the use of digital certificates into their applications.

Key Differentiators   *BBN Safekeyper Signer:* BBN Safekeyper Signer is a hardware number generator; the private component of a key pair never leaves the unit in cleartext form. Tamper resistance is provided by having the activation of unit signing controlled by one or more Cryptographic Ignition Keys (CIKs).

BBN CAW: The CAW offers high availability and key loss protection. There are 150+ CAWs deployed worldwide. The CAW is a stand-alone system, the only MISSI-compliant CA system that programs Fortezza cards.

Enterprise CMS: This system can operate up to 10 CAs, offers the ability to administer certificates either centrally or distributed and in a hierarchical or flat administration structure, is scalable, permits plug-and-play customization, and has no fee-per-certificate or per-user pricing philosophy. The system provides configurability of policies and process.

Compact CMS: This system is a lower-cost version of Enterprise CMS.

List of Major Partners/Customers   BBN's customers include banks, mutual funds agencies, brokerages, and insurance companies. Liberty Financial, a diversified asset management organization, is the only customer BBN can publicly disclose at this time. BBN has also sold approximately 200 SafeKeyper Signer units for a wide variety of applications, from code signing and software licensing to certificate signing. In the government market, BBN is supplying the NSA CAW to major programs like the Defense Message System.

Future Directions   BBN's future includes expanded token management support, including smart cards; additional certificate profiles such as Netscape, PKIX, and FEDPKI; support for additional platforms, such as Windows NT; additional certificate management interfaces; enhancements to SafeKeyper Signer to increase speed; additional browser support; expanded cross-certification support; and additional algorithms, such as ECDSA.

CertCo

55 Broad Street - Suite 22
  New York, NY 10004
  (212) 709-8900 (voice)
  (212) 709-6754 (fax)
  http://www.certco.com

Company Background   CertCo was founded to enable banks and other financial institutions to provide a trustworthy infrastructure capable of supporting large-scale, international, secure electronic commerce. In December 1996, CertCo was spun out of Bankers Trust, the seventh largest U.S. bank and the world's fourth largest clearer of money. The spin-off coincided with completion of a $30 million financing agreement. Investors included Marsh & McLennan Risk Capital Holdings, Addison Fischer, members of the Tisch family, and other undisclosed financial institutions and technology investors. All offered business contributions as well as funding. Bankers Trust retains an equity interest.

CertCo believes that no single technology company can meet all the challenges of assuring secure and reliable transactions over the Internet. Chips, computers, smart cards, software, and networks must work seamlessly together. Therefore, CertCo has assembled a staff made up of leading professionals in cryptography, risk management, law, technology, and banking, and is developing strategic alliances with other companies in relevant business areas.

Products   *RelyAble CA Product Group:* RelyAble CA enables financial institutions and other substantial entities to provide electronic commerce assurance services to their customers. To facilitate such services, CertCo provides the product and service suites for certification; they also provide certificate repository services. RelyAble CA enables a certifier to manage its risk by clearly defining and assessing the risk, minimizing it to the greatest extent practicable, and spreading the residual risk among similarly situated risk bearers so that insuring against a catastrophic loss is reduced to a moderate, predictable expense.

Microcommerce Product Group: A payment system that enables bank customers to make fast and secure electronic payments easily over the Internet at an extremely low cost per transaction.

Key Differentiators   To help minimize a certifier's risk, CertCo's token-based Multi-Step Signing technology heightens security by creating a certifier's digital signatures through joint action of a defined group, each of which holds a fragment of a private key. To create a digital signature, all or a prescribed quorum of private key holders must act, but without ever bringing their private key fragments together in one place. Token-based Multi-Step Signing enables distributed security capabilities and eliminates the possibility of a single point of failure.

Cylink Corporation

910 Hermosa Court
   Sunnyvale, CA 94086
   (408) 735-5800 (voice)
   (408) 735-6643 (fax)
   http://www.cylink.com
   Cylink's Fax-on-Demand System:

USA and Canada: (800) 735-6614
All other countries: (415) 596-4499

Company Background   Cylink Corporation (NASDAQ: CYLK), founded in 1984, is a recognized leader of information security solutions, providing a comprehensive portfolio of public key cryptographic hardware and software products. Cylink recently had a successful IPO on February 15, 1996. Cylink's products enable secure data transmissions over LANs, WANs, public packet-switched networks such as the Internet, intranet, ATM, and frame relay networks. Cylink's information security products incorporate encryption security technologies based on digital signatures and certificates, public key cryptography, and sophisticated data-encryption algorithms. Cylink is helping encryption hardware and software vendors export strong encryption technology by providing companies with the design for its government-approved key recovery mechanism, CyKey. Cylink also provides security training and consultation.

Cylink is headquartered in Sunnyvale, CA, with offices, distributors, and customer support worldwide. Cylink's U.S. branch offices are located in Los Angeles, Denver, Marietta, GA, Schaumburg, IL, Wood Dale, IL, Kansas City, Jersey City, Rye, NH, Irving, TX, Layton, UT, and Vienna, VA. Cylink's international offices are located in Beijing, England, New Dehli, Karachi, Moscow, and Singapore. Cylink customers include Fortune 500 companies, multi-national financial institutions, agribusiness, construction, petro-chemical, and U.S. and international government agencies.

Products   The SecureAccess product line enables telecommuters, mobile workers, consultants, and business partners to access the corporate network securely.

SecureGate Remote Access Server (serial): This product is a remote-access security server that secures dial-in access to the corporate network. It provides cryptographic authentication using X.509 certificates, privacy for data transmission with the Data Encryption Standard (DES), complete audit records of all call attempts, and departmental call accounting. It can scale up to hundreds of thousands of callers. SecureGate Server will support Triple DES by the end of June.

SecureGate-IP: This product enables the road warrior, mobile worker, or telecommuter to connect securely into the enterprise via the Internet. Dialing into the corporate LAN via an independent ISP, the remote client can be authenticated and can securely access corporate information. The SecureGate IP is a server-based IP gateway integrating the remote-access features of the existing SecureGate products and the use of certificate-based encrypted IP traffic. The SecureGate IP will provide an end-to-end secure IP session between the remote user and the SecureGate Server. It provides cryptographic authentication using X.509 certificates, privacy for data transmission with the DES, complete audit records of all call attempts, and departmental call accounting. It can scale up to hundreds of thousands of callers.

SecureTraveler for Windows: This product is a software security solution for telecommuters and road warriors who need to share critical information over open, public-enterprise remote-access networks. As part of Cylink's SecureAccess System, SecureTraveler for Windows is installed in the remote PC. The SecureTraveler for Windows is a security driver for Microsoft Windows that provides authentication and encryption using X.509 certificates, public key cryptography, and DES or a Cylink exportable encryption algorithm. It works transparently with all Windows communications applications. SecureTraveler for Windows will support Triple DES by the end of June.

SecurePocket Traveler: This is a small RS232 encryption unit that installs between any host and modem. It will authenticate and encrypt calls from other SecurePocket Travelers, calls from SecureTraveler for Windows, and calls into the SecureGate Server. Because it uses X.509 certificates and public key encryption, thousands of units can be in use at one time.

TrustPoint Data: This is a Windows application that provides file encryption and digital signatures. It protects documents stored on portable computers during e-mail transmissions, and allows the user to verify the author and integrity of signed documents. TrustPoint Data is easy to use, with drag-and-drop security and automatic e-mail and browser integration. TrustPoint Data will be available for shipment in late 1997.

Partners/Customers   Cylink's business partners include the Cisco Systems, Mitsui, GTE Government Systems, JavaSoft/Sun Microsystems, and Cygnus. Cylink customers include S.W.I.F.T., AT&T, Boeing, the U.S. Army, and Concert (a joint venture between MCI and British Telecom).

Key Differentiators   Over the past 13 years, Cylink has built multiple cryptographic and public key hardware and software solutions that have never been breached. In the future, Cylink plans to leverage its cryptographic and public key assets from network through application and management layers for end-to-end information security solutions.

Cylink is working to expand into vertical industries as we have done with the banking and telecommunications industries.

Entrust Technologies Inc.

2 Constellation Crescent, 4th Floor
   Nepean, Ontario
   CANADA
   K2G 5J9
   (919) 992-5525 (USA)
   (613) 765-5607 (Canada)
   (613) 765-3520 (fax)
   http://www.entrust.com

Company Background In response to the need for data security software for corporate enterprises, Northern Telecom (Nortel) established Nortel Secure Networks in 1993. In 1996, Nortel spun out Nortel Secure Networks as a majority-owned subsidiary called Entrust Technologies Inc. Entrust Technologies' Entrust family of software products is designed to provide customers with public key infrastructures and technologies, and helps guarantee privacy and authenticity of data communications for corporate networks, intranets, and the Internet. Entrust Technologies has 78 employees with offices in Ottawa, Ontario, New York, California, North Carolina, and the United Kingdom. In 1996, Entrust software received the *InfoSecurity News* Readers' Trust Award and was named "Editor's Choice" by *Network Computing*.

Products *Entrust/Lite:* Entrust/Lite is a stand-alone workgroup CA tool designed for groups of up to 100 users. Entrust/Lite supports the same applications and platforms as the full Entrust, offering a seamless upgrade path from Entrust/Lite.

Entrust/Web CA: Entrust/Web CA enables organizations and individuals offering web-based services to act as their own certification authority (CA) and issue X.509 certificates to all parties with whom they do business over the Internet and intranets. With Entrust/Web CA, web site owners can convey sensitive information with confidence and positively identify who is accessing their servers.

Key Differentiators   As a public key security product, Entrust gives organizations a single security infrastructure to which all applications can connect for their security requirements. With Entrust, organizations administer security once for a broad range of applications—such as electronic mail, file transfer, and database transactions—rather than administering security separately for each individual application. The product family provides an integrated solution for data security enterprise-wide on Windows, Macintosh, and UNIX systems.

List of Major Partners/Customers   Entrust's many customers include Wall Street firms, government agencies, high-tech companies, and other corporations, including IBM, Hewlett-Packard, and Tandem.

GTE CyberTrust Solutions Incorporated

77 A Street
   Needham Heights, MA 02194-2892
   (800) 487-8788
   (617) 455-5031
   http://www.cybertrust.gte.com

Company Background   With revenues of more than $21 billion in 1996, GTE is one of the largest publicly held telecommunications companies in the world. In the U.S., GTE offers local and wireless service in 29 states, and long-distance service in all 50 states. GTE was the first among its peers to offer one-stop shopping for local, long-distance, and Internet access services. Outside the U.S., where GTE has operated for more than 40 years, the company serves over 6.5 million customers. GTE is also a leader in government and defense communications systems and equipment, directories and telecommunications-based information services, and aircraft-passenger telecommunications. Additional information about GTE can be found on the Internet at http://www.gte.com.

Products   *CyberTrust Certification Authority Product:* This CA product provides a complete digital certificate solution for organizations that wish to own and operate their own certification authority system, including application software with a license to issue digital certificates; system documentation; and operational training. All root keys are hardware-generated to ensure the highest levels of security. CyberTrust CA can be configured to generate digital certificates that comply with the X.509 Secure Sockets Layer (SSL) standards or the Secure Electronic Transactions (SET) protocol. The SSL certificates currently interoperate with the Microsoft Internet Explorer 4.0 and Netscape Navigator 3.0 browsers, and the Microsoft Internet Information Server, Netscape Enterprise Server, and the Open Market Secure Webserver.

CyberTrust Customer-Branded Service: This service is designed for companies seeking to outsource their certificate management system while still maintaining control of who receives certificates. It enables customers to issue digital certificates under their own brand through CyberTrust's proven, highly reliable certificate-management system. A web-based interface is used for issuing and managing certificates. Both the interface and the certificates can be tailored to meet the specific needs of the customer and to promote the customer's brand. Certificate authorization, renewal, and revocation decisions can be managed from within the customer's organization through a web-based registration authority or by GTE using customer-provided authorization criteria. In either case, the customer controls who receives a branded certificate and the privileges associated with each certificate.

CyberTrust Partner Forum: This is a development and testing service for use by technology providers, systems integrators, and business partners. The Partner Forum provides a platform for interoperability testing of public key-enabled applications and digital certificate systems prior to release or implementation. Support includes X.509 standards and S/MIME standards, as well as the SET protocol, electronic payments, and access control.

Key Differentiators CyberTrust digital certificates can be configured to comply with either the SET protocol or X.509 standards, and feature customizable certificate extensions, customer branding options, and a web-based interface for certificate management. GTE offers a clear migration path for customers that elect to start with the CyberTrust Customer-Branded Service and migrate to the CyberTrust CA product at a later date.

With more than 15 years' ongoing experience developing and managing public key-based systems for the U.S. government, GTE is one of the world's most experienced providers of security solutions for electronic information. The GTE CyberTrust Certificate Management System operates from a highly secure facility, featuring redundant operating systems and Internet connections, multiple electronic, biometric, and physical security systems, and an experienced team of information security experts. In addition, all CyberTrust and customer-branded root keys are hardware-generated by an offline system to protect the root keys from potential network tampering.

Major Customers and Partners   GTE's major customers and partners include American Express, the Commonwealth of Massachusetts, CyberCash, CyberTrust Japan, Inc., GTE Telephone Operations, Maithean, Inc., MasterCard International, Microsoft, Netscape, Oracle Corporation, Security Dynamics, SPYRUS, Terisa Systems, VeriFone, Wells Fargo Bank, First Union Bank, GlobeSet, Hewlett-Packard, Mellon Bank, and V-One.

Additional information on customers and partners can be found on the Internet at http://www.cybertrust.gte.com/partnerforum/PFPartnersCustomers.html

What the Future Holds   Future projects for GTE include the development of systems to support corporate transactions (purchasing and Internet/ID access, time stamping, trust broker, key recovery), electronic payments, EDI, S/MIME-enabled certificates, and smart-card applications.

International Business Machines Corporation (IBM)

Electronic Payments & Certification Department
  Internet Division
  3190 Fairview Park Drive
  Falls Church, VA 22042
  (703) 205-5670 (voice)
  (703) 205-6151 (fax)
  http://ww.internet.ibm.com/commercepoint/registry

Company Background   International Business Machines (IBM), with revenues of almost $76 billion in 1996, is one of the world's largest providers of computer hardware, software, and services. The company makes a broad range of computers, including desktop, midrange, and mainframe computers and servers. Its peripheral products include printers and devices for networking, storage, and telecommunications. IBM also provides information technology services such as consulting and systems integration. Among its Internet operations are the online shopping mall World Avenue and the online information service infoMarket. IBM owns software pioneer Lotus, developer of the Lotus Notes messaging system. Nearly 60 percent of IBM's sales are to foreign customers.

Products   *IBM World Registry:* This is a complete public key infrastructure provided as a service. IBM World Registry is a web-based service operated by IBM for organizations requiring a certificate and key management infrastructure, but without CA and directory operations responsibilities. IBM is not in the business of issuing certificates directly to the general public. The features include IBM personal vault space (which provides individual web vault boxes, i.e., personal web space for user and CA applications, key storage and secure directory access, a tailorable web end-user interface for registration, key management, security, and cryptography service requests, and for modifying "personal" directory entries), a full suite of security and cryptography services including the ability for web access control, encryption, and digital signing to enable secure and trusted applications, and registration authority (RA) web user interface for registration and key management services. Policy publication, directory services, and support for multiple CAs are also included.

IBM Registry: This is a flexible public key infrastructure solution targeted toward meeting the needs of medium-to-large institutions (e.g., governments, Fortune 500 corporations) wishing to deploy a comprehensive PKI and security solution with robust administrative features. Highlights of the IBM Registry include comprehensive application programming interfaces (APIs) and the capability to allow third-party applications to take advantage of the security infrastructure and provide encryption and digital signature capabilities to users. Certificate information is maintained in a powerful, integrated Telstar X.500 directory. The Registry supports a broad scope of applications on multiple platforms; it supports multiple registration authorities' APIs, which support store-and-forward applications, such as e-mail forms, and online, real-time applications, such as remote access.

IBM Registry (SET Compliant): This is a software product that is intended to· fill the need for a certificate authority for secure use of credit and other payment cards over the Internet. With IBM Registry (SET Compliant), digital certificates enable a buyer to verify that a merchant is bonafide. It also enables the merchant to verify that the credit card is being used by the legitimate user. The public key infrastructure allows these digital certificates to be instantly exchanged, checked, and validated for every transaction made over the Internet. The mechanics of this operation are transparent, simple, and quick.

Key Differentiators   IBM has a clear focus on securing networked applications. Organizations demand strong security and a clear understanding of how their applications can be aided through the use of digital certificates. The Registry family provides that, and allows organizations to, through the use of public key encryption, extend trust to their relationships on the net. The Vault Deposit Server provides a secure web space that will allow the safe deposit and retrieval of keys, documents, etc. It can also act as a secure buffer for accessing data on legacy systems.

Netscape Communications

501 E. Middlefield Rd.
   Mountain View, CA 94043
   (415) 937-2555 (voice)
   (415) 528-4124 (fax)
   http://www.netscape.com

Company Background   Netscape Communications Corporation was founded in April of 1994 by Jim Clark and Marc Andreesson. They develop client, server, and commercial applications software for information exchange and commerce over the Internet and private IP networks. These products allow individuals and organizations to use the Internet for activities such as Internet commerce, catalog development, and information and service delivery. The company's software allows organizations to extend their internal information systems and enterprise applications to geographically dispersed facilities, remote offices, and mobile employees. Netscape is a publicly traded company. It is best known for its browser, Netscape Navigator, which is the most popular web browser in the world. Netscape also produces secure web servers that are discussed, along with their browser, in the next chapter.

Products   *Netscape Certificate Server:* This software product allows a company to create, sign, and manage standard-based public key certificates. Netscape Certificate Server sends updates about certificates to Netscape Directory Server via LDAP over SSL. Features include support for X.509v3, SSL, HTML, HTTP, PKCS, and LDAP, a built-in relational database, customizable policy templates, and remote administration.

VeriSign

1390 Shorebird Way
  Mountain View, CA 94043
  (415) 961-7500 (voice)
  (415) 961-7300 (fax)
  http://www.verisign.com
  http://digitalid.verisign.com (Digital ID Center)

Company Background   VeriSign was founded in April of 1995 as a spin-off of RSA Data Security. Its purpose is to provide public key—based certification services and products to enable applications to robustly authenticate users for both Internet and intranet usage. VeriSign is a privately held company. Its principal investors include Ameritech, AT&T, Bessemer Venture Partners, Cisco, Comcast, First Data Corp, Intuit, Kleiner Perkins Caufield & Byers, Merrill Lynch, Microsoft, Mitsubishi, RSA Data Security, Security Dynamics, Softbank, Reuters, and VISA International. VeriSign was the first CA to offer certificates that they call Digital IDs for both individuals and corporations over the Internet.

The goal of VeriSign's offerings is to give consumers, merchants, and corporations a trusted third party for certificate management, establishing the confidence necessary to conduct electronic commerce worldwide. The initial focus at VeriSign is on providing full-featured certificate authority solutions for customers, including complete technology, infrastructure, and practices capabilities. Companies can elect to either use VeriSign's public certificate services for individuals and corporations, or they can contract with VeriSign to build, run, and maintain customized services to meet their specific needs.

Products/Services   VeriSign's offerings are divided into three lines of business: public Digital ID Services (publicly available identity certificates), Private-Label Certificate Services (application/market or company-specific certs), and Certificate Management Products.

Class 1 Digital ID: The Class 1 Digital ID is a low-assurance public key certificate that simply verifies the user's e-mail address, but does not do more robust identity authentication. This type of certificate, available worldwide, is useful for casual web authentication and e-mail. A trial certificate of this type is available for free. The standard version includes the NetSureSM Protection Plan, which protects the user from up to $1,000 of loss due to theft or fraud. Standard version cost is $9.95/year.

Class 2 Digital ID: This product is a higher-assurance public key certificate with stronger measures added for identity verification via an online consumer database from Equifax and a physical mail back for verification. Additional assurance is gained through the use of a hardware unit to actually sign the certificate. This type of certificate is useful for low-risk transactions, software validation, e-mail, and online subscriptions. It includes $25,000 of NetSure Protection (insurance against misuse). The cost of this certificate is $19.95.

Class 3 Digital IDs for Individuals: This type of certificate provides important assurances of the identity of individual subscribers by requiring their personal (physical) appearance before an authorized agent (e.g., a notary) along with specific proofs of identity. These certificates will be available in late 1997.

Class 3 Digital IDs for Organizations: These public key certificates provide assurance of the existence and name of organizations. Validation includes review of authorization records provided by the applicant or third-party business databases (e.g., Dun and Bradstreet), and independent call-backs to the organization. They are used by VeriSign customers primarily for certain electronic commerce applications such as electronic banking, electronic data interchange (EDI), software validation, and membership-based on line services. Prices for Class 3 organizational Digital IDs start at $290.

Private Label Certificate Services: These services constitute a customized CA developed for a particular organization's authentication, branding, and security needs. They are appropriate for such companies as financial institutions or corporations that are planning high-volume deployments. Customizations include web pages, certificates and extensions, authorization process, practices, reporting, and management based on a company's own requirements. Prices range from $100,000 to $1 million+.

NOTE: VeriSign also provides a customized CA service for smaller organizations or organizations initiating pilot programs that starts at less than $5,000. This service allows full customization and includes the ability to maintain a company's own local registration authority for authentication.

SET Services: A customized CA service for financial services companies wishing to provide high-volume SET-compliant certificates to their constituents.

Certificate Management Products: Some companies might want to manage and maintain their own CA. For these companies, VeriSign will be releasing CA products in 1997.

Key Differentiators   VeriSign was first to market with all major categories of certificates: SSL server certs, SSL client certs, S/MIME certs,

SET test certs, Authenticode certs, and warranted certs (NetSure), and vow to continue to be first to market in the future. They have partnerships with key industry players including Microsoft, Cisco, Visa, Netscape, and AT&T. VeriSign published the industry's first Certification Practice Statement establishing the necessary standards for trust.

VeriSign has scalable systems that have been proven by the issuance of over one million certs in the first year of service, with systems scalable to tens or hundreds of millions. VeriSign has experienced practices, public key, and business teams, including industry-known individuals like Michael Baum, Warwick Ford, Peter Williams, Jim Brandt, and others. They are a provider of full-lifecycle solutions (technology, infrastructure, and practices).

Future Directions   Smart-card/token support, cross-certification, signing services, additional protocol support, additional cryptographic algorithm support, and additional application integration support.

List of Major Partners/Customers   VeriSign's major customers include America Online, Apple Computer, Banyan Systems, BBN, C2Net Software, Inc., Compuserve/Spry, Computer Software, Connect, ConnectSoft, Consensus Development, Coordinate.com, CyberCash, Deming Software, Epoch Networks, FTP Software, Frontier Technologies, Gemplus, GLACI, Gradient, Hiway Technologies, I/NET, IBM, Industrial Technology Research Institute (ITRI), Information Builders, Information Hyperlink, InterNIC, Iserver, Litronic, Lotus Development, Luckman Interactive, Maithean, Manufaktur, Microsoft, NetCentric, Netscape, Novell, O'Reilly & Associates, Open Market, OpenSoft, Oracle, Premenos, Process Software, PSINet, Quarterdeck, RSA Data Security, Schlumberger, Sirius, Spyglass, Stratus, TERISA Systems, Thawte Consulting, The Internet Factory, Transarc, Trintech, UUNet, V-One, VeriFone, VISA International, and Worldtalk.

Xcert Software Inc.

1001-701 West Georgia Street
   PO Box 10145, Pacific Centre
   Vancouver, BC
   V7Y 1C6
   (604) 640-6210 (voice)
   http://www.xcert.com

Company Background   Xcert Software Inc. was founded with the mission to provide a ubiquitous public key infrastructure (PKI) technology for the Internet. Xcert's products provide a platform for organizations and developers to seamlessly integrate open and standards-based PKI technology into existing and new applications for the Internet. Xcert's products enable organizations to:

- Act as their own certification authority and manage their own trust relationships without having to use a third-party certification service.

- Communicate and interoperate with unrelated certification authorities using standards-based cross-authentication, thereby extending business-to-business trust relationships to the Internet.

Xcert's founders are early implementers and proselytizers of public key cryptography. Xcert was incorporated in April 1996 as the vehicle to further the development of these technologies and derived products, and to take them into the marketplace. Xcert's first major investor was Addison Fischer, owner of Fischer International Systems Corporation and largest shareholder of Security Dynamics, which recently purchased RSA. Addison has been a convincing PKI advocate for decades.

Products   Xcert's basic offering includes secure directory services, PKI, and a suite of applications that leverage this technology. Xcert provides a powerful technology for building Internet security infrastructures by enabling organizations to seamlessly handle the authentication and distribution of enterprise resources.

Xcert Universal Database API (XUDA): XUDA is best seen as a toolkit or library of programs that isolates applications from the complexities of public key cryptography. It encapsulates secure database access and strong authentication via public key certificates, and employs SSL and Lightweight Directory Access Protocol (LDAP) to query remote databases using certificates presented during an SSL transaction. XUDA was built to use the cryptography of other vendors. This allows Xcert to provide customers with the cryptography of their choice, including all PKCS#11-compliant smart cards and hardware tokens.

Sentry CA: Sentry CA is a certification authority product that facilitates the creation, management, and widespread distribution of certificates for use with secure protocols such as SSL and secure applications such as S/MIME. This product enables validated time-stamped transactions for internal auditing or to meet external legal requirements. It includes support for X-Parse, an HTML-based scripting language, which allows web developers to quickly customize the Xcert Sentry line of products to create tailor-made secure web commerce applications. X-Parse provides the tools for the flexible integration of Sentry CA to a diverse range of secure commercial web applications, such as pay-per-view, online shopping, product ordering systems, software distribution, banking applications, and more.

Client Side XUDA: This tool is an *application programming interface* (API) for a client-side public key cryptography infrastructure. This infrastructure is based on XUDA and provides client-side public key cryptography (including CRLs), public key cryptography functionality for existing unmodified desk-top applications, multiple application interoperability for single key pairs, multiple certificate enrollment for single key pairs, application-independent hardware tokens, optional software emulation of hardware tokens, and full escrow key support.

Key Differentiators   Xcert is the first public key cryptography vendor to provide a full LDAP architecture and API. By leveraging their commitment to an open and ubiquitous directory service technology, Xcert's public key cryptography can interoperate with any other distributed, LDAP-based, public key cryptography in real time.

Xcert is the first vendor to offer cross-authentication, or *Online Certificate Status Protocol* (OCSP), as a standard feature of their public key cryptography. This means that certificate attributes (including certificate revocation) can be stored in a secure back-end database and queried by any distributed server during certificate verification.

List of Major Partners/Customers   Xcert's customers include Fischer International, C2Net, the Food and Drug Administration, Public Works and Government Services Canada, and the GE Research Center.

CHAPTER 15

Application and Toolkit Vendors

Because public key cryptography is just beginning to gain broad acceptance, the number of applications that incorporate this technology are relatively few. Because this is a fluid area, there are sure to be companies that have been omitted. For a more up-to-date list, see the book's web site.

The companies covered in this chapter fall into two broad categories: applications, and toolkits that can be used to build applications. Within the applications, there are three main types discussed: EDI over the Internet, S/MIME and web browsers, and servers.

E-Stamp Corporation

4009 Miranda Ave.
  Suite 225
  Palo Alto, CA 94304-1218
  (415) 843-8000
  http://www.estamp.com

Company Background   E-Stamp Corporation was founded in 1994 and is a privately held company. Its vision is to create a series of branded products and services to unite the physical and electronic communication needs of the worldwide information economy. The company has been working with the United States Postal Service (USPS) for several years on developing a PC postage solution that prints digital stamps. Digital stamps, represented by a bar code, can be printed onto a mailpiece using a PC and printer, and are functionally equivalent to traditional postage stamps.

Since 1847, when the USPS created the first postage stamp, only four companies have been granted the right to create U.S. postage. In 1997, E-Stamp expects to become the fifth company to secure this approval, and, shortly thereafter, E-Stamp will deploy a worldwide secure infrastructure for buying and selling digital postage over the Internet.

In the fourth quarter of 1997, E-Stamp plans to introduce its first product, code-named *E-Stamp SoHo,* a software and hardware combination aimed at addressing the needs of small businesses and home offices (SoHos). E-Stamp SoHo allows anyone with a PC and printer to purchase and download digital postage over the Internet and print USPS-approved digital stamps on envelopes, labels (for packages), and letters.

A key part of E-Stamp's business strategy is to broadly license its technology to software and hardware companies. Using the E-Stamp Postage

API, other companies can postage-enable their applications so that digital stamps can be printed simultaneously with the recipient address directly on letters, checks, invoices, and other documents. Revenues will be generated from recurring sources including subscription and digital postage refill transaction fees.

Products/Services Offered   *E-Stamp SoHo (code name):* This is E-Stamp's first product offering. It is a software and hardware solution that enables users to purchase digital postage quickly and easily via E-Stamp's Internet Post Office web site, using a variety of secure payment options. Once purchased, the postage is secured and stored in an electronic vault, called the E-Stamp Postal Security Device (PSD), attached to a PC. Users print the recipient address and USPS-approved digital stamps on envelopes, labels (for packages), and letters all in one quick and easy step. The computer not only queues a printing request, it also debits an account set up in the PSD. The PSD stores the amount of postage available to the user and the RSA private key used to digitally sign each stamp it dispenses. The PSD is a very secure, tamper-resistant device about the size of three stacked dimes. It attaches to the printer port of the PC, which deletes the private key and any remaining postage if it detects malicious tampering. The first version of E-Stamp SoHo is expected to be available by the end of 1997 pending USPS approval, and should cost less than $300. Initially, product availability will be limited to the San Francisco Bay Area and Washington, DC, but a nationwide rollout is expected in 1998.

Internet Post Office: This tool is the only convenient way for Internet users to make secure online purchases of digital postage and other post-related products and services.

Key Differentiators   What makes E-Stamp's offering unique from competitors? E-Stamp expects E-Stamp SoHo to be the first product of its kind that allows users to purchase digital postage via the Internet and print digital stamps using their PCs.

Future Directions   E-Stamp plans to leverage its secure payment platform by offering digital postage solutions for international markets, medium-to-large enterprises, and high-volume mailing markets. In addition, it plans to offer other products and services such as certified e-mail, digital IDs, and mail tracking.

List of Major Partners/Customers   None announced yet.

Harbinger

1055 Lenox Park Blvd.
  Atlanta, GA 30319
  (800) 555-2989
  http://www.harbinger.com

Company Background   Harbinger Corporation, founded by C. Tycho Howe in March 1983, is a leading provider of EDI software and solutions, with over 38,000 customers. Harbinger merged with Supply Tech Inc. in early 1997. Harbinger has more than 680 employees worldwide. Its corporate headquarters are located in Atlanta, Georgia, with its Supply Tech division located Ann Arbor, Michigan, and the Enterprise Solutions Division in Dallas, Texas. The company also has operations in the Netherlands, Germany, the United Kingdom, Italy, and Mexico. Additionally, Harbinger has relationships with an international network of more than 20 value-added resellers to market and support its software worldwide. Harbinger is a publicly traded company.

Products   *TrustedLink Commerce Internet:* This product enables companies to exchange business documents with a single trading partner, or send and receive EDI transactions directly from business applications securely over the Internet. Receipt notification and secure public key cryptography guarantee confidentiality, authentication, integrity, and nonrepudiation of all transmissions.

TrustedLink Guardian: This product enables secure, reliable, and cost-effective delivery of EDI transactions over the Internet and value-added networks. It interoperates with third-party translators and works seamlessly with the entire TrustedLink product family, including all desktop and enterprise versions.

Harbinger Express: This is a ground-breaking World Wide Web service that enables any company with Internet access to gain the full benefits of EDI. Harbinger Express allows users to send and receive EDI documents using any industry-standard browser, such as Netscape Navigator or Microsoft Internet Explorer. Authorization from a participating trading partner is required.

TrustedLink Procurement: Harbinger's electronic catalog solutions automate the extensive task of managing suppliers, distributors, and purchasing agents. Users can access a centralized multivendor catalog with a browser via the Internet or company intranet. The Java-based client interface and robust search engine expedite navigation even over a 28.8-bps connection. Harbinger offers a solution that links multiple MRO suppliers into a centralized purchasing system and a solution that offers suppliers a web-based catalog solution for product distribution or sales. Hosting services and many management capabilities (including sales channel management across multiple buyers) are available.

TrustedLink INP: This product provides an easy way to make an order-ready web storefront. It includes everything needed to build and maintain an order-ready web site without programming.

Premenos Technology Corporation

1000 Burnett Ave.
   Concord, CA 94520
   (510) 602-2000
   (800) 426-3836
   33-1-47-78-1645 (Paris)
   44(0) 1344-382-071 (London)
   http://www.premenos.com

Company Background   Premenos (NASDAQ: PRMO) was incorporated in 1989. Premenos Corporation develops and markets business-to-business electronic commerce software and related services for Fortune 1000 and mid-size companies that need to lower costs, shorten trading cycles, and increase competitive advantage. Premenos delivers traditional EDI translators, forms-based products for smaller trading partners, and complimentary standards-based applications that add security and the ability to use TCP/IP networks and emerging web technologies. Premenos was the first to market with Templar, a standard-based server software to support secure EDI over the Internet and other TCP/IP networks. Premenos products support MVS, AS/400, IBM RS/6000, HP 9000, Sun SPARC, and Windows NT and 95 platforms.

Products   Premenos software applications enable businesses to electronically execute over 150 types of business transactions, including essential commercial functions such as purchasing, invoicing, shipping and notification, and funds transfer. Their software is interoperable, provides communication options, and easily integrates business information.

PReMO Templar: Templar, unveiled in May 1995, is the first commercially available authentication agent to provide secure, auditable business-to-business EDI over open networks. Templar software is a layer between the transport agent, such as SMTP and MIME, and the EDI translation software to ensure confidentiality, integrity, authentication, and nonrepudiation of both origin and receipt of messages. Templar software also provides operations management, including trading partner set-up, designation of communication and security requirements, key management, and transaction tracking. Price: $1,500 to $30,000.

PReMO WebDox: This tool enables expansion of existing EDI programs onto the World Wide Web. WebDox permits rapid deployment of powerful and inexpensive applications to the desktop of your trading partners. WebDox provides the ability to combine offline operation as well as mix document exchange with other nondocument activities (e.g., viewing informational web pages). WebDox is flexible and well suited to solutions requiring high volumes and advanced capabilities. WebDox is a structured electronic commerce trading system that consists of two components: 'WebDox Central, which resides on the server at the 'hub' location, and 'WebDox Remote, a Windows-based module installed on the 'spoke' or trading partner's PC. Price: Server: $25,000 to $40,000. Price for remote trading partner: $299.

PReMO Prime Factors: Information security solutions for financial, commercial, and government applications. Prime Factors is a wholly owned subsidiary of Premenos Corporation. Prices range from $6,000 to $50,000 depending on product and requirements.

Premenos also offers professional and educational services.

Key Differentiators   Premenos is known for its technology vision. They were:

- First to introduce a mapping function for EDI.
- First to fully support UN EDIFACT standards in products.
- First to provide a GUI for midrange translators.
- First to provide secure EDI over the Internet.
- First in customer service as rated by independent surveys.

Premenos products will work with any major network (VAN) or the Internet. They boast strong application product integration with well-known partners such as SAP/BAAN, etc.

Future Directions   Premenos will continue to provide electronic commerce technology and contribute the necessary expertise to empower businesses to lower costs, shorten trading cycles, and increase their competitive advantage. Premenos will continue to partner with major network services, Extranet outsource services, application vendors, web EC system integrators, and hardware providers.

List of Major Partners/Customers   Here is a partial list of Premenos partners: BAAN, JDEdwards, SAP, Informix, Oracle, Sybase, HP, IBM, Microsoft, SUN, AT&T, IBM, and Kleinschmidt. Premenos has over 6,000 customers. See their web site for details.

RSA Data Security, Inc., a Security Dynamics Company

100 Marine Parkway
Suite 500
Redwood City, CA 94065
(415) 595-8782 (voice)
(415) 595-1873 (fax)
http:/www.rsa.com

Company Background   Founded in 1982 by the inventors of the RSA Public Key Cryptosystem, RSA Data Security, Inc. (http://www.rsa.com), a wholly owned subsidiary of Security Dynamic Technologies, Inc. (http://www.securid.com), is a brand name for cryptography. There are more than 80 million copies of RSA encryption and authentication technologies installed and in use worldwide. RSA technologies are part of existing and proposed standards for the Internet and World Wide Web, CCITT, ISO, ANSI, and IEEE. Their encryption engines are in many of the world's most popular software products, such as Lotus Notes, Netscape Navigator and Communicator, Microsoft NT, WebTV, IBM Secure Way, and Novell Netware.

RSA develops and markets platform-independent developer's kits and end-user products, and provides comprehensive cryptographic consulting services, with six cryptographic toolkits and security solutions: BSAFE for general-purpose crypto, TIPEM for general-purpose messaging security, BCERT for certificate processing, S/MAIL for secure PC mail and messaging development, S/PAY for secure credit and payment card applications and services, and J/SAFE, RSA's toolkit for building Java security. RSA SecurPC is a file-encryption product for Windows 95, 97, and NT.

Products *S/PAY 1.0:* For secure electronic payment card transactions over the Internet, RSA's S/PAY toolkit is specifically designed for developing Secure Electronic Transactions (SET) security applications and services. The S/PAY developer's kits provide a full implementation of all of the cryptographic and messaging constructs required for quickly building SET-compliant products. The S/PAY developer's kits also include sample code to illustrate the capabilities of the cardholder, merchant, and payment gateway (acquirer) components, as well as test-tools to road test and debug SET applications.

S/MAIL 1.0: This toolkit is a complete solution for building secure, interoperable messaging applications. S/MAIL is RSA's high-level cryptographic API designed for S/MIME-compliant secure mail and messaging development. Developers save time (an estimated 8-12 man-months) by using S/MAIL's high-level libraries to quickly create, format, and parses complex PKCS #7 and #10 messages automatically inside the toolkit. S/MAIL includes all of RSA's core cryptographic enveloping, signing, and authentication algorithms required for S/MIME secure mail applications.

JSAFE 1.0: JSAFE is RSA's set of security building blocks for Java developers. JSAFE is RSA's first cryptographic toolkit designed specifically for Java developers. JSAFE provides developers with a state-of-the-art implementation of the most important privacy, authentication, and data integrity routines—all in Java. JSAFE uses the same Java Security API developers are used to. The toolkit also includes source code for sample applications and easy-to-use self-test modules. This means proven security and shorter time-to-market for new Java projects.

BSAFE 3.0: This tool is RSA's general-purpose software developer's kit for cryptography. BSAFE, the encryption "engine" used by the developers of products like Windows 97, Netscape Communicator, and WebTV, is now available in a major new release. BSAFE 3.0 is a portable C toolkit that allows developers to integrate privacy and authentication features into virtually any application. BSAFE 3.0 modules can be used to construct anything from RSA Digital Signatures to complex key exchange, encryption, or key-negotiation schemes. BSAFE 3.0 provides the programmer with a complete palette of crypto algorithms, including RSA, DES, Triple-DES, the exportable RC2 and RC4 ciphers, Diffie-Hellman, Bloom-Shamir secret sharing, and many more.

TIPEM 2.0: This is a low-level, full-featured, flexible development kit for PKCS #7 message creation and formatting. RSA's public key cryptography standards (PKCS) were developed by an industry consortium to standardize encryption and authentication implementations, cryptographic message formatting, and certificate requesting, issuing, and private key storage. It enables developers to easily implement PKCS #7, the standard for secure messaging development. RSA's TIPEM allows programmers to develop secure, interoperable messaging, mail, workflow, and forms applications. TIPEM gives the developer access to many crypto algorithms and constructs, such as RSA Digital Envelopes, Digital Signatures, and DES or RC2 encryption.

BCERT 1.0: This toolkit is designed for adding sophisticated X.509 certificate issuing and key management features applications. BCERT provides full support to the industry standard, X.509 v3 certificate extensions, and contains all the cryptographic support necessary to generate certificate requests, sign certificates, and create and distribute certificate revocation lists.

Pricing: A comprehensive list of RSA pricing for toolkits can be found on their web site or by calling them.

Key Differentiators RSA is set apart by the RSA patents, RSA's 15 years of experience providing security technologies, RSA Labs, RSA's new innovations in message digests, stream and block ciphers, and faster, stronger implementations of the RSA algorithm. Over 290 of the world's leading software and hardware companies have chosen the RSA public key algorithm for their cryptographic needs. RSA has been the chosen algorithm for almost every major Internet standard in place today, from secure commerce in SET, to secure e-mail with SMIME, secure networks with IPSEC and SWAN, and secure Internet connections through SSL.

Future Directions RSA is looking at new security algorithms for privacy, user authentication, and data integrity and support for the SecurID family of user authentication products.

List of Major Partners/Customers RSA has over 290 licensees. See their web site or call them for details.

S/MIME Products

S/MIME is a proposed standard that adds authentication, privacy, message integrity, and nonrepudiability to Multipurpose Internet Mail Extensions (MIME), the Internet standard that specifies how to handle non-text files in e-mail messages. There are three other specifications for handling secured e-mail: PGP, which was mentioned earlier, Privacy Enhanced Mail (PEM), which has been around the longest, and MOSS, a relatively new specification. PEM has the problem of not being able to deal with non-text files, which are now commonly sent over the Internet. MOSS was intended to overcome the problems of PEM, but its very richness of options makes interoperability between different mailers difficult. Because most modern mailers now support MIME, S/MIME is easier to support, with fewer options, but still able to get the job done. There are now several vendors that offer S/MIME mailers or plug-in options that enable existing mailers to support S/MIME. These products and vendors are:

MailSecure

(works with any Microsoft Exchange products)
  Baltimore Technologies Ltd.
  IFSC House
  International Financial Services Centre
  Custom House Quay
  Dublin 1, Ireland
  +353 1 605 4399 (voice)
  +353 1 605 4388 (fax)
  E-mail: info@baltimore.ie
  http://www.baltimore.ie/mailsecure.htm

E-mail Connection (for Windows systems)

ConnectSoft
  11130 NE 33rd Place
  Bellevue, WA 98004-1448
  (800) 889-3499
  (206) 827-6467
  (206) 822-9095 (fax)
  E-mail: ddolson@connectsoft.com (USA)
  marco@connectsoft.com (international)
  http://www.connectsoft.com

Intranet Genie (for Windows 95/NT)

Frontier Technologies
  10201 N. Port Washington Road
  Mequon, WI 53092
  (414) 241-4555

(800) 929-3054
(414) 241-7084 (fax)
E-mail: Info@FrontierTech.Com
http://www.frontiertech.com

Internet Explorer 4.0 (for Windows 95/NT)

Microsoft
One Microsoft Way (map)
Redmond, WA 98052-6399
(206) 882-8080 (voice)
(206) 936-7329 (fax)
http://www.microsoft.com/ie/

Netscape Communicator 4.0 (most platforms)

See previous chapter for contact information.

ExpressMail (for Windows)

OpenSoft
319 Avenue C, Suite 10F
New York, NY 10009
(800) 996-OPEN (voice)
(212) 249-5806 (voice)
(212) 396-4963 (fax)
E-mail: sales@opensoft.com
http://www.opensoft.com/products/expressmail/

Secure Messenger (for Microsoft Exchange and Eudora (Windows))

Deming Internet Security (a division of Worldtalk)
13122 NE 20th St., Suite C
Bellevue, WA 98005
(206) 882-8861 (voice)
(206) 882-8060 (fax)
E-mail: info@worldtalk.com
http://www.deming.com/sm.htm

SET Vendors

SET is in its early deployment stages, so the list of vendors with SET products will grow. This list includes both application and toolkit vendors. Generally, companies choose payment systems for other characteristics, but this list will help companies know that vendors either currently ship or plan to ship SET-compliant products. Over 300 organizations have requested a copy of the reference implementation, which suggests that this list will grow dramatically.

COST Computer Security Technology AB

CyberCash
    2100 Reston Pkwy., Ste. 430 (map)
    Reston, VA 22091
    (703) 620-4200 (voice)
    (703) 620-4215 (fax)
    http://www.cybercash.com

GlobeSET, Inc. (formerly Interval Systems)

1250 Capital of Texas Hwy. So.
    Building One, Suite 300
    Austin, TX 78746
    (512) 427-5111 (voice)
    (512) 427-5101 (fax)

IBM Corporation

See previous chapter for contact information.

Open Market, Inc.

245 First St.
    Cambridge, MA 02142
    (617) 949-7000

RSA Data Security, Inc. (toolkit)

See above for contact information.

Terisa Systems, Inc. (toolkit)

See below for contact information.

VeriFone, Inc.

3 Lagoon Dr., Ste. 400 (map)
 Redwood City, CA 94065-1561
 (415) 591-6500
 (415) 598-5504
 http://www.verifone.com

Terisa Systems, Inc.

4984 El Camino Real
 Los Altos, CA 94022
 (415) 919-1770
 (415) 919-1760
 http://www.terisa.com

Company Background Terisa Systems develops products and toolkits to enable secure Internet commerce. Terisa was founded in the summer of 1995 funded by investments of both cash and technology from America Online, CompuServe, IBM, Motorola, Netscape Communications, RSA, and VeriFone/EIT. In May 1997, they announced that they were being acquired by SPYRUS, subject to shareholder approval. SPYRUS of San Jose, California, makes smart cards, software libraries, and cryptographic service toolkits.

Products Offered *SecureWeb Documents:* This product is a browser plug-in and server add-on that enable dynamic, real-time signing of documents, providing users with message-level privacy, authentication of all parties, and nonrepudiation of message content. This unique solution's ability to store, retrieve, and manipulate documents dynamically differentiates it from present store-and-forward e-mail technologies that primarily handle only static documents. SecureWeb Documents runs on most standard web platforms, and complements and extends existing certification and message security technologies by providing document signing, which is not currently available through standard web protocols. Pricing: the browser plug-in is free to individuals. Redistribution licenses range start at $2,000. The web server add-on is $3,000.

Web Browser and Server Vendors

Most web browsers available today support SSL, the primary security protocol for the web. The real question that companies should ask is what version of SSL the web browser supports. As mentioned earlier, version 2 of SSL does not support client authentication, so companies wanting to use this function need to purchase browsers with SSL version 3 supported. The most popular browsers are Netscape and Microsoft. See above for contact information.

Virtually all commercial web servers support SSL, so no list is provided. As with S/MIME and SET, companies will generally choose a server based on other characteristics, not SSL support, since most offer this. For more details on the long list of companies that offer web servers, see http://www.webcompare.com.

This site lists all the major web servers (over 50) and their features in a series of charts that highlight what functionality each server offers. In many cases pricing is included. For simple lists of vendors that offer browsers and servers, see: http://www.yahoo.com/Computers_and_Internet/Software/Internet/World_Wide_Web/.

PART 5

What the Future Holds

This section covers some of the possible applications using public key cryptography that could be seen in the future, and the impact that public key infrastructure could have on businesses in the future. The applications are in differing stages. A few are in testing. Some of these systems are currently in research or prototype. Others are only a dream today. But with all of them, public key cryptography and certificates play an important role. These applications depend on the robust authentication, message integrity, and nonrepudiation that public key cryptography provides, combined with strong symmetric cryptography for privacy.

What will be the impact of all these new applications? Will they change the way companies do business? What impact will they have on society as a whole? These are the questions that this last section attempts to answer.

CHAPTER 16

Future
Applications

The applications can be divided into the general categories of:

- Remote authentication
- Internet VAN
- Remote trusted device
- Distributed applications
- Signed instruments

Each of these uses public key crypto for a slightly different purpose. Some of them already have examples today, while others are simply ideas that have emerged from various sources.

Remote Authentication

Remote authentication is the same category as discussed in the Chapter 6 case studies. The difference for the future is in scale and availability. In the future, there will be many of these types of applications that use public key certificates for authentication and the breadth of coverage could be worldwide. Governments will make their services available on-line, just as the state of Massachusetts is beginning to do with their banking application. Citizens will be able to apply for any type of service, pay taxes, and apply for government grants, all over the Internet using public key certificates.

For banks and other financial service firms, remote authentication will be used for more than just home banking. In the future, the commercial (not consumer) interface of choice will most likely travel over the Internet and be enabled by the use of public key certificates, so that organizations will be able to manage their cash flow with a degree of minute control never possible before. There might even come a day when voting will be done completely online. Intra-bank transfers, netting, and corporate intranets will all use the Internet. Any relationship that a business or consumer has with an organization will be able to be serviced online. This will mean tremendous cost savings for the organizations, and increased access for their customers.

Internet VAN

Diamond Shamrock, Mellon Bank, and others are beginning to use the Internet to expand their internal networks or replace their private networks. The tremendous cost savings this brings will drive more and more organizations to move to the Internet for business transactions. When the costs of usage are as little as a tenth the cost of a private network, this is understandable. But there are capabilities that corporations need that the Internet does not provide, such as message confirmation, time-stamping, service guarantees, etc. These needs are becoming the basis of business plans for new companies around the world, and are causing many large VANs to consider how to add value in this new Internet-worked world.

The Federal Reserve in the USA is considering Internet usage for transactions and communication. According to statistics compiled by the author, twelve banks went online every week in 1996. Although they are not currently making use of the Internet for high-value transactions, they will in the future. The other advantage of an Internet VAN is that more parties can play, because it isn't as expensive as a typical value-added network. Because Internet connections can be used for many different things, the costs of access can be spread over many different business functions.

Remote Trusted Devices

Remote authentication will also move beyond the authentication of people to the authentication of objects. Microsoft has proposed a standard called Authenticode, which allows a software publisher to sign the software package that they allow to be downloaded over the Internet. This signature provides authentication and message (program) integrity for the downloader, so they know that the software package has not maliciously or inadvertently been altered since the manufacturer created it. There is also a similar effort from Netscape called Netscape Signed Objects, and Java, the programming language that will enable many of these future applications, also has functionality that will allow digital signatures and authentication.

Copyright protection might also begin to use sophisticated systems to track usage of copyrighted materials. Imagine a system that would find any significant instance of copyrighted text or media on the Internet and be able to immediately tell if it was an authorized usage. This could revolutionize the industry and provide much-needed relief to businesses who fear piracy when they place their materials online.

Perhaps the most interesting type of future application is that which is exhibited by the E-Stamp case study: remote trusted devices that enable an organization to load value into remote devices on the network. There are many possibilities for this, including metered usage of databases, stored value cards, micropayment, and application usage. Because the organization charging for the product or service can do so remotely, it completely changes the costing structure. This can either save companies money, or enable them to offer services for lower fees.

Distributed Applications

Java is a programming language that was designed with platform independence, security, and distributed usage in mind. Many of the applications of the future will be written using Java. How distributed applications work was discussed earlier, but the types of distributed applications of tomorrow have as much similarity to those of today as a commercial jet has to a paper airplane. As more and more trust is established in public key cryptography, the uses could become quite startling. One of my favorite was spelled out by Bruce Schneier at the 1997 RSA conference; his presentation was something like this:

A business wants to purchase a series of widgets and doesn't want to spend more than a certain price. They notify potential bidders of their needs. Let's say that this is a commodity product, with no additional characteristics to influence choice. The buyer enters a sealed range of prices that the company is willing to pay and enters it into a distributed application that manages bid procurement. The bidders all do the same thing. The application then compares the bids and, based on agreed-upon stipulations, awards the contract to the lowest bidder. If no bidder is within the buyer's range, the buyer is notified and can re-enter a new range. The system protects both the bidders and the buyer's price range, but still resolves the transaction. This type of mechanism could also be applied to auctions, raffles, and many different types of applications.

Signed Instruments

Systems will be developed in the future with different types of instruments encapsulated and authenticated with public key cryptography, coupled with symmetric-key crypto. An example of this type of signed instrument is in pilot using the Financial Services Technology Consortium's (FSTC) E-check project. E-check uses smart cards and public key cryptograpy to create a signed, nonrepudiable, electronic version of a check. After its creation, the E-check is sent to the recipient, who endorses it electronically and sends it to the bank, which then sends it through the financial networks for settlement.

According to an article in *American Banker*, the Treasury Department is planning to use this solution to pay up to fifty contractors electronically. This is not a small project: The pilot would generate hundreds of E-checks, worth about $1 million, daily. Although this is small potatoes compared with the funds it disburses via other mechanisms, this is a very interesting development. The checks would be much more cost-effective than paper checks, saving money and effort on the part of the Treasury for both check issuance and postage to send the check. This doesn't even include the costs savings to the payees.

The Impact of Certificates and Digital Signatures on Business

Today, the impact of public key cryptography on businesses is virtually nil. Few companies use it, but the potential for impact in the future is great. As companies begin to deploy applications over the Internet that reduce costs and increase competitiveness, there could be a dramatic impact on the business models of existing companies, as well as creating new markets of opportunity for companies yet to be formed. The telephone revolutionized business, allowing people to talk to others in organizations around the world. The Internet has created a similar sort of revolution for business, but up until now, it has primarily been used for marketing and support functions, due to the big problems discussed in Chapter 2. Public key cryptography and the use of public key certificates will provide the basis for yet another industrial revolution.

This is not without costs. Public key cryptography requires a tremendous amount of infrastructure that does not exist today. The rules have yet to be written about what digital signatures mean in a particular business context. Risks aren't understood, and only time can bring that understanding. There are no international agreements about digital signatures; corporations and consumers don't understand the technology at all, and the lack of familiarity will cause consumer usage to lag. Businesses will be there first, but consumers will eventually follow.

Another battle lurking in the curtains is who the mega-certification authorities will be. There are three primary candidates today: banks, telecommunication companies, and governments. It is uncertain that any will emerge as the preeminent "trusted third party" that issues the certificates "everyone" trusts. Perhaps a dark horse, like VeriSign, will end up winning the race. It is impossible to tell. The one thing that is certain is that people around the world will use, even if they don't understand, public key cryptography in the near future.

Closing Notes

When I started writing this book, I did it because I thought it was a book that needed to be written. It was an interesting project, but the topic didn't evoke much excitement for me. I wrote it because the topics I wanted to write about have already been covered *ad nauseum*. During the course of the book's composition, however, I had a change of heart. As I located case studies and talked to people in product companies, I caught their enthusiasm for the possibilities. The more I wrote, the more I came to believe that this technology will make a dramatic difference in the way we conduct business in the future. I hope that some of this enthusiasm, along with a better understanding of the technology, has rubbed off on the readers as well.

APPENDIX I

Hobbes' Internet Timeline v3.1

Hobbes' Internet Timeline Copyright©1993-7 by Robert H. Zakon. Permission is granted for use of this document in whole or in part for non-commercial purposes as long as appropriate credit is given to the author/maintainer. A copy of the material the Timeline appears in is appreciated. For commercial uses, please contact the author first.

The author wishes to acknowledge the Internet Society for hosting this document, and the many Net folks who have contributed suggestions and helped with the author's genealogy search.

Additional information about the Internet may be found at Hobbes' Internet World.

1950s

1957

USSR launches Sputnik, first artificial earth satellite. In response, U.S. forms the Advanced Research Projects Agency (ARPA) within the Department of Defense (DoD) to establish U.S. lead in science and technology applicable to the military (:amk:)

1960s

1962

Paul Baran, RAND: "On Distributed Communications Networks"

- Packet-switching (PS) networks; no single outage point

1965

ARPA sponsors study on "cooperative network of time-sharing computers"

- TX-2 at MIT Lincoln Lab and Q-32 at System Development Corporation (Santa Monica, CA) are directly linked (without packet switches)

1967

ACM Symposium on Operating Principles

■ Plan presented for a packet-switching network

■ First design paper on ARPANET published by Lawrence G. Roberts

National Physical Laboratory (NPL) in Middlesex, England, develops NPL Data Network under D. W. Davies

1968

PS-network presented to ARPA

1969

ARPANET commissioned by DoD for research into networking

■ First node at UCLA [Network Measurements Center - SDS SIGMA 7:SEX] and soon after at: [legend = function - system:os]

■ Stanford Research Institute (SRI) [NIC - SDS940/Genie]

■ UCSB [Culler-Fried Interactive Mathematics - IBM 360/75:OS/MVT]

■ U of Utah [Graphics (hidden line removal) - DEC PDP-10:Tenex]

■ Use of Information Message Processors (IMP) [Honeywell 516 mini computer with 12K of memory] developed by Bolt Beranek and Newman, Inc. (BBN)

First Request for Comment (RFC): "Host Software" by Steve Crocker
U of Michigan, Michigan State, and Wayne State U establish X.25-based Merit network for students, faculty, alumni (:sw1:)

1970s

Store-and-forward networks

■ Used electronic mail technology and extended it to conferencing.

1970

ALOHAnet developed by Norman Abrahamson, U of Hawaii (:sk2:); connected to the ARPANET in 1972
ARPANET hosts start using Network Control Protocol (NCP)

1971

15 nodes (23 hosts): UCLA, SRI, UCSB, U of Utah, BBN, MIT, RAND, SDC, Harvard, Lincoln Lab, Stanford, UIU(C), CWRU, CMU, NASA/Ames
Ray Tomlinson of BBN invents e-mail program to send messages across a distributed network. The original program was derived from

two others: an intra-machine e-mail program (SNDMSG) and an experimental file transfer program (CPYNET) (:amk:irh:)

1972

International Conference on Computer Communications with demonstration of ARPANET between 40 machines and the Terminal Interface Processor (TIP) organized by Bob Kahn

InterNetworking Working Group (INWG) created to address need for establishing agreed upon protocols. Chairman: Vinton Cerf

Telnet specification (RFC 318)

1973

First international connections to the ARPANET: University College of London (England) and Royal Radar Establishment (Norway)

Bob Metcalfe's Harvard PhD Thesis outlines idea for Ethernet (:amk:)

Bob Kahn poses Internet problem, starts internetting research program at ARPA. Vinton Cerf sketches gateway architecture in March on back of envelope in hotel lobby in San Francisco (:vgc:)

Cerf and Kahn present basic Internet ideas at INWG in September at U of Sussex, Brighton, UK (:vgc:)

File Transfer specification (RFC 454)

1974

Vint Cerf and Bob Kahn publish "A Protocol for Packet Network Intercommunication," which specified in detail the design of a Transmission Control Program (TCP). [IEEE Trans Comm] (:amk:)

BBN opens Telenet, the first public packet data service (a commercial version of ARPANET) (:sk2:)

1975

Operational management of Internet transferred to DCA (now DISA)

"Jargon File," by Raphael Finkel at SAIL, first released (:esr:)

Shockwave Rider written by John Brunner (:pds:)

1976

Elizabeth II, Queen of the United Kingdom, sends out an e-mail (various Net folks have e-mailed dates ranging from 1971 to 1978; 1976 was the most submitted and the only found in print)

UUCP (Unix-to-Unix CoPy) developed at AT&T Bell Labs and distributed with UNIX one year later

1977

THEORYNET created by Larry Landweber at U of Wisconsin providing electronic mail to over 100 researchers in computer science (using a locally developed e-mail system and TELENET for access to server)

Mail specification (RFC 733)

Tymshare launches Tymnet

First demonstration of ARPANET/Packet Radio Net/SATNET operation of Internet protocols with BBN-supplied gateways in July (:vgc:)

1979

Meeting between U of Wisconsin, DARPA, NSF, and computer scientists from many universities to establish a Computer Science Department research computer network (organized by Larry Landweber)

USENET established using UUCP between Duke and UNC by Tom Truscott, Jim Ellis, and Steve Bellovin. All original groups were under net.* hierarchy

First MUD, MUD1, by Richard Bartle and Roy Trubshaw at U of Essex

ARPA establishes the Internet Configuration Control Board (ICCB)

Packet Radio Network (PRNET) experiment starts with DARPA funding. Most communications take place between mobile vans. ARPANET connection via SRI

1980s

1981

BITNET, the "Because It's Time NETwork"

- Started as a cooperative network at the City University of New York, with the first connection to Yale (:feg:)
- Original acronym stood for 'There' instead of 'Time' in reference to the free NJE protocols provided with the IBM systems
- Provides electronic mail and listserv servers to distribute information, as well as file transfers

CSNET (Computer Science NETwork) built by a collaboration of computer scientists and U of Delaware, Purdue U, U of Wisconsin, RAND Corporation, and BBN through seed money granted by NSF to provide networking services (specially e-mail) to university scientists with no access to ARPANET. CSNET later becomes known as the Computer and Science Network (:amk,lhl:)

Minitel (Teletel) is deployed across France by France Telecom

True Names written by Vernor Vinge (:pds:)

1982

DCA and ARPA establishes the Transmission Control Protocol (TCP) and Internet Protocol (IP) as the protocol suite, commonly known as TCP/IP, for ARPANET (:vgc:)

- This leads to one of the first definitions of an "internet" as a connected set of networks, specifically those using TCP/IP, and "Internet" as connected TCP/IP internets
- DoD declares TCP/IP suite to be standard for DoD (:vgc:)
  EUnet (European UNIX Network) is created by EUUG to provide e-mail and USENET services (:glg:)
- Original connections between the Netherlands, Denmark, Sweden, and UK

External Gateway Protocol (RFC 827) specification. EGP is used for gateways between networks

1983

Name server developed at U of Wisconsin, no longer requiring users to know the exact path to other systems

Cutover from NCP to TCP/IP (1 January)

CSNET/ARPANET gateway put in place

ARPANET split into ARPANET and MILNET; the latter became integrated with the Defense Data Network created the previous year

Desktop workstations come into being, many with Berkeley UNIX, which includes IP networking software

Need switches from having a single, large time-sharing computer connected to Internet per site to connection of an entire local network

Internet Activities Board (IAB) established, replacing ICCB

Berkeley releases 4.2BSD incorporating TCP/IP (:mpc:)

EARN (European Academic and Research Network) established. Very similar to the way BITNET works with a gateway funded by IBM

FidoNet developed by Tom Jennings

1984

Domain Name Server (DNS) introduced

Number of hosts breaks 1,000

JUNET (Japan Unix Network) established using UUCP

JANET (Joint Academic Network) established in the UK using the Coloured Book protocols; previously SERCnet

Moderated newsgroups introduced on USENET (mod.')

Neuromancer written by William Gibson

1985

Whole Earth 'Lectronic Link (WELL) started

100 years to the day of the last spike being driven on the cross-Canada railroad, the last Canadian university is connected to BITNET in a one-year effort to have coast-to-coast connectivity (:kf1:)

1986

NSFNET created (backbone speed of 56Kbps)

■ NSF establishes 5 super-computing centers to provide high-computing power for all (JVNC@Princeton, PSC@Pittsburgh, SDSC@UCSD, NCSA@UIUC, Theory Center@Cornell)

■ This allows an explosion of connections, especially from universities

NSF-funded SDSCNET, JVNCNET, SURANET, and NYSERNET operational (:sw1:)

The first Freenet (Cleveland) comes online July 16 under the auspices of the Society for Public Access Computing (SoPAC). Later Freenet program management assumed by the National Public Telecomputing Network (NPTN) in 1989 (:sk2, rab:)

Network News Transfer Protocol (NNTP) designed to enhance Usenet news performance over TCP/IP

Mail Exchanger (MX) records developed by Craig Partridge allow non-IP network hosts to have domain addresses

The great USENET name change; moderated newsgroups changed in 1987

BARRNET (Bay Area Regional Research Network) established using high-speed links. Operational in 1987

1987

NSF signs a cooperative agreement to manage the NSFNET backbone with Merit Network, Inc. (IBM and MCI involvement was through an agreement with Merit). Merit, IBM, and MCI later founded ANS

UUNET is founded with Usenix funds to provide commercial UUCP and Usenet access. Originally an experiment by Rick Adams and Mike O'Dell

1000th RFC: "Request For Comments reference guide"

Number of hosts breaks 10,000

Number of BITNET hosts breaks 1,000

1988

1 November - Internet worm burrows through the Net, affecting ~6,000 of the 60,000 hosts on the Internet (:ph1:)

CERT (Computer Emergency Response Team) formed by DARPA in response to the needs exhibited during the Morris worm incident

Year	Reports	Advisories
1988	x	1
1989	x	7
1990	12	130

Year	Reports	Advisories *(Continued)*
1991	23	x
1992	21	800
1993	1,300	18
1994	2,300	15
1995	2,412	18

DoD chooses to adopt OSI and sees use of TCP/IP as an interim. U.S. Government OSI Profile (GOSIP) defines the set of protocols to be supported by government-purchased products (:gck:)

Los Nettos network created with no federal funding, instead supported by regional members (founding: Caltech, TIS, UCLA, USC, ISI)

NSFNET backbone upgraded to T1 (1.544Mbps)

CERFnet (California Education and Research Federation network) founded by Susan Estrada

Internet Relay Chat (IRC) developed by Jarkko Oikarinen (:zby:)

First Canadian regionals join NSFNET: ONet via Cornell, RISQ via Princeton, BCnet via U of Washington (:ec1:)

FidoNet gets connected to the Net, enabling the exchange of e-mail and news (:tp1:)

Countries connecting to NSFNET: Canada, Denmark, Finland, France, Iceland, Norway, Sweden

1989

Number of hosts breaks 100,000

RIPE (Reseaux IP Europeens) formed (by European service providers) to ensure the necessary administrative and technical coordination to allow the operation of the pan-European IP Network (:glg:)

First relays between a commercial electronic mail carrier and the Internet: MCI Mail through the Corporation for the National Research Initiative (CNRI), and Compuserve through Ohio State U (:jg1, ph1:)

Corporation for Research and Education Networking (CREN) is formed by the merge of CSNET into BITNET

Internet Engineering Task Force (IETF) and Internet Research Task Force (IRTF) come into existence under the IAB

AARNET - Australian Academic Research Network - set up by AVCC and CSIRO; introduced into service the following year (:gmc:)

Cuckoo's Egg written by Clifford Stoll tells the real-life tale of a German cracker group that infiltrated numerous U.S. facilities

Countries connecting to NSFNET: Australia, Germany, Israel, Italy, Japan, Mexico, Netherlands, New Zealand, Puerto Rico, UK

1990s

1990

ARPANET ceases to exist

Electronic Frontier Foundation (EFF) is founded by Mitch Kapor

Archie released by Peter Deutsch, Alan Emtage, and Bill Heelan at McGill

Hytelnet released by Peter Scott (U of Saskatchewan)

The world comes online (world.std.com), becoming the first commercial provider of Internet dial-up access

ISO Development Environment (ISODE) developed to provide an approach for OSI migration for the DoD. ISODE software allows OSI application to operate over TCP/IP (:gck:)

CA*net formed by 10 regional networks as national Canadian backbone with direct connection to NSFNET (:ec1:)

The first remotely operated machine to be hooked up to the Internet, the Internet Toaster (controlled via SNMP), makes its debut at Interop.

Countries connecting to NSFNET: Argentina, Austria, Belgium, Brazil, Chile, Greece, India, Ireland, South Korea, Spain, Switzerland

1991

Commercial Internet eXchange (CIX) Association, Inc. formed by General Atomics (CERFnet), Performance Systems International, Inc. (PSInet), and UUNET Technologies, Inc. (AlterNet), after NSF lifts restrictions on the commercial use of the Net (:glg:)

Wide Area Information Servers (WAIS), invented by Brewster Kahle, released by Thinking Machines Corporation

Gopher released by Paul Lindner and Mark P. McCahill from the U of Minnesota

World Wide Web (WWW) released by CERN; Tim Berners-Lee developer (:pb1:)

PGP (Pretty Good Privacy) released by Philip Zimmerman (:ad1:)

US High Performance Computing Act (Gore 1) establishes the National Research and Education Network (NREN)

NSFNET backbone upgraded to T3 (44.736Mbps)

NSFNET traffic passes 1 trillion bytes/month and 10 billion packets/month

Start of JANET IP Service (JIPS), which signaled the changeover from Coloured Book software to TCP/IP within the UK academic network. IP was initially 'tunneled' within X.25 (:gst:)

Countries connecting to NSFNET: Croatia, Czech Repulic, Hong Kong, Hungary, Poland, Portugal, Singapore, South Africa, Taiwan, Tunisia

1992

Internet Society (ISOC) is chartered

Number of hosts breaks 1,000,000

First MBONE audio multicast (March) and video multicast (November)

IAB reconstituted as the Internet Architecture Board and becomes part of the Internet Society

Veronica, a gopherspace search tool, is released by U of Nevada

World Bank comes online

Internet Hunt started by Rick Gates

Countries connecting to NSFNET: Cameroon, Cyprus, Ecuador, Estonia, Kuwait, Latvia, Luxembourg, Malaysia, Slovakia, Slovenia, Thailand, Venezuela

1993

InterNIC created by NSF to provide specific Internet services: (:sc1:)

- directory and database services (AT&T)

- registration services (Network Solutions Inc.)

- information services (General Atomics/CERFnet)

U.S. White House comes online (http://www.whitehouse.gov/):

- President Bill Clinton: president@whitehouse.gov

- Vice-President Al Gore: vice-president@whitehouse.gov

- First Lady Hillary Clinton: root@whitehouse.gov (-:rhz:-)

Worms of a new kind find their way around the Net - WWW Worms (W4), joined by Spiders, Wanderers, Crawlers, and Snakes ...

Internet Talk Radio begins broadcasting (:sk2:)

United Nations (UN) comes online (:vgc:)

US National Information Infrastructure Act

Businesses and media really take notice of the Internet

Mosaic takes the Internet by storm; WWW proliferates at a 341,634% annual growth rate of service traffic. Gopher's growth is 997%

Countries connecting to NSFNET: Bulgaria, Costa Rica, Egypt, Fiji, Ghana, Guam, Indonesia, Kazakhstan, Kenya, Liechtenstein, Peru, Romania, Russian Federation, Turkey, Ukraine, UAE, Virgin Islands

1994

ARPANET/Internet celebrates 25th anniversary

Communities begin to be wired up directly to the Internet (Lexington and Cambridge, Mass., USA)

US Senate and House provide information servers

Shopping malls arrive on the Internet

First cyberstation, RT-FM, broadcasts from Interop in Las Vegas

The National Institute for Standards and Technology (NIST) suggests that GOSIP should incorporate TCP/IP and drop the "OSI-only" requirement (:gck:)

Arizona law firm of Canter & Siegel "spams" the Internet with e-mail advertising green card lottery services; Net citizens flame back

NSFNET traffic passes 10 trillion bytes/month

Yes, it's true - you can now order pizza from the Hut online

WWW edges out telnet to become 2nd most popular service on the Net (behind ftp-data) based on % of packets and bytes traffic distribution on NSFNET

Japanese Prime Minister online (http://www.kantei.go.jp/)

UK's HM Treasury online (http://www.hm-treasury.gov.uk/)

New Zealand's Info Tech Prime Minister online (http://www.govt.nz/)

First Virtual, the first cyberbank, opens up for business

Radio stations start rockin' (rebroadcasting) round the clock on the Net: WXYC at UofNC, WJHK at UofKS-Lawrence, KUGS at Western WA U

Trans-European Research and Education Network Association (TERENA) is formed by the merge of RARE and EARN, with representatives from 38 countries as well as CERN and ECMWF. TERERNA's aim is to "promote and participate in the development of a high quality international information and telecommunications infrastructure for the benefit of research and education"

Countries connecting to NSFNET: Algeria, Armenia, Bermuda, Burkina Faso, China, Colombia, French Polynesia, Jamaica, Lebanon, Lithuania, Macau, Morocco, New Caledonia, Nicaragua, Niger, Panama, Philippines, Senegal, Sri Lanka, Swaziland, Uruguay, Uzbekistan

1995

NSFNET reverts back to a research network. Main U.S. backbone traffic now routed through interconnected network providers

Hong Kong police disconnect all but one of the colony's Internet providers in search of a hacker. 10,000 people are left without Net access (:api:)

RealAudio, an audio streaming technology, lets the Net hear in near real-time

Radio HK, the first 24 hr., Internet-only radio station starts broadcasting

WWW surpasses ftp-data in March as the service with greatest traffic on NSFNet based on packet count, and in April based on byte count

Traditional online dial-up systems (Compuserve, American Online, Prodigy) begin to provide Internet access

A number of Net-related companies go public, with Netscape leading the pack with the 3rd largest ever NASDAQ IPO share value (9 August)

Thousands in Minneapolis-St. Paul (USA) lose Net access after transients start a bonfire under a bridge at the U of Minn. causing fiber-optic cables to melt (30 July)

Registration of domain names is no longer free. Beginning 14 September, a $50 annual fee has been imposed, which up until now was subsidized by NSF. NSF continues to pay for .edu registration, and on an interim basis for .gov

The Vatican comes online (http://www.vatican.va/)

The Canadian Government comes online (http://canada.gc.ca/)

The first official Internet wiretap was successful in helping the Secret Service and Drug Enforcement Agency (DEA) apprehend three individuals who were illegally manufacturing and selling cell phone cloning equipment and electronic devices

Operation Home Front connects, for the first time, soldiers in the field with their families back home via the Internet

Richard White becomes the first person to be declared a munition, under the USA's arms export control laws, because of an RSA file security encryption program emblazoned on his arm (:wired 496:)

Technologies of the Year: WWW, Search engines

Emerging Technologies: Mobile code (JAVA, JAVAscript), Virtual environments (VRML), Collaborative tools

1996

Internet phones catch the attention of U.S. telecommunication companies who ask the U.S. Congress to ban the technology (which has been around for years)

The controversial U.S. Communications Decency Act (CDA) becomes law in the USA in order to prohibit distribution of indecent materials over the Net. A few months later a three-judge panel imposes an injunction against its enforcement. Supreme Court rules it unconstitutional in 1997.

9,272 organizations find themselves unlisted after the InterNIC drops their name service as a result of not having paid their domain name fee

Various ISPs suffer extended service outages, bringing into question whether they will be able to handle the growing number of users. AOL (19 hours), Netcom (13 hours), AT&T WorldNet (28 hours - e-mail only)

New York's Public Access Networks Corp (PANIX) is shut down after repeated attacks by a cracker using methods outlined in a hacker magazine, 2600

Various U.S. government sites are hacked into and their content changed, including CIA, Department of Justice, Air Force

MCI upgrades Internet backbone adding ~13,000 ports, bringing the effective speed from 155Mbps to 622Mbps.

The Internet Ad Hoc Committee announces plans to add 7 new generic Top Level Domains (gTLD): .firm, .store, .web, .arts, .rec, .info, .nom. The IAHC plan also calls for a competing group of domain registrars worldwide

A cancelbot is released on USENET wiping out more than 25,000 messages

The WWW browser war, fought primarily between Netscape and Microsoft, has rushed in a new age in software development, whereby new releases are made quarterly with the help of Internet users eager to test upcoming (beta) versions

Restrictions on Internet use around the world:

- China: requires users and ISPs to register with the police

- Germany: cuts off access to some newsgroups carried on Compuserve

- Saudi Arabia: confines Internet access to universities and hospitals

- Singapore: requires political and religious content providers to register with the state

- New Zealand: classifies computer disks as "publications" that can be censored and seized

- source: Human Rights Watch

vBNS additions: Baylor College of Medicine, Georgia Tech, Iowa State U, Ohio State U, Old Dominion U, UoCA, UoCO, UoChicago, UoIL, UoMN, UoPA, UoTX, Rice U

CERT advisories: 27, reports: 2573

Country domains registered: Qatar (QA), Vientiane (LA), Djibouti (DJ), Niger (NE), Central African Republic (CF), Mauretania (MF), Oman (OM), Norfolk Island (NF), Tuvalu (TV), French Polynesia (PF), Syria (SY), Aruba (AW), Cambodia (KH), French Guiana (GF), Eritrea (ER), Cape Verde (CV), Burundi (BI), Benin (BJ) Bosnia-Hercegovina (BA), Andorra (AD), Guadeloupe (GP), Guernsey (GG), Isle of Man (IM), Jersey (JE), Lao (LA), Maldives (MV), Marshall Islands (MH), Mauritania (MR), Northern Mariana Is

Technologies of the Year: Search engines, JAVA, Internet Phone

Emerging Technologies: Virtual environments (VRML), Collaborative tools, Internet appliance (Network Computer)

1997

2000th RFC: "Internet Official Protocol Standards"

71,618 mailing lists registered at Liszt

The American Registry for Internet Numbers (ARIN) is established to handle administration and registration of IP numbers to the geographical areas currently handled by Network Solutions (InterNIC), starting March 1998

CERT advisories thus far: 18

Country domains registered: Falkland Islands (FK), East Timor (TP), Congo (CG), Christmas Island (CX), Gambia (GM), Guinea-Bissau (GW), Haiti (HT), Iraq (IQ), Lybia (LY), Malawi (MW), Martinique (MQ), Montserrat (MS), Myanmar (MM), French Reunion Island (RE), Seychelles (SC), Sierra Leone (SL), Sudan (SD), Turkmenistan (TM), Turks and Caicos Islands (TC)

Technologies of the Year: Push, Multicasting

Emerging Technologies: Push, Streaming Media (:twc:)

Growth

Internet growth:

Date	Hosts	Date	Hosts	Networks	Domains
1969	4	07/89	130,000	650	3,900
04/71	23	10/89	159,000	837	
06/74	62	10/90	313,000	2,063	9,300
03/77	111	01/91	376,000	2,338	
08/81	213	07/91	535,000	3,086	16,000
05/82	235	10/91	617,000	3,556	18,000
08/83	562	01/92	727,000	4,526	
10/84	1,024	04/92	890,000	5,291	20,000
10/85	1,961	07/92	992,000	6,569	16,300
02/86	2,308	10/92	1,136,000	7,505	18,100
11/86	5,089	01/93	1,313,000	8,258	21,000
12/87	28,174	04/93	1,486,000	9,722	22,000
07/88	33,000	07/93	1,776,000	13,767	26,000
10/88	56,000	10/93	2,056,000	16,533	28,000
01/89	80,000	01/94	2,217,000	20,539	30,000
		07/94	3,212,000	25,210	46,000
		10/94	3,864,000	37,022	56,000
		01/95	4,852,000	39,410	71,000
		07/95	6,642,000	61,538	120,000

Internet growth: (*Continued*)

Date	Hosts	Date	Hosts	Networks	Domains
		01/96	9,472,000	93,671	240,000
		07/96	12,881,000	134,365	488,000
		01/97	16,146,000		828,000
		07/97	19,540,000		1,301,000

Worldwide networks growth: (I)nternet (B)ITNET (U)UCP (F)IDONET (O)SI

Date	# Countries I	B	U	F	O	Date	# Countries I	B	U	F	O
09/91	31	47	79	49		08/93	59	51	117	84	31
12/91	33	46	78	53		02/94	62	51	125	88	31
02/92	38	46	92	63		07/94	75	52	129	89	31
04/92	40	47	90	66	25	11/94	81	51	133	95	
08/92	49	46	89	67	26	02/95	86	48	141	98	
01/93	50	50	101	72	31	06/95	96	47	144	99	
04/93	56	51	107	79	31	06/96	134		146	108	

WWW growth:

Date	Sites	Date	Sites	Date	Sites
06/93	130	08/96	342,081	04/97	1,002,612
12/93	623	09/96	397,281	05/97	1,044,163
06/94	2,738	10/96	462,047	06/97	1,117,255
12/94	10,022	11/96	525,906	07/97	1,203,096
06/95	23,500	12/96	603,367	08/97	1,269,800
01/96	100,000	01/97	646,162		
06/96	252,000	02/97	739,688		
07/96	299,403	03/97	883,149		

USENET growth:

Date	Sites	~MB	~Posts	Groups
1979	3		2	3
1980	15		10	
1981	150	0.05	20	
1982	400		35	
1983	600		120	
1984	900		225	
1985	1,300	1.0	375	

USENET growth: (*Continued*)

Date	Sites	~MB	~Posts	Groups
1986	2,200	2.0	946	2
1987	5,200	2.1	957	2
1988	7,800	4.4	1933	3
1992	63,000	42	17,556	
1993	69,000	50	19,362	
1994	190,000	190	72,755	

~approximate: MB - megabytes per day, Posts - articles per day

Additional growth charts (square root, logarithmic) available from http://www.is-bremen.de/~mhi/inetgrow.htm.

Hobbes' Internet Timeline FAQ

1. Why did you compile Hobbes' Internet Timeline?
For use in the Internet courses I taught: Introduction to the Internet, Internet Tools Administration, and Net Surfing 101.

2. How do I get Hobbes' Internet Timeline?
The Timeline is archived at: http://info.isoc.org/guest/zakon/Internet/History/HIT.html. If you prefer a copy via e-mail, send a blank message to timeline@hobbes.mitre.org. For comments/corrections please use hobbes@hobbes.mitre.org.

3. What do you do at MITRE?
I design the soccer shoe of the future (wrong MITRE :-). Actually, I wear the following hats: Net Evangelist, HCI Engineer, Systems Integrator, Information Engineer, NIDR Administrator, Lead Scientist, Instructor, He with the Most Toys.

4. Why don't you list the number of Internet users?
This is too controversial, and relatively inaccurate, an issue which the author does not want to get flamed or spammed for. His guess would be between 1 (himself) and 5 billion (but then again, one never knows if you're a dog on the Net).

5. Is your license plate really NET SURF?
Yes, and there is a frame around it with INTERNET at the top, and my e-mail address at the bottom. (My wife is too embarrassed to drive it:) Oh, and the bumper sticker says "I'd Rather Be Net Surfing."

6. Can I reprint the Timeline or use parts of it for ... ?

Drop me an e-mail. The answer is most likely (though don't assume) 'yes' for nonprofit use, and 'maybe' for for-profit; but to be sure you are not going to break any copyright laws, drop me an e-mail and wait for a reply. [I realize the question below is outdated, but I leave it as proof of my prediction powers :-]

7. Who do you think is going to win the '94 World Cup?
Brasil, of course! (I was born in Rio de Janeiro ...)

8. Peddie (Ala Viva!), CWRU (North Side), Amici Usque Ad Aras (OH Epsilon)
E-mail me if you know.

Sources

Hobbes' Internet Timeline was compiled from a number of sources, with some of the stand-outs being:

Cerf, Vinton (as told to Bernard Aboba). "How the Internet Came to Be." This article appears in "The Online User's Encyclopedia," by Bernard Aboba. Addison-Wesley, 1993.

Hardy, Henry. "The History of the Net." Master's Thesis, School of Communications, Grand Valley State University. http://www.ocean.ic.net/ftp/doc/nethist.html.

Hardy, Ian. "The Evolution of ARPANET email." History Thesis, UC Berkeley. http://server.berkeley.edu/virtual-berkeley/email_history.

Hauben, Ronda and Michael. "The Netizens and the Wonderful World of the Net." http://www.columbia.edu/~hauben/netbook/.

Kulikowski, Stan II. "A Timeline of Network History." (author's e-mail on page 221)

Quarterman, John. "The Matrix: Computer Networks and Conferencing Systems Worldwide." Bedford, MA: Digital Press. 1990.

"ARPANET, the Defense Data Network, and Internet." Encyclopedia of Communications, Volume 1. Editors: Fritz Froehlich, Allen Kent. New York: Marcel Dekker, Inc. 1991.

Internet growth summary compiled from:

- zone program reports maintained by Mark Lottor at:

ftp://ftp.nw.com/pub/zone/

- connectivity table maintained by Larry Landweber at:

ftp://ftp.cs.wisc.edu/connectivity_table/

WWW growth summary is available from:

- web growth summary page by Matthew Gray of MIT:

http://www.mit.edu/people/mkgray/net/web-growth-summary.html

USENET growth summary compiled from Quarterman and Hauben sources above, and news.lists postings. Lots of historical USENET postings also provided by Tom Fitzgerald (fitz@wang.com).

Many of the URLs provided by Arnaud Dufour

(arnaud.dufour@hec.unil.ch)

Contributors to Hobbes' Internet Timeline have their initials next to the contributed items in the form and are:

ad1   Arnaud Dufour (arnaud.dufour@hec.unil.ch)

amk   Alex McKenzie (mckenzie@bbn.com)

ec1   Eric Carroll (eric@enfm.utcc.utoronto.ca)

esr   Eric S. Raymond (esr@locke.ccil.org)

feg   Farrell E. Gerbode (farrell@is.rice.edu)

gck   Gary C. Kessler (kumquat@hill.com)

glg   Gail L. Grant (grant@glgc.com)

gmc   Grant McCall (g.mccall@unsw.edu.au)

gst   Graham Thomas (G.S.Thomas@uel.ac.uk)

irh   Ian R Hardy (hardy@uclink2.berkeley.edu)

jg1   Jim Gaynor (gaynor@agvax.ag.ohio.state.edu)

kf1   Ken Fockler (fockler@hq.canet.ca)

lhl   Larry H. Landweber (lhl@cs.wisc.edu)mpc - Mellisa P. Chase (pc@mitre.org)

pb1   Paul Burchard (burchard@cs.princeton.edu)

pds   Peter da Silva (peter@baileynm.com)

ph1   Peter Hoffman (hoffman@ece.nps.navy.mil)

rab   Roger A. Bielefeld (rab@hal.cwru.edu)

sc1   Susan Calcari (susanc@is.internic.net)

sk2   Stan Kulikowski (stankuli@uwf.bitnet) - see sources section

sw1   Stephen Wolff (swolff@cisco.com)

tp1   Tim Pozar (pozar@kumr.lns.com)

vgc   Vinton Cerf (vcerf@isoc.org) - see sources section

zby   Zenel Batagelj (zenel.batagelj@uni-lj.si)

Help the Author

The author is on an eternal genealogical search. If you know of some-one whose last name is Zakon or could spare 1 minute to check your local phonebook, please e-mail any info (i.e., name, phone, address, city) to torhz@po.cwru.edu; your help is greatly appreciated.

Help update: Thanks to Net folks, 39 new Zakon's have been found so far, making the current total around 175! (this after a decade of research)

Archive-name: Hobbes' Internet Timeline v3.1

Archive-location:

http://info.isoc.org/guest/zakon/Internet/History/HIT.html

Last updated: 25 August 1997

Maintainer: Robert "Hobbes" Zakon, zakon@info.isoc.org

Description:

An Internet timeline highlighting some of the key events and tech-nologies that helped shape the Internet as we know it today.

APPENDIX II

Digital Signature Trading Partner Agreement

NOTE: This document was written by Maureen Dorney of Gray, Cary, Ware and Friendenrich. Readers should be aware that this agreement assumes that the parties have already entered into an EDI agreement.

PLEASE NOTE: This document is based in part on the Model Trading Partner Agreement drafted by the ABA Information Security Committee.

Digital Signature Trading Partner Agreement

This Digital Signature Trading Partner Agreement ("Agreement") is made by and between _____ ("Seller"), a _____ corporation, having its principal place of business at _____, and _____ ("Purchaser"), a _____ corporation, having its principal place of business at _____. The effective date of this Agreement shall be the latest date set forth on the signature page of this Agreement (the "Effective Date").

Recitals

WHEREAS, the parties have previously entered into a paper-based trading partner agreement dated _____ (the "Trading Partner Agreement") governing the terms and conditions whereby Seller and Purchaser conduct certain transactions electronically; and

WHEREAS, the parties desire to begin to utilize to digital signature technology to conduct such transactions.

NOW THEREFORE, the parties agree as follows:

Agreement

1. Definitions. The terms used in this Agreement shall have the following meanings.

1.1 Asymmetric Cryptosystem. "Asymmetric Cryptosystem" means an algorithm or series of algorithms which provide a secure key pair.

1.2 Certificate. "Certificate" means a computer-based record which: (a) identifies the certification authority issuing it; (b) names or identifies its subscriber; (c) contains the subscriber's Public Key; and (d) is digitally signed by the certification authority issuing such Certificate.

1.3 Correspond. "Correspond" means, with reference to key pairs, to belong to the same key pair.

1.4 Digital Signature. "Digital Signature" means the transformation of a message using Asymmetric Cryptosystem technology such that a person having the initial document and the signer's Public Key can accurately determine: (a) whether the transformation was created using the private key that corresponds to the signer's Public Key; and (b) whether the document has been altered since the transformation was made.

1.5 Key Pair. "Key Pair" means a Private Key and its Corresponding Public Key in an Asymmetric Cryptosystem, which keys have the property that the Public Key can Verify a Digital Signature that the Private Key creates.

1.6 Paper-Based. "Paper-Based" means documents not transmitted electronically, and which are manually signed by the party to be charged.

1.7 Private Key. "Private Key" means the key of a Key Pair used to create a Digital Signature.

1.8 Public Key. "Public Key" means the key of a Key Pair used to Verify a Digital Signature.

1.9 Recommended Reliance Limit. "Recommended Reliance Limit" means the monetary amount recommended by the issuing party for reliance on a Certificate.

1.10 Repository. "Repository" means the system for storing and retrieving Certificates and other information related to Digital Signatures as described in references contained in the Appendix.

1.11 Revoke a Certificate. "Revoke a Certificate" means to make a Certificate ineffective permanently from a specified time forward.

1.12 Standards. "Standards" shall mean uniform specifications for effective and reliable use of Digital Signatures for the interchange of business communications including provisions for the issuance, verification, revocation and suspension of Certificates as well as the minimum standards for Key management which are described in the Appendix. Standards may include identification and authentication policies, technical and security policies and key management policies.

1.13 Suspend a Certificate. "Suspend a Certificate" means to make a Certificate ineffective temporarily for a specified time forward.

1.14 Transaction Sets. "Transaction Sets" shall mean the types of data which the specified electronic transmission must contain and the format in which the data must appear as described in the Trading Partner Agreement.

1.15 Trustworthy System. "Trustworthy System" means computer software and hardware which: (a) are reasonably secure from intrusion and misuse; (b) provide a reasonable level of availability, reliability and correct operation; and (c) are reasonably suited to perform their intended functions.

1.16 Verify. "Verify" means, in relation to a given Digital Signature, message and Public Key, to determine accurately that: (a) the Digital Signature was created by the Private Key corresponding to the Public Key; and (b) the message has not been altered since its Digital Signature was created.

2. Documents and Standards.

Each party may use Digital Signatures electronically transmitted over the Internet to or receive from the other party any of the Transaction Sets listed in the Trading Partner Agreement and Transaction Sets which the parties by Paper-Based written agreement add to the Trading Partner Agreement (collectively "Documents"). Each party will specify for each Document which party(ies) may be a "Sender" of such Document. Any transmission of data which is not a Document shall have no force or effect between the parties. All Documents shall be transmitted in accordance with the Standards referenced in the Appendix. The provisions of this Agreement, including any terms in the Appendix, shall control in the event of any conflict with any Standards listed in the Appendix.

3. Third Party Service Providers.

3.1 Documents will be transmitted electronically to each party either directly or through any third party Internet service provider ("Provider") acceptable to the other party with which either party may contract. Either party may modify its election to use, not use, or change a Provider upon 30 days prior paper-based written notice.

3.2 Each party shall be responsible for the costs of any Provider with which it contracts, unless otherwise set forth in the Appendix.

3.3 Each party shall be liable for the acts or omissions of its Provider while the Provider is transmitting, receiving, storing, or handling Documents, or performing related activities for such party; provided, that if both the parties use the same Provider to effect the transmission and receipt of a Document, the originating party shall be liable for the acts or omissions of such Provider as to such Document.

4. System Operations.

Each party, at its own expense, shall provide and maintain a "Trustworthy System" as specified by the Standards. The obligation to "maintain" requires the parties to mutually agree upon reasonable updates to the description of the Trustworthy System contained in the Standards as necessary to assure that effective and reliable communications are maintained in accordance with prevailing commercial practices and technology.

5. Security Procedures.

Each party shall properly use the security procedures specified in the Standards referenced in the Appendix. Each party is liable for any unauthorized transmissions originating from such party.

6. Signatures.

Each party shall adopt Digital Signature identification for authorized employees using Asymmetric Cryptosystem technology which is applied to each Document transmitted by such party ("Digital Signatures"). The Public Key for each authorized employee will be contained in a Certificate issued by a Certification Authority acting in compliance with Standards. Each party agrees that any Digital Signature of such party affixed to or contained in any transmitted Document shall be sufficient to Verify such party originated such Document. Neither party shall disclose to any unauthorized person the Signatures of the other party.

7. Receipt.

7.1 Acceptance. If the acceptance of a Document is required under the terms of the Trading Partner Agreement, any such Document signed with a Digital Signature which has been properly received shall not give rise to any obligation unless and until the party initially transmitting such Document has properly received in return a Document in the form specified in such Trading Partner Agreement and such Document is also signed with a Digital Signature.

7.2 Garbled Transmissions. If any transmitted Document is received in an unintelligible, altered or garbled form, the receiving party shall promptly notify the originating party (if the originating party is identifiable from the received Document) in a reasonable manner. A transmitted Document is unintelligible or garbled if it is incapable of having effective meaning or is missing material components. "Unintelligible", "altered" or "garbled" does not include transmissions that contain information in human readable form which the receiving party knows is incorrect. Upon receipt of such notice from the receiving party, the originating party shall promptly inform the receiving party of the correct contents of the transmitted Document by facsimile.

7.3 Reliance. [COMPANY] and [COMPANY] shall have the right to legally rely upon any Digitally Signed information properly received by the Trustworthy System.

8. Transaction Terms.

8.1 Terms and Conditions. This Agreement is to be considered part of any other Paper-Based written agreement expressly incorporating it by reference. Paper-Based written agreements or paper-based standard printed forms referenced in the Appendix will be considered part of this Agreement. The terms of this Agreement shall prevail in the event of any inconsistency or conflict with any paper-based terms and conditions applicable to any transaction included as part of the Transaction Sets.

8.2 Confidentiality. No information contained in any Document or otherwise exchanged between the parties shall be considered confidential, except to the extent provided by a paper-based written agreement between the parties, or by applicable law.

8.3 Validity and Enforceability.

8.3.1 This Agreement has been executed by the parties to evidence their mutual intent to create binding obligations pursuant to the electronic transmission and receipt of Documents using Digital Signatures.

8.3.2 Any Document properly transmitted pursuant to this Agreement shall be considered, in connection with any, and/or this Agreement, to be a "writing" or "in writing"; and any such Document when containing, or to which there is affixed, a Digital Signature ("Signed Documents") shall be deemed for all purposes (a) to have been "signed" and (b) to constitute an "original" when printed from electronic files or records established and maintained in the normal course of business.

8.3.3 The conduct of the parties pursuant to this Agreement, including the use of Signed Documents properly transmitted and received pursuant to this Agreement, shall, for all legal purposes, evidence a course of dealing and a course of performance accepted by the parties in furtherance of any transaction authorized by the Trading Partner Agreement, any other Paper-Based written agreement and/or this Agreement.

8.3.4 The parties agree not to contest the validity or enforceability of Signed Documents under the provisions of any applicable law relating to whether certain agreements are to be in writing or signed by the party to be bound thereby. Signed Documents, if introduced as evidence on paper in any judicial, arbitration, mediation or administrative proceedings, will be admissible as between the parties to the same extent and under the same conditions as other business records originated and maintained in documentary form. Neither party shall contest the admissibility of copies of Signed Documents under either the business records exception to the hearsay rule or the best evidence rule on the basis that the Signed Documents were not originated or maintained in documentary form.

9. Miscellaneous.

9.1 Termination. This Agreement shall remain in effect until terminated by either party with not less than thirty (30) days prior Paper-Based written notice, which notice shall specify the effective date of termination; provided, however, that any termination shall not affect the respective obligations or rights of the parties arising under any Documents or under the terms of this Agreement prior to the effective date of termination.

9.2 Limitation of Damages. Neither party shall be liable to the other for any special, incidental, exemplary or consequential damages arising from or as a result of (i) any delay, omission or error in the electronic transmission or receipt of any Documents pursuant to this Agreement (even if caused by a Provider as described in Paragraph 3.1), (ii) the breach of Paragraph 5 ("Security Procedures") or (iii) the breach of Paragraph 6 ("Signatures"), even if either party has been advised of the possibility of such damages.

9.3 Liability. Nothing in this Agreement is intended to expand, alter or in any way affect the liability of either party, or the applicable limitations of either party's liability, as determined under applicable Paper-Based agreements and forms, including but not limited to liability for carriage of cargo as determined under the bill of lading.

9.4 Force Majeure. No party shall be liable for any failure to perform its transmission or receipt obligations in connection with any Transaction or any Document, where such failure results from any act of God or other cause beyond such party's reasonable control (including, without limitation, acts or omission by a Provider, any mechanical, electronic or communications failure) which prevents such party from transmitting or receiving one or more Documents. The party who is prevented from performing by force majeure (i) shall be obligated within a period not to exceed five (5) days after the occurrence or detection of any such event or cause, to give notice to the other party setting forth in reasonable detail the nature thereof and the anticipated extent of the delay, and (ii) shall use its reasonable efforts to remedy such cause and to perform.

9.5 Severability. Any provision of this Agreement which is determined to be invalid or unenforceable will be ineffective to the extent of such determination without invalidating the remaining provisions of this Agreement or affecting the validity or enforceability of such remaining provisions.

9.6 Governing Law. This Agreement shall be governed by and interpreted in accordance with the laws of the United States of America and the State of California. Nothing in this Agreement is intended to expand, alter or in any way affect the governing law or forum choices, if any, expressed in the terms of the applicable Paper-Based bill of lading.

9.7 Entire Agreement. This Agreement and the Appendix constitute the complete agreement of the parties relating to the subject matter specified in this Agreement and supersede all prior or contemporaneous representations or agreements, whether oral or written, with respect to such subject matter. No oral modification or waiver of any of the provisions of this Agreement shall be binding on either party. This Agreement shall not be modified unless done so in a Paper-Based writing signed by an authorized representative of each of the parties. No obligation to enter into any Transaction is to be implied from the execution or delivery of this Agreement. This Agreement is for the benefit of, and shall be binding upon, the parties and their respective successors and assigns.

IN WITNESS WHEREOF, each party has caused this Agreement to be properly executed on its behalf and this Agreement shall be effective as of the date last written below.

[CLIENT]:	[COMPANY]:
[CLIENT]	[COMPANY]
By:	By:
Name:	Name:
Title:	Title:
Date:	Date:

APPENDIX III

Digital Signature Legislation

—by Maureen S. Dorney

Gray Cary Ware & Freidenrich
400 Hamilton Avenue
Palo Alto, CA 94301-1825

Derived from an Article that was funded by CommerceNet.

I. Introduction

The explosive growth of the World Wide Web has sparked intense interest among companies in engaging in electronic commerce. Currently, however, businesses are concerned that the technical and legal infrastructure does not exist to make electronic commerce practical. How can you determine who is communicating with you and how can you tell that an electronic message that you receive is unaltered by a third party? How can consumers and businesses be confident that the sender of an electronic message will be legally bound to stand by the text of his or her message? The resolution of these issues requires the application of both law and technology.

This White Paper will examine existing law regarding writings and signatures and discuss the nature and status of legislation in the United States designed to promote the adoption and use of digital signatures in electronic commerce.

II. The Law of Signatures

Legal systems have traditionally regulated certain types of transactions by requiring the use of a writing or a signature to establish a legally enforceable agreement. Methods for authenticating written documents have evolved over time. In medieval England, because of widespread illiteracy, documents were commonly authenticated by using a seal, not by

231

signature.[1] Gradually, the convention of authenticating a document by the application of a written signature replaced the use of the seal, both in England and in the United States. Writings and signatures serve several functions including: (1) the evidentiary function, i.e., providing evidence of the existence and terms of a contract; (2) the cautionary function, i.e., alerting the signer to the significance of his or her act and thus deterring rash actions; (3) the deterrent function, deterring the signer from entering into transactions of doubtful utility; and (4) the channeling function, i.e., distinguishing transactions that are meant to be enforceable from tentative expressions of intent that are not intended to be binding.[2]

The classic example of a law requiring a "writing" for a contract to be enforceable is the "statute of frauds." The Statute of Frauds developed under English common law and it requires that certain categories of contracts be in writing in order to be enforceable.[3] The Statute of Frauds traditionally required that a writing be signed by the person against whom enforcement of the contract was sought, or by that person's lawfully authorized representative. Today, in the United States, the laws of virtually all states[4] include a statute of frauds provision for contracts concerning the following types of transactions:

- Suretyship contracts (contracts to be responsible for the debt of another)[5]
- Contracts made upon consideration of marriage
- Contracts for the sale of an interest in land

1. Restatement (Second) of Contracts, § 94, Topic 3 (1981).

2. Id. at § 72, Comment (c). This list of functions is not exhaustive. For one author's description of other functions performed by signed writings, see Joseph M. Perillo, "The Statute of Frauds in the Light of the Functions and Dysfunctions of Form," 43 Fordham L. Rev. 39 (1974).

3. Arthur L. Corbin, Corbin on Contracts, § 275 (1950). With the exception of the Republic of China and Japan, most legal systems have rules, customs or regulations similar to the statute of frauds. See Perillo, supra note 2, at 40-41.

4. The state legislatures in Louisiana, Maryland and New Mexico have not enacted a general statute of frauds. However, in Maryland and New Mexico, courts recognize and enforce a common law statute of frauds. E. Allan Farnsworth, Farnsworth on Contracts, § 6.1, n.5 (1990).

5. Examples of Suretyship agreements include the promise of the executor of a will to pay the debts of the deceased out of the executor's own funds and an agreement to guarantee a loan made to a third party.

- Contracts that, by their terms, cannot be performed within one year
- Contracts for the sale of goods which exceed a certain value.

The last application of the statute of frauds is the most important for electronic commerce because it affects the greatest number of transactions. This requirement is imposed by Section 2-201 of Article 2 of the Uniform Commercial Code (the "UCC") which applies to transactions in "goods." Section 2-201 requires a writing for transactions with a value of $500 or more. Article 2 has been adopted by all states except Louisiana. Goods are very broadly defined as "all things (including specially manufactured goods) which are moveable at the time of identification to the contract of sale."[6] Article 2 does not apply to transactions for services, such as house painting or investment advice. The determination of what constitutes a "good" and what is a "service" has not always been clear. For example, until the late 1980s, the application of Article 2 to software was in dispute. Today, courts generally agree that all software are "goods" for Article 2 purposes. As with the common law statute of frauds, the writing under the UCC must be signed by the party against whom enforcement is sought or by his authorized agent or broker. The UCC also imposes writing requirements on other types of transactions: the sale of certain personal property, sale or return transactions, the sale of securities and most security agreements.[7] Ironically, the statute of frauds has been repealed for many years in the United Kingdom, the original source for the statute of frauds in the United States.

In addition to these traditional categories, many states have extended signature and writing requirements to other types of contracts: contracts to make or revoke provisions in a will and certain types of contracts authorizing a real estate agent or broker to sell property.[8] State legislatures have also extended the writing requirement to other areas, such as government contracts, arbitration agreements, cohabitation agreements concerning property and agreements relating to medical prognoses.[9]

---

6. UCC § 2-105(1).

7. James J. White and Robert B. Summers, Uniform Commercial Code, § 2-2 (1995). UCC §§ 1-206, 2-326, 8-319 and 9-203.

8. See, e.g., Cal. Prob. Code § 150; Cal. Civ. Code § 1624(d).

9. See, e.g., 31 U.S.C. § 1501; 9 U.S.C. § 2; Minn. Stat. § 513.075; Ohio Rev. Code § 1335.05.

The location of the signature is rarely critical, although some statutes require that the writing be subscribed, which means that a signature must be located at the end of the document. Generally, however, the test that a contract has been "signed" is whether the party seeking enforcement reasonably believes that the signer's intent was to authenticate the writing. Thus, courts have interpreted the meaning of "signature" to include symbols that are typed, stamped, or printed. Under most statutes, the signature requirement can be met by the signature of a person acting for another, an "agent." The agent can be an agent of one party or an agent of both parties.

Over time, courts have required fewer formalities and technicalities to comply with the statute of frauds. For example, courts have found that the "writing" itself can take various forms: they have held that telegraphs, telexes and mailgrams can satisfy the statute of frauds.[10] Various courts have reached conflicting conclusions, however, regarding whether audiotape recordings constitute "writings."[11] The UCC has encouraged this decrease in formalities by adopting a liberal definition of what constitutes a signature. The Official Comments to Section 2-201 define "signed" as including "any authentication which identifies the party to be charged." The general provisions of the UCC also define "signed" to include "any symbol executed or adopted by a party with a present intention to authenticate a writing." The Official Comment to this definition explains that:

> [t]he inclusion of authentication in the definition of 'signed' is to make clear that as the term is used in this Act a complete signature is not necessary. Authentication may be printed, stamped or written; it may be by initials or by thumbprint. It may be on any part of the document and in appropriate cases may be found in a billhead or letterhead. No catalog of possible authentications can be complete and the court must use common sense and commercial experience in passing upon these matters. The question always is whether the symbol was executed or adopted by the party with present intention to authenticate the writing.

The UCC also makes a significant change to the common law writing requirement if both parties are merchants. A party can satisfy the writing requirement if: (1) such party sends the other party a written confir-

---

10. Benjamin Wright, The Law of Electronic Commerce, § 16.4.1 (1995).

11. Id. at § 16.4.4.

mation meeting certain requirements and (2) the receiving party does not provide written notice of objection within ten days after receipt.[12]

The challenge for digital signatures is to satisfy the four main functions currently performed by written signatures (i.e., evidentiary, cautionary, deterrent and channeling). These traditional functions have been reformulated in discussing digital signatures to three basic functions: signer authentication, non-alteration and non-repudiation. This paper will use these terms to be consistent with other discussions of this topic.

III. Digital Signature Technology

A "digital signature" is not merely a digital version of an actual signature: it is a process that transforms an electronic message in a manner that is unique to each user. Digital signatures are created and verified by using a particular type of cryptography. Cryptography is defined as the "art of writing in or deciphering secret code." In traditional "symmetric" electronic cryptographic methods, cypher text is created and deciphered using a mathematic algorithm in conjunction with a key. The holder of such a key had to distribute that key to any individual whom he wanted to be able to read his encrypted transmission. This process has two significant problems: (1) the encryption scheme will be compromised if an unauthorized third party obtains the "key" and poses as an authorized sender of such messages; and (2) the key is not unique to a particular individual or company, so symmetric encryption cannot perform the function of non-repudiation (in other words, its use cannot signify the sender's intention to be legally bound).

Public key or "asymmetric" cryptography reduces these risks by using two mathematically related keys.[13] The keys are generated using a known algorithm. One key is the "private" key which is used to "sign" the message and for decryption. The private key is under the sole control of the owner of that key. The second key is mathematically related to the private key but it is a public key, i.e., it is used for encryption and to verify the digital "signature." These keys are based on a known algorithm, but they are secure because, for practical purposes, the private key cannot be

---

12. UCC § 2-201(2).

13. For a more detailed explanation of digital signatures and public key encryption, see Bruce Schneier, E-mail Security: How to Keep Your Electronic Messages Private (1995).

derived from the public key. This last qualifier is important: the basic security of public key encryption is based on the strength of the algorithm and the key length of the key pair. Even with a strong algorithm, a public key pair with a short key length may be "cracked" by the brute force approach consisting of the random generation of all of the possible public/private key pair combinations for a given public key until the third party discovers the correct private key. The greater the length of the key, the greater the number of possible key pairs and the harder it is to randomly discover the correct key pair. In fact, the security of all public key encryption is relative: it depends on the amount of computing power available, the randomness of the generation of the key pair and the state of decryption techniques. Professional cryptographers point out that no encryption scheme is completely invulnerable.[14] With enough time, money and computing power, and with future advances in technology, it may be theoretically possible to crack any key pair within a limited time. However, by making certain assumptions about computing power and encryption technology, a key pair with a long key may require thousands of years to crack using a brute force approach. Several leading cryptographers suggest that keys generated for the RSA algorithm with a key length of 1024 bits are satisfactory for commercial use. An integral part of the security of any digital signature procedure is security for the private key. If the private key is disclosed or otherwise compromised, the strength of the algorithm and the key length become irrelevant. For example, if a private key is stored on a hard disk, the theft of the computer can defeat the most theoretically secure system. Although public key encryption has its limits, written signatures also have vulnerabilities, such as forgery or alteration.

The most commonly used algorithms are those from RSA Data Securities. These algorithms are the basis for most of the commonly available commercial encryption including Pretty Good Privacy ("PGP") and Privacy Enhanced Mail ("PEM"). The other well-known digital signature algorithm is the Digital Signature Algorithm ("DSA"). DSA was created by the Federal government and some cryptographers have expressed concern that the algorithm has not been sufficiently reviewed by the cryptology community and may contain a trapdoor. The National Institute of Science and Technology has approved DSA for electronic signatures as a federal digital signature standard.

---

14. Bruce Schneier, Applied Cryptography (1994); S. Levy, "Wisecrackers," Wired, p. 128 (March 1996).

The use of public key encryption for digital signatures is rather complicated. Public key encryption is relatively slow, so when signing a document, rather than encrypt an entire document, public key encryption is generally used to encrypt a "hash result" of the entire document. The "hash result" is a unique representation of the message, a kind of digital fingerprint. The hash result provides a method to verify the authenticity of a document. The "hash result" is created by running an arbitrary length message through a one-way hash routine to produce a short fixed length hash. The one-way hash function does not have a key and no secrecy is involved. The recipient of the message also creates a "hash result" of the message by using the same hash function. If the message has been altered by a third party after it left the sender, the decrypted "hash result" and the "hash result" created by the recipient will not match. However, like public key encryption, a cracker could generate hash values for numerous messages to try to determine the original message. Two of the most common one-way hash functions are: MD5 (Message Digest) which was invented by Ron Rivest (one of the founders of RSA Data Securities, Inc.) and SHA (Secure Hash Algorithm) invented at the National Security Agency. MD5 produces a 128-bit value hash, which many cryptographers believe is the minimum size necessary for security. SHA produces a 160-bit hash and is considered more secure than MD5.

If two parties wish to exchange a message that has been digitally signed, they will follow certain steps. These steps are invisible to the user because they are performed automatically by the software. Let us assume that Harry wishes to send a signed document to Dianne. Harry will take the following steps:

1. Harry composes the document.

2. Harry runs the document through a one-way hash function (such as MD5) to create a "hash result."

3. Harry signs the "hash result" of the document using his private key and employing public key encryption technology such as RSA.

4. Harry combines the document with the signature to obtain a new signed document.

5. Harry sends the signed document to Dianne.

Upon receipt of the document, Dianne can read the document, but cannot be sure that the document has not been altered or that it comes from Harry. To confirm that the document comes from Harry and has not been altered, she takes the following steps:

1. Dianne separates the document from the signature.

2. Dianne runs the document through the same one-way hash function (such as MD5) used by Harry to obtain a "hash result" for the document.

3. Dianne gets Harry's public key either from a key ring on the Internet or from a Certification Authority (see below).

4. Dianne uses Harry's public key to decrypt Harry's signature (once again a public key encryption algorithm, such as RSA).

5. Dianne compares the "hash result" derived from decrypting Harry's digital signature with the "hash result" for the document which she generated herself. If the "hash results" are the same, then she can be confident that the document was sent by Harry and that it has not been altered. However, if the "hash result" is different, then she rejects the document.

As this example indicates, a digital signature has advantages over a written signature: a digital signature is linked to the document itself and will vary depending on the document. On the other hand, a written signature may be copied from one document to another one.

This example assumes that Harry has chosen not to "encrypt" the document so that in the example, the document is readable by anyone. If Harry chose to encrypt the text of the document, he would generally use "symmetric" encryption to encrypt the text of the document (remember that public key encryption is very slow) and use public key encryption to encrypt the symmetric "key" (similar to the encryption of the "hash result").

An example of a digitally signed document is set forth below:

```
<Signed SigID=1>

     Promissory Note

I, Jon Peters, promise to pay to the order of Old
Eastern Shore Bank fifty thousand dollars ($50,000)
on or before January 1, 2000 with interest at the
rate of nine percent (9%) per annum.

                                     Jon Peters

Maker

</Signed>

<Signature SigID=1 PsnID=peters031>
DE2AB79457ACC20774C1622D3998B
2302B249C17746D39622DC1622D399
533024B2349802DE212990C1622D39
917746D39622DC </Signature>
```

IV. Verifying Owners of Public Key Pairs

To send a document using a digital signature, the recipient of a document must be able to obtain the sender's public key and confirm that such key corresponds with the sender's private key. With transactions that take place remotely over the Internet or through on-line services, such identification is not a simple task because it is impossible to use normal methods of verifying identity such as a driver's license or fingerprints. The recipient may be unwilling to simply accept the sender's representation that a particular key is in fact the public key of a particular individual. The use of public key encryption technology for digital signatures requires that a method be adopted to verify the identity of the "owner" of the key pair.[15]

"Certification Authorities" are one potential answer to this problem. They are organizations that serve to verify and authenticate individuals' or companies' digital signatures, after requiring that the individual or company provide the Certification Authority with reliable evidence of identity. (For convenience, such individuals or companies will be referred to as "Subscribers.") The Certification Authority could also serve as a trusted repository of the public keys. Recipients of documents or messages bearing digital signatures could contact the proper Certification Authority and obtain a time-and-date stamped electronic certificate that would verify that the particular public key belonged to a particular individual or company and that the key pair is currently valid. The Subscriber would notify the Certification Authority if the confidentiality of his or her private key has been compromised and the Certification Authority would then revoke the certificate. For example, if Harry wants to send Dianne an encrypted message, Dianne can assure herself that she has Harry's public key by either obtaining it from Harry and verifying with the Certification Authority that the public key Harry gave her is indeed his key, or Dianne can obtain Harry's public key directly from the Certification Authority. The certificate might include an amount that would be the "recommended

---

15. Currently, a number of companies have begun to provide Certification Authority Services, including VeriSign (http://www.Verisign.com), IBM (http://www.internet.ibm.com/commercepoint) and GTE's CyberTrust (http://www.cybertrust.com). The U.S. Post Office has also announced plans to begin acting as a Certification Authority.

reliance limit." Under the Utah Digital Signature Act, the recommended reliance limit would represent the liability limit of an issuing Certification Authority for its negligence in issuing an inaccurate certificate or for failing to revoke a certificate when a private key is compromised.

The combined use of public key encryption technology and of Certification Authorities is intended to ensure that digital signatures can achieve the same degree of reliability offered by a signed writing, i.e., (1) signer authentication: unless the signer has lost control of the private key, the digital signature serves as verification of the identity of the sender; (2) non-alteration: the recipient is assured that the message was not altered after it was "signed" with a private key; and (3) non-repudiation: like a traditional written signature, by applying his digital signature, the sender of the message has indicated that he intends to be legally bound by the terms in the document.

An alternative to the use of Certification Authorities is a system where the holder of a key pair would choose friends to act as "introducers," i.e., individuals who would certify the sender's public key. This method has been promoted by the PGP ("Pretty Good Privacy") encryption system.[16] This system is very informal and is not likely to be adopted as the legal standard for key pair verification.

Several groups oppose the widespread adoption of digital signatures based on public key encryption.[17] Some critics believe that it is too early to adopt universal technological standards for a technology that is likely to evolve over time. Others complain that the infrastructure needed to implement digital signatures is too expensive and too cumbersome. For example, public key encryption necessarily depends on the sender of electronic messages keeping his private key private, i.e., not disclosing it to any third parties. Since the keys are too long to be remembered, they must be stored on the hard drives of computers or on devices such as PCMCIA cards or smart cards, thus necessitating the purchase of additional hardware. Moreover, these devices can be stolen or misplaced, so, to ensure security, they must be password protected, which adds another step to the process of sending a "digitally signed" electronic document.

---

16. This method obviously has its limits in that it depends on trusting that the introducers are trustworthy and have accurately ascertained the sender's identity.

17. For a detailed criticism of the adoption of the public key encryption system described above, see Wright, supra note 10, at § ET1.1, et seq. (1995).

In addition, critics complain that the implementation of a system of Certification Authorities requires the creation and maintenance of an unnecessarily complex and expensive bureaucracy. Because certificates can be lost, suspended or revoked, the recipient of an encrypted message must check with the Certification Authority to determine if a certificate has been suspended or revoked each time a public key is used to verify a message. This procedure can be time consuming and costly.[18]

The government has considered whether it should establish a central Federal Certification Authority.[19] A number of groups are concerned about the concept of the government acting as a universal certification authority. Would all citizens be entitled to access to certification services and would the government be prohibited from denying such access without affording each citizen due process of law? To what extent would law enforcement have access to the records of the Certification Authority?

V. Legal Considerations

A digital signature is a technical concept. The legal significance of a digital signature will depend on whether it constitutes a "signature" under the applicable law. Under current law, the legal effect of a digital signature would be determined by looking at the circumstances surrounding a transaction, including whether the party applying the digital signature intended to be legally bound. Although it is possible that a digital signature would be found to be a "signature" under either current common law or statute, the result is very uncertain. Consequently, many state legislatures have either enacted or are considering enacting statutes that would provide that digital signatures are legally valid and binding under certain circumstances. Such legislation needs to address a number of important policy issues, such as:

---

18. For instance, as of June 1997, an initial certificate purchase from VeriSign might cost an organization as much as $300 plus $100 for each additional Certificate.

19. For a general analysis of the legal and policy problems posed by the creation of a Federal Certification Authority, see Michael S. Baum, Federal Certification Authority Liability and Policy: Law and Policy of Certificate-Based Public Key and Digital Signatures, National Institute of Standards and Technology, NIST-GCR-94-654 (June 1994). The author of this study recommended that the federal government proceed with the implementation of a federal certification authority including the establishment of an appropriate liability scheme. Id. at 380.

(1) the legal consequences when a Subscriber loses control over the private key;

(2) the responsibilities of a Certification Authority to verify the identity of individuals and companies to ensure that they are who they claim to be;

(3) the responsibility of a Certification Authority to verify the status of certificates and maintain accurate records;

(4) the liability for errors by a Certification Authority, such as issuing a certificate which is based on fraud (i.e. the person is not who he or she claims to be), issuing a certificate with an error (such as a "reliance limit" of $10,000 instead to $1,000) or the failure to revoke a certificate when a private key is lost or compromised;

(5) the ability of the Certification Authority to limit its liability, either by contract or other means, to its Subscribers;

(6) the legal consequences and procedures to be followed if a Certification Authority goes out of business;

(7) the potential limits on the types of entities which can act as Certification Authorities;

(8) the limits, if any, on the type of technology which can be used to create digital signatures because some technologies may not provide adequate security;

(9) the methods of changing legal rules for digital signatures as the technology evolves; for example, formerly "approved technology" is no longer secure due to advances in cryptography or computing power;

(10) who, if anyone, should regulate Certification Authorities and the scope of such regulation; and

(11) the legal status to be accorded to certificates from Certification Authorities from other states which may have different regulatory regimes.

The following scenarios illustrate the types of issues which digital signature laws must address.

Certification Authority Grants Key in Error   Jon applies to a Certification Authority ("CA") for a digital signature pair. CA asks several questions of Jon, but does not request a driver's license or other appropriate identification. CA issues him a certificate in the Subscriber name of John X. Another subscriber has a certificate under the name John X ("Second Subscriber").

Jon digitally signs an invoice for the purchase of $100,000 worth of computers from General Retail ("GR"). GR has customer accounts for both individuals. GR sends the computers to the Second Subscriber. The Second Subscriber is surprised to receive the computers and refuses to accept them. On the other hand, when Jon does not receive the computers, he orders the computers from Universal Retailer ("UR"), but they cost him $150,000. He sues CA for the $50,000 difference. Is CA liable? Is the answer different if the "reliance limit" on the certificate for Jon is $40,000 (i.e., neither GR nor UR should have relied on the certificate for an order exceeding $40,000)? Should Jon be liable for not properly identifying himself? Is Jon liable to GR?

Subscriber Loses Her Private Key   Mary obtains a key pair from a Certification Authority ("CA"). Mary keeps her private key on a notebook computer. Her notebook computer is stolen by Jay. Mary does not suspend or revoke the certificate. Before the expiration of the certificate, Jay hires Hal to assist him in using the private key. Hal is able to use the private key to transfer funds to his own account in a foreign bank. Although Hal and Jay are obviously liable, should Mary also be liable for failure to report the loss of her private key? Would the answer be different if Mary had undertaken special security measures to protect her key on the notebook computer, such as password protection, but Hal had been able to overcome these security measures?

Failure to Confirm Status of Key Pair   Mary obtains a key pair from a Certification Authority ("CA"). Mary keeps her private key on a notebook computer. Her notebook computer is stolen by Jay on May 13 and Mary notifies CA on May 15. CA revokes the certificate on May 16. On May 17, Jay uses the private key to sign a check for an airline ticket to Europe on Saber Airlines. Because Mary has used Saber Airlines in the past, Saber Airlines only checks their local collection of certificates to confirm Mary's signature and does not check with CA to confirm the validity of the certificate. When Mary receives her bank statement, she contests the debit to her account for the forged check. Should Saber Airlines bear the expense of the plane ticket? Should the result be different if CA does not revoke the certificate until May 18 (even though Saber Airlines did not check with CA)? Should the result be different if Jay buys the ticket on May 14?

VI. Overview of Liability

An important aspect of the implementation of the widespread use of digital signatures is the establishment of the duties and liabilities of Subscribers and of Certification Authorities. Through its laws, each state establishes liabilities for engaging in certain activities. The law approaches the apportioning of liability in two ways: fault-based liability, which apportions liability based on the performance or non-performance of certain responsibilities; and activity based liability, which apportions liability based on a determination of who should appropriately bear the risk of a particular activity.[20] In the absence of statutory provisions apportioning the respective liability of Subscribers and Certification Authorities, it is likely that liability would be determined by contract and by the general tort law principles of negligence and willful misconduct. Significant damage could be caused by relying on a revoked, carelessly issued or fraudulent verification certificate issued by a Certification Authority, but the application of general tort law concepts to these issues is difficult due to conflicting policy concerns. For example, should the individual Subscriber bear all of the risk of loss of his private key or should he only be liable if he was negligent? Consequently, many states have enacted or are currently considering enacting statutes that establish the respective duties of Subscribers and Certification Authorities and also apportion their respective liabilities.[21]

A critical policy question is whether such rules should be implemented as statutes or as regulations. A statute is passed by the legislature and can only be amended by the legislature. A regulation, on the other hand, is developed by an administrative agency and can be changed more easily. A statute permits the legislature to allocate risks and responsibilities very clearly, but is not effective in governing a rapidly evolving area. Regulations, on the other hand, permit much more detailed fact finding and more rapid changes to accommodate changing needs. Regulations do not permit the allocation of risk and responsibility to be decided by the elected representatives of the citizens and may be influenced by the industry being regulated. Both approaches have their advantages and both have been adopted by different states. Given the mixture of impor-

---

20. W. Page Keeton, et al., Prosser and Keeton on the Law of Torts, § 75 (1984).

21. Utah Code §§ 46-3-301-310. See also proposed Illinois Electronic Commerce Security Act §§ 501-503, 601-608, 701-705 (January 13, 1997 Draft).

tant policy choices and rapidly evolving technology involving digital signatures, a combination of these approaches is probably advisable.[22]

VII. Liability for the Loss or Compromise of the Private Key by Subscribers

A critical issue is the extent of the liability that Subscribers should bear for allowing unauthorized third parties to gain access to their private key.[23] Several models exist for apportioning this type of liability in the various statutes that address the liability of the holder of financial instruments, such as credit cards or checks, for their unauthorized use.

The credit card statutes generally adopt the "activity based" model of liability. The law assumes that banks are better able to bear the liability for this type of loss. The owner of a lost or stolen credit card is only liable for up to $50 of charges incurred by an unauthorized use of the card before the cardholder gives notice of the loss or theft to the credit card company.[24] A similar law applies to lost or stolen automatic teller cards.[25]

For forged or altered checks, liability is based on both "activity" and "fault" based models. Under most circumstances, banks bear the liability for accepting forged checks.[26] However, if the account holder fails to exercise ordinary care in a manner that contributes to an alteration or the forging of a signature on a check, then the account holder can be held

---

22. For examples see the Utah Code and Proposed Regulations (http://www.commerce.state.ut.us/web/commerce/digsig/dsmain.htm) and the California Legislation, 1995 California A.B. 1577, and Proposed Digital Signature Regulations (http://www.ss.ca.gov/digsig/digsig.htm).

23. A subscriber could be held responsible for any authorized use of his private key on the theory that the user was acting as the agent of the subscriber. See Martin v. American Express, Inc. 361 So.2d 597 (Ala. Civ. App. 1978).

24. 15 U.S.C. § 1643.

25. 15 U.S.C. § 1693g. Normally, liability for the loss of an automatic teller card is also limited to $50.00. However, in the absence of extenuating circumstances, if the consumer fails to notify the bank within two days after the consumer becomes aware of the loss of the card, the consumer's potential liability is increased to $500.

26. See UCC § 3-403.

liable for the loss instead of the bank.[27] Generally, it is considered appropriate for banks to bear the risk associated with lost or stolen financial instruments. This conclusion reflects the public policy that banks are engaged in an activity where it is appropriate that they bear the risk of loss from the unauthorized use of financial instruments. However, in certain instances, the customers of banks can be held liable for the failure to exercise reasonable care with respect to a financial instrument under their control. These exceptions to the general rule impose a degree of fault based liability on consumers and further the policy of encouraging consumers to safeguard their financial instruments.

The success of public key encryption schemes depends on the Subscriber keeping his or her private key confidential and not allowing others access to the private key. Digital signature legislation could address this issue by imposing fault based liability on a Subscriber; the Subscriber would be liable if he failed to exercise reasonable care in preventing access to his private key. On the other hand, the legislation could adopt a higher standard of care and impose liability on the Subscriber for any loss of his private key, whether or not he took reasonable steps to protect it. As with the statutes relating to credit cards and checks, this liability could be limited to losses incurred prior to the Subscriber's notification to the Certification Authority that the private key had been compromised. To encourage the prompt reporting of such an occurrence, digital signature legislation might also impose a duty on Subscribers of prompt reporting and provide penalties for failing to report in a prompt manner.

VIII. Liability of Certification Authorities

Certification Authorities will be responsible for: (1) accurately determining a Subscriber's identity, (2) issuing a certificate containing correct information, and (3) promptly revoking a certificate upon notice from the Subscriber indicating that the private key has been compromised or that the Subscriber no longer wishes to rely on the certificate. The failure to comply with any of these responsibilities could potentially sub-

---

27. UCC § 3-406.

ject Certification Authorities to liability under contract or tort law, depending on the circumstances.

Digital signature legislation needs to address the duties and liabilities that should be borne by Certification Authorities. Without specific legislation, Certification Authorities could face potential liability to third parties who rely on a certificate only to discover that the certificate was inaccurate, either due to the negligence of the Certification Authority or negligence or fraud on the part of the Subscriber.[28] In the absence of relevant legislation, the liability of Certification Authorities would be determined by general contract or tort law principles on a case by case basis. Due to the uniqueness of the issues, these decisions would probably be inconsistent for many years.

Contract law principles would be relevant if the Certification Authority attempted to limit its exposure to liability by entering into contracts with persons and companies using its services. Such an agreement would attempt to set forth the conditions under which the Certification Authority could face liability for losses incurred due to the reliance on a false or misleading certificate.[29] To the extent that contract law governs a transaction between a third party and a Certification Authority, a Certification Authority will only face liability if it breaches (fails to perform) an express or implied obligation assumed under the terms of the contract.[30]

The monetary damages that might be recoverable in suits against Certification Authorities for breach of contract include: (1) direct damages, which are intended to put the non-breaching party in the same position that would have existed if the breaching party had fully performed

---

28. For a very detailed discussion of the potential liabilities faced by Certification Authorities, see Baum, supra note 19, at 79-378.

29. Common law and certain state and federal statutes impose restrictions on the extent to which businesses can use contracts to limit their liability to consumers, so not all disclaimers and limitations on liability contained in a contract will be upheld by a court.

30. Depending on whether transactions with Certification Authorities are found to be "goods" or "services," the general contract principles of Article 2 of the UCC may also play a role in determining the liabilities of Certification Authority. The UCC provides rules for obligations that are created by express promises (or "warranties") in a contract relating to "goods." The UCC also provides that, unless disclaimed in the contract, every contract contains certain implied promises (or warranties). The most important of these are the implied warranties of merchantability and fitness for a particular purpose. See Baum, supra note 19, at 109-116. It may seem unlikely that Certification Authority services would be considered to be "goods." However, courts have held that many unusual types of transactions were sales of goods, including "leases" of personal property and the granting of communications licenses. Id.

its obligations under the contract; (2) consequential damages, which typically include lost profits and loss of business opportunities[31]; (3) reliance damages, which include the costs incurred in reliance upon the contract; and (4) punitive damages, which are only awarded when the defendant has done something wrong beyond merely breaching the contract (e.g., fraud). In addition to monetary damages, the non-breaching party might seek specific performance (a ruling by a court ordering the breaching party to perform its obligations under the contract).

Certification Authorities could also face liability under tort law principles. "Broadly speaking, a tort is a civil wrong, other than a breach of contract, for which the court will provide a remedy, in the form of an action for damages."[32] Tort liability can be imposed if one of three circumstances exist: (1) the defendant intended to interfere with the plaintiff's interest; (2) the defendant was negligent (i.e., failed to exercise reasonable care); or (3) strict liability, where the defendant can be held liable without "fault."[33] Generally, except for reliance damages and specific performance, the same remedies would be available in a tort claim as in a contract claim.

Unfortunately, due to conflicting policy concerns, it is difficult to predict how these issues would be decided in the absence of a digital signature law. One of the core functions of the Certification Authority is the issuance and verification of certificates. An error in issuing a certificate could result in damages far exceeding the fees which a Certification Authority could charge: in the first example, in which the Certification Authority mistakenly issued a certificate, the liability could be $50,000. Although the Certification Authority could try to control this liability with its Subscribers through contract, many of the potentially damaged parties would not be Subscribers and the Certification Authority's liability to such third parties would be unlimited. However, companies may not be willing to act as Certification Authorities if their liability is unlimited. One approach would be to permit a Certification Authority to shift the liability contractually to a Subscriber who misidentifies himself. On the other hand, a digital signature law could impose such liability directly on the Subscriber. Such a law could also permit the use of "reliance limits" (limits on the amount

---

31. To be recoverable, consequential damages must be a reasonably foreseeable consequence of the breach.

32. Keeton, supra note 20, at § 1.

33. Id. at § 7.

which can be legally obligated under a particular certificate), which would be part of the certificate and limit the liability of the Certification Authority to the amount of the reliance limit. Digital signature laws would need to balance the incentive such unlimited liability would create for Certification Authorities to ensure that their records are accurate with the potential harm that would be caused by imposing liability of unlimited and unpredictable amounts on Certification Authorities.

Legislatures may also wish to limit the ability of the Certification Authority to shift risks to the Subscriber. For example, if the legislature decides that private keys should be treated like credit cards for liability purposes, it would want to prevent the Certification Authority from imposing greater liability on its Subscribers by contract. Digital signature laws could also establish minimum standards to be followed in the issuance and revocation of a certificate, such as warranties that the certificate as issued does not include any statements known by the Certification Authority to be false and a commitment to revoke a certificate within a specified period after appropriate notice. These minimum standards could be very important, because many Subscribers would not have the bargaining power to negotiate them with the Certification Authority. The potential liability for the cancellation of a certificate includes both the failure of the Certification Authority to revoke a certificate after notice and the incorrect revocation of a certificate which should still be valid. Although the Certification Authority will clearly wish to limit its liability with the Subscriber contractually in both circumstances, such limitations could be contrary to public policy because they would not encourage the Certification Authority to handle revocation promptly and carefully. Finally, such legislation could also deal with specific situations such as the effect of death of a Subscriber on the validity of a certificate. For example, should the executor of the estate of the deceased be able to use the certificate?

IX. Regulatory Oversight of Certification Authorities

If the potential liability of Certification Authorities is left largely unregulated, responsible companies may be deterred from becoming Certification Authorities because of the uncertainty of the extent of their potential liability. Therefore, many commentators have recognized the need to pass legislation (or regulations) that addresses the liability of Certification Authorities as well as other issues related to digital signatures. Because of the importance of the role of Certification Authorities in the digital signature process, legislatures may wish to specify which individuals or companies could qualify to act as Certification Authorities, e.g., banks, lawyers or state agencies, and what financial criteria they must meet.[34] Legislation could also specify who would be responsible for the licensing and regulation of Certification Authorities. Licensing would ensure that the prospective Certification Authority had both the capability (such as staff and appropriate administrative procedures) and the financial means to serve in this function. The financial criteria might also include the posting of a bond in a reasonable amount to deal with the uncertainty of the risks in this new business. Such legislation could also establish minimum standards for the procedures that must be followed for the issuance or revocation of certificates verifying "key pairs." In addition, digital signature statutes could specify the procedures to be followed to adequately determine a Subscriber's identity, what information should be contained in a certificate and the qualifications that must be met to act as a Certification Authority. Regulatory oversight could also address the procedure for dealing with an insolvent Certification Authority. Because many Subscribers will be depending on the existence of a Certification Authority, the insolvency of a Certification Authority could have consequences similar to the failure of a bank or other financial institution. This risk could be reduced by imposing upon Certification Authorities specific record keeping requirements, regular audits and requirements for giving minimum notice prior to cessation of operations. The effect of such a cessation of operations on valid certificates could also be addressed either in the statute or accompanying regulations. Finally, digital signature legislation could mandate appropriate technological standards.

X. Technological Standards

In part, the widespread adoption of digital signature technology depends on the adoption of uniform technological standards. Several

---

34. While the Utah Code sets forth such requirements explicitly (Utah Code § 46-3-201-204), other states leave the licensing procedures up to the Secretary of State. See the Florida Electronic Signature Act of 1996; 1996 Florida H.B. 1023, Florida S.B. 942.

international standards have been proposed for digital signatures. The International Consultative Committee on Telegraphy and Telephony (now the International Telecommunication Union) set the basic foundations for digital signature authentication in its X.500 series of standards, including X.509. The Internet Activities Board has adopted similar standards in RFC 1421 through 1424. The American National Standards Institute is considering adopting standards X9.30 and X9.31 and its enhancement, X9.55. The American Society of Testing and Materials Subcommittee on Electronic Authentication of Health Information has also drafted guidelines which are referred to as ASTM E1.20. The Internet Engineering Task Force has produced a draft standard known as PKIX. Recently, Visa and MasterCard circulated for public comment a draft of the SET (Secure Electronic Transactions) specifications, which provide formal specifications for digital signature systems for credit card transactions.

There will continue to be further development of standards for digital signature technology. Some groups believe that digital signature legislation should promote the use of digital signatures by specifying the technological standards that may be used, while others feel that it is premature to adopt specific standards because the technology will continue to evolve.

XI. Digital Signature Legislation

A committee of the American Bar Association ("ABA") has been working on the issues arising in the implementation of digital signature legislation. The ABA Digital Signature Guidelines ("ABA Guidelines") are intended to establish guiding principles that can be followed by the drafters of digital signature legislation and regulations. A draft of the ABA Guidelines was released for public comment on October 5, 1995.[35] After a period for comment, the final version of the ABA Guidelines was released in August 1996. The ABA Guidelines provide a tutorial on digital signatures and guidelines with comments. They were developed to provide a framework to facilitate discussion of digital signature statutes and identify a number of policy choices. On the

---

35. Information Security Committee, Science and Technology Section, American Bar Association, Digital Signature Guidelines (October 5, 1995 draft).

whole, the drafting committee sought to extend existing legal doctrines to deal with the issues surrounding the use of digital signatures.

Utah   Several members of the ABA committee drafted a digital signature statute for the Utah legislature before the ABA Guidelines were complete. In May of 1995, Utah became the first jurisdiction to enact legislation regulating digital signatures (the "Utah Act").[36] An amendment to amend the Utah Act to conform to the final version of the ABA Guidelines became law in March of 1996.[37] Regulations implementing the Utah Act have not yet been adopted. The Utah Department of Commerce expects to license its first Certification Authority by October of 1997.[38] The Utah Act is intended to provide a comprehensive legal framework for digital signatures sufficient to allow the widespread adoption and use of digital signatures in commerce. The Utah Act limits who can qualify to act as a licensed Certification Authority to attorneys, financial institutions, title insurance companies and the State of Utah. It also requires that licensed Certification Authorities post a guaranty in the form of a bond or letter of credit. Nothing in the Utah Act prohibits unlicensed Certification Authorities from operating in Utah. Unlicensed Certification Authorities, however, do not enjoy limited liability under the Utah Act.

The Utah Act provides for the regulation of Certification Authorities by the Utah Department of Commerce. The Utah Act specifies what constitutes adequate record keeping procedures and provides for the regular audit of Certification Authorities. The Utah Act also provides the procedures that Certification Authorities must follow when they go out of business or otherwise cease to act as a Certification Authority and when issuing, revoking or suspending a certificate. In particular, the Utah Act specifies in great detail what information must be included in the certificate.

The Utah Act addresses many of the policy issues discussed above. With regard to the Subscriber, the Utah Act imposes a duty upon a Subscriber to indemnify the Certification Authority for loss or damage caused by a Subscriber's false or negligent misrepresentations of a material fact in connection with the issuance of the key pairs and of certifi-

---

36. Utah Code § 46-3-101, et seq.

37. 1996 Utah S.B. 188.

38. The proposed regulations may be found at
http://www.commerce.state.ut.us/web/commerce/digsig/rule.htm.

cates concerning such key pairs. The Utah Act also imposes a duty on Subscribers to "exercise reasonable care in retaining control of the private key and keeping it confidential." The Utah Act does not expressly address what constitutes reasonable care or the liability of the Subscriber for failing to exercise reasonable care. Significantly, unlike the statutes regarding lost credit cards or forged checks, the Utah Act does not place any limits on the potential liability of a Subscriber for the loss of his or her private key.

The Utah Act does limit the liability of licensed Certification Authorities in two important ways. First, licensed Certification Authorities are not liable for losses caused by a false or forged digital signature if, with respect to that signature, it complied with the requirements of the Utah Act. Second, licensed Certification Authorities' liability for their own errors or negligence is limited to the amount specified in the certificate as the recommended reliance limit.

The Utah Act also provides that a digitally signed document is as "valid as if it had been written on paper" and creates a rebuttable legal presumption that the application of a digital signature to an electronic message (if the public key is valid and accessible) establishes that the sender of that electronic message intended to be legally bound by its contents.[39] This provision eliminates the necessity of expressly amending each Utah statute that provides a writing or signature requirement to recognize the use of digital signatures.

Currently, a bill to amend the Utah Act to conform to the current draft of the ABA Guidelines is before the Utah Legislature.[40] The amendments are largely technical. They are intended to give Utah more flexibility in adopting new technological standards and in establishing procedures for the Certification Authorities. The Utah Act has not yet formally taken effect because implementing regulations have yet to be promulgated.

California   A bill similar to the Utah Act was introduced in the California legislature in 1995. It met with vigorous opposition from members of the computer industry who were concerned that the proposed legislation would lock California into adopting technological standards that would become obsolete and who believed that California should wait for the final report of the ABA committee before enacting

---

39. Utah Code §§ 46-3-401, 46-3-402.
40. 1996 Utah S.B. 188.

comprehensive legislation. The bill was dramatically amended because of such criticism. In accordance with the amendment, California enacted a much more limited statute in 1995.[41] This legislation simply authorized the use of digital signatures in connection with electronic communications with the State of California. It did not specify any particular technological standards. On April 22, 1997, the California Secretary of State released proposed Digital Signature Regulations for comment.[42] Although the regulations provide a list of "acceptable technologies" for digital signature creation (currently only public key encryption and "signature dynamics"), they also establish procedures by which new technologies may be added to that list. The Secretary of State, uncertain of its authority, chose not to address liability concerns in the regulations, leaving them to be addressed by the legislature or resolved contractually between the parties.

Other States   As of this writing (June 1997), at least twenty states have enacted some form of digital signature legislation, ranging from comprehensive bills resembling the Utah Act to minor amendments of existing legislation. Although public key cryptography appeared to be the method of choice as the facilitating technology in early legislation, the new trend seems to be a definition of digital signatures which leaves the question of implementing technology open. In addition, although some legislation apportions liability and creates evidentiary presumptions, many proposed or enacted laws appear to be avoiding such specificity.

Washington was the first state after Utah to adopt major digital signature legislation.[43] The Washington Act looks a great deal like the Utah Act in that it is limited to public key cryptography and it creates certain evidentiary presumptions and sets statutory liability limits. The recently passed Minnesota Act also creates presumptions and sets liability limits.[44] Other states have adopted a more modified Utah model. For instance, the Mississippi Act doesn't specify a liability limit for Certification Authorities.[45] And the Oklahoma Act, while containing provisions

41. 1995 California A.B. 1577.

42. The proposed regulations may be found at http://www.ss.ca.gov/digsig/digsig.htm.

43. Washington Digital Signature Act; 1996 Washington S.B. 6423 and 1997 Washington S.B. 5308.

44. Minnesota Electronic Authentication Act; 1997 Minnesota S.B. 173 and 1997 Minnesota H.F. 56.

45. Mississippi Digital Signature Act of 1997; 1997 Mississippi H.B. No. 752.

for the licensing and regulation of Certification Authorities, doesn't make validation of digital signatures dependent on them.[46]

But other states have taken a less prescriptive and regulatory approach. These states tend to define a signature in a more open, less technologically specific, manner.[47] For instance, after the failure of Utah based legislation to pass, Georgia successfully passed an Act that adopts a more open definition of "electronic signature" similar to that used in the California legislation.[48] The same approach was used in Kansas, Indiana and Virginia.[49] Texas enacted a technology neutral definition of digital signature, much like California; but unlike the California law, the requirements of a digital signature listed in the Texas Act are "suggested" rather than "required" elements.[50] And none of the above legislation creates any presumptions or apportions any liability.

A few states have taken a more limited approach by incorporating the concept of "digital" or "electronic" signature into existing legislation without actually defining it.[51] And at the time of this writing, at least sixteen additional states are considering or have introduced some type of digital signature legislation.[52]

Federal   Recently, the first federal legislation relating to digital signatures was introduced in the Senate by Senator Leahy. The proposed bill

---

46. Oklahoma Electronic Signature Act; 1997 Oklahoma H.B. 1690.

47. For instance, Florida defines an "electronic signature" as "any letters, characters, or symbols manifested by electronic or similar means, executed or adopted by a party with an intent to authenticate a writing." Florida Statutes 282.72(4). Florida Electronic Signature Act of 1996; 1996 Florida S.B. 942.

48. Georgia Electronic Records and Signatures Act; 1997 Georgia S.B. 103. The California Act provides that "a digital signature shall have the same force and effect as the use of a manual signature if and only if it embodies all of the following attributes:
   (1) It is unique to the person using it.
   (2) It is capable of verification.
   (3) It is under the sole control of the person using it.
   (4) It is linked to data in such a manner that if the data is changed, the digital signature is invalidated.
1997 California AB 1577; Section 1, 16.5(a).

49. Kansas Digital Signature Act; 1997 Kansas H.B. 2059; 1997 Virginia S.B. No. 923; 1997 Indiana S.B. 5a.

50. 1997 Texas H.B. 984.

51. 1996 Arizona H.B. 2444; General Statutes of Connecticut Sections 19a-25a (1994); 1995 Delaware S.B. 458; West's Louisiana Revised Statutes Annotated Section 40:2144 (1995); 1997 Nevada S.B. 42; 1997 Tennessee H.B. 1718; Wyoming Statutes 9-1-306.

52. The states are, in alphabetical order: Colorado, Hawaii, Illinois, Iowa, Maryland, Massachusetts, Michigan, Nebraska, New Hampshire, New York, North Carolina, North Dakota, Ohio, Oregon, Rhode Island, Vermont.

is entitled the Encrypted Communications Privacy Act of 1996.[53] This bill would restrict the unauthorized release of "decryption keys"[54] to law enforcement officers pursuant to a warrant or court order. The bill provides for fines and imprisonment for violations of its provisions.[55] The proposed bill fails to address other privacy issues that arise in connection with digital signatures. For example, Certification Authorities will likely keep records identifying who obtains or verifies the public key of each subscriber. Like phone records, this information reveals a great deal of information about the activities of a Subscriber. Presently, there are no restrictions on the dissemination of this type of information.

Even more recently, the Clinton Administration released the first draft of the proposed government regulated key escrow system.[56] The legislation seeks to "enable the development of a key management infrastructure for public-key-based encryption . . . that will assure that individuals and businesses can transmit and receive information electronically with confidence in the information's confidentiality, integrity, availability, and authenticity, and that will promote lawful government access." The Act provides for the registration of Certification Authorities by the Secretary of Commerce; however, public keys may be issued under the Act only if the private key allowing for decryption of a message encrypted with that key is stored with a key recovery agent. Under the EDSA, access to a private key may be gained by a government agency acting pursuant to a duly authorized warrant or court order or a national government security agency.

In a more limited scope, the U.S. Food and Drug Administration released regulations that would allow the FDA to accept electronic signatures as they would accept handwritten ones.[57]

International Countries outside of the United States have begun to consider enacting legislation relating to digital signatures. The Chilean

---

53. 104th Congress, S. Res. 1587.

54. The bill defines "decryption keys" to mean "the variable information used in a mathematical formula, code, or algorithm, or any component thereof, used to decrypt wire or electronic communications that have been encrypted."

55. The proposed bill would also relax the current export restrictions on encryption technology by allowing the export of such technology as long as it is already generally available abroad.

56. The Electronic Data Security Act of 1997 (March 12, 1997 Draft).

57. Regulations on Electronic Records; Electronic Signatures — 21 CFR Part 11 (March 20, 1997) (URL:http://www.fda.gov/cder/esig/part11.htm).

Department of Justice plans to introduce implementing legislation regarding digital signatures in March of 1996. Germany has made public a final draft law that is limited in scope and that leaves the regulation of Certification Authorities to future legislation. It is expected to become law in August 1997. The Certification Authority Working Group Electronic Commerce Promotion Council of Japan (ECOM) has just released its Certification Authority Guidelines (Alpha version), which seeks to provide guidance in the establishment of a Certification Authority in Japan. In addition, legislation regarding the use of public key encryption or digital signatures is being considered in France, Italy, the U.K. and Malaysia. More broadly, UNCITRAL (United Nations Commission on International Trade Law) has begun early work on a model digital signature law.

In addition, the United States Council for International Business is proposing the creation of a quasi-public office, known as the Cyber-Notary, with responsibilities similar to the greater role of notaries in civil law jurisdictions. The CyberNotary would use public key encryption technology to certify international transactions that originate in the United States.[58]

XII. Conclusion

To foster the growth of electronic commerce, government and private industry should continue to work together to adopt a comprehensive legal framework for the use of digital signatures. Basic legal issues, such as the validity of digital signatures and the apportionment of liability in a system employing Certification Authorities, should be resolved by legislation because the failure to do so will result in unpredictable decisions by different courts. Because technological and administrative issues (such as appropriate technological standards and procedures for qualifying to act as a Certification Authority) will evolve over time, such issues should be addressed in regulations instead of being included in statutes.

---

58. See The CyberNotary® Home Page.

APPENDIX IV

Summary of Legislation Relating to Digital Signatures, Electronic Signatures, and Cryptography
   (as of June 6, 1997)
   To submit additions or corrections, or to obtain further information, contact Thomas J. Smedinghoff at smedinghoff@mbc.com.

Important Note: This is an excerpt in time from a very active, constantly updated web site. It is included for people without access to the web. For the most recent version, see://www.mbc.com/ds_sum.html.

State Legislation and Regulations

1. Alabama

2. Alaska

3. Arizona

1996 Arizona Session Laws 213. Arizona amended Section 41-121 of Arizona Revised Statutes on April 18, 1996, to provide limited use of digital signatures. The amendment provides that the Secretary of State shall "[a]pprove for use by all other state agencies, and accept digital signatures for documents filed with the office of the Secretary of State" and gives the Secretary of State authority to adopt rules to achieve this purpose. "The term digital signatures" is not defined.

4. Arkansas

5. California

California Government Code Section 16.5 (1995). On October 4, 1995, California adopted digital signature legislation significantly narrower than that of Utah. It governs only digital signatures affixed to communications with public entities. The Act provides that a digital signature shall have the same force and effect as a manual signature if: (1) it is unique to the person using it; (2) it is capable of verification; (3) it is under the sole control of the person using it; (4) it is linked to data in such a manner that if the data are changed, the digital signature is invalidated; and (5) it conforms to regulations adopted by the Secretary of State.

Digital Signature Regulations. On April 22, 1997, the Secretary of State released California's proposed Digital Signature Regulations for comment. The proposed regulations provide for the following:

1. Digital signatures must be created by an acceptable technology, as specified in the regulations.

2. The criteria for determining if a digital signature technology is acceptable for use by public entities are set forth in the regulation (and essentially includes the five requirements set forth in the statute, plus a requirement that the technology must create digital signatures that are able to satisfy California's requirements for introducing writings into evidence).

3. The regulations provide that acceptable technologies are:
  (a) Public key cryptography
  (b) Signature dynamics

4. The regulations provide a procedure for adding new technologies to the list of acceptable technologies.

With respect to digital signatures, the regulations impose upon a person who holds a key pair a duty to exercise reasonable care to retain control of the private key and prevent its disclosure to any person not authorized to create the subscriber's digital signature. The regulations also establish an approved list of certificate authorities authorized to issue certificates for digitally signed communications with public entities in California. To qualify as an approved certification authority, a CA must undergo a performance audit in accordance with AICPA Statement on Auditing Standards No. 70 (S.A.S. 70) to ensure that the CA's practices and policies are consistent with the requirements of the statute. In lieu of completing such audit, a CA may provide proof of accreditation by an international accreditation body acceptable to the state.

Finally, the regulations do not address liability concerns because the Secretary of State deemed that it did not have the authority to do so through California State regulations. It anticipates that some of the liability concerns can be addressed contractually with the service providers, but recognize that other issues need to be addressed by the legislature.

Public hearings on the regulations will be held on July 15, 1997. Written comments are due by June 17, 1997.

California Assembly Bill 44. This Bill requires the Secretary of State to assign a task force to study the creation of a digital electoral system and to report its findings by March 1, 1999. The Bill was introduced in December 1996 and amended March 31, 1997.

LEXIS: 1997 CA A.B. 44.

Electronic Filing Disclosure Act; 1997 California Senate Bill 49. This Bill would require the Secretary of State to develop a process whereby reports and statements that are required under the Act to be filed with the Secretary of State could be filed electronically and viewed by the public at no cost by way of the largest and non-proprietary, cooperative public computer network. The Act also requires the Secretary of State to develop a system for the electronic transfer of the data specified in the Act that utilizes public and private keys in connection with digital signatures. It was amended on April 14, 1997.

LEXIS: 1997 CA S.B. 49.

Campaign and Lobbying Electronic Disclosure Act of 1997; 1997 California Senate Bill 7. This legislation is similar to California Senate Bill 49. It was amended on April 14, 1997.

LEXIS: 1997 CA S.B. 7.

1995 Cal. A.B. 2755. On September 24, 1996, California enacted legislation (1995 CA A.B. 2755) permitting the use of an electronic signature, or other indicator of authenticity, approved by the state registrar in lieu of a manual signature on certificates of death by embalmers and by persons attesting to the accuracy of the certificate. The act also authorizes the use of such signature substitutes by local registrars in registering certificates of death.

6. Colorado

1997 Colorado S.B. 155. Engrossed on February 7, 1997, this Bill relates to the State's central indexing system for financing statements. It

provides that financing statements may be filed electronically provided they include an electronic signature.
LEXIS: 1997 CO S.B. 155.

7. Connecticut

General Statutes of Connecticut Sections 19a-25a (1994). Connecticut has promulgated legislation directing the Commissioner of Public Health and Addiction Services to adopt regulations for the use of electronic signatures for certain medical records. The statute, however, does not make specific reference to digital signatures.

1997 Connecticut Senate Bill 1308. This legislation establishes a task force to study the use of digital signatures. The task force is charged with examining digital signature technology, including digital signature creation, signer authentication and digital verification, and the relationship of such processes to the legal concept of signature. The task force is to submit its findings and recommendations by January 1, 1998. The Bill was introduced on March 19, 1997.
LEXIS: 1997 CT S.B. 1308.

8. Delaware

1995 DE S.B. 458. On July 12, 1996, Delaware enacted legislation to amend Title 29 of the Delaware Code, which relates to state budget, accounting and payroll policies and procedures, to allow for the use of electronic signatures with respect to documents created pursuant to Title 29. The bill broadens the scope of the term "signature" as it applies to the signing of checks or drafts by the state treasurer by dispensing with the requirement that a check-signing machine be used if the check or draft is not signed by hand. Furthermore, the bill authorizes the use of an "electronic approval" by state officers in approving payment for services.

9. Florida

Electronic Signature Act of 1996; 1996 Florida Senate Bill 942. This Bill creates the "Electronic Signature Act of 1996." It authorizes the

Secretary of State to be a certification authority to verify electronic signatures and requires it to conduct a study of the use of electronic signatures for commercial purposes. It became law without the Governor's signature on May 25, 1996. To be codified at Fla. Statutes & sect; 1.01(4).

1996 Digital Signature Advisory Committee Report. On November 30, 1996, the Florida Digital Signature Advisory Committee issued its report titled Electronic Commerce in Florida: Report to the Joint Legislative Committee on Information Technology Resources, from the Florida Department of State. Their report concluded that while licensure of private certification authorities is likely to be necessary in the future, there is not an immediate demand for digital signature services, and as such, comprehensive legislation would be inappropriate. Instead, the report recommends that the legislature authorize the Secretary of State to establish a voluntary system of licensure and regulation for private certification authorities, at such future time when it is clear that such a program has become necessary. The features of this future program would include voluntary licensure, funding by licensees through licensing fees and audit charges, identification of standards and specific requirements for licensure, audit procedures to assure program compliance, insurance, reserve, or bonding requirements, and procedures for license revocation or suspension. The report also recommends that the Secretary of State be authorized to enter into reciprocity agreements with other jurisdictions to allow the fullest possible recognition of digital signatures executed in Florida.

The Report also recommends the creation of a special class of attorneys, who are authorized under Florida law with the Secretary of State's approval, to act as international attorney-notaries to authenticate and execute international transactions.

Electronic Notarization; 1997 Florida House Bill 1413. Enacted on May 30, 1997, this Bill authorizes the Secretary of State to provide commissions for notaries public to perform electronic notarizations. It also authorizes the Secretary of State to establish a voluntary licensure program for private certification authorities, and the commissioning of international notaries (e.g. "cybernotaries"). It grants rulemaking authority to the Secretary of State.
LEXIS: 1997 FL H.B. 1413.

Electronic Notarization; 1997 Florida House Bill 957. Introduced on March 4, 1997, revised on April 1, 1997, and sent to the Senate Committee on Governmental Reform and Oversight on April 24,

1997, this Bill authorizes the Secretary of State to provide commissions for notaries public to perform electronic notarizations. It also authorizes the Secretary of State to establish a voluntary licensure program for private certification authorities, and the commissioning of international notaries (e.g. "cybernotaries"). It grants rulemaking authority to the Secretary of State.

LEXIS: 1997 FL H.B. 957.

Electronic Notarization; Florida Senate Bill 998. This Bill was also introduced on March 4, 1997, and is similar to House Bill 957.

LEXIS: 1997 FL S.B. 998.

10. Georgia

Georgia Electronic Records and Signatures Act; 1997 Georgia Senate Bill 103. This Bill was enacted and signed by the governor on April 22, 1997. It defines the term "electronic signature" using the same five requirements as the California legislation. It provides that any person "may, but shall not be required to" accept or agree to be bound by an electronic record executed or adopted with an electronic signature. It further provides that where a person agrees to be bound by an electronic record executed or adopted with an electronic signature, then applicable writing and signature requirements shall be deemed satisfied.

The legislation also expresses the General Assembly's desire to encourage state government agencies and private sector entities to conduct their business and transactions using electronic media, and to that end authorizes all state agencies to establish pilot projects to serve as models for the application of technology such as electronic signatures, and to provide a proof of concept for same. The statute also provides that "one such pilot project may involve digital signatures and the use of a public key infrastructure established by a service provider."

Finally, the legislation creates an Electronic Commerce Study Committee composed of twelve members to issue findings and recommendations for proposed legislation by 12/15/97.

1997 Georgia House Bill 487. This Bill was enacted on April 14, 1997. It amends the Georgia statutes relating to motor vehicles and traffic to authorize the use of digital signatures under certain circumstances. It grants the Commissioner the authority to authorize use of a digital signature as an alternative to a handwritten signature as long as appropriate security measures are implemented which assure security and verification of the digital signature process. The Act defines a digital signature as a digital or electronic method executed or adopted by a party with an intent to be bound or to authenticate a record, which is (1) unique to the person using it; (2) capable of verification; (3) under the sole control of the person using it; and (4) linked to the data in such a manner that if the data are changed, the digital signature is invalidated.

LEXIS: 1997 GA H.B. 487.

11. Hawaii

Hawaii Rev. Statutes, Chapter 601.   Enacted on June 17, 1996, this Bill provides that the state judiciary shall convene a task force in consultation with the Department of Commerce and Consumer Affairs to explore a program for computer-based digital and electronic filing of court documents. The judiciary and the Department of Commerce and Consumer Affairs shall submit a joint report to the legislature on an annual basis regarding the status and results of the program. A special fund is created for implementation of the program. The Bill is to be repealed on June 30, 2000. 1995 HI S.B. 2401.

Hawaii Digital Signature Act; 1997 Hawaii Senate Bill 961.   The Hawaii Digital Signature Act was introduced on January 17, 1997, and amended on February 28, 1997. It was sent to the House Committees on Comsumer Protection and Commerce and the Judiciary on March 6, 1997. It provides for the licensing and regulation of certification authorities by the Hawaii Department of Commerce and Consumer Affairs. To obtain a license, a certification authority must be either an attorney, a financial institution, a title insurance company, or a department or division of the state government. CAs must employ at least one notary public, and must file a suitable guarantee with the Department. The legislation also provides for performance audits and investigations or licensed CAs, and publication of certification authority disclosure records containing information about CAs. The Bill also provides that the Department will be a certification authority, and will provide for an online repository.

LEXIS: 1997 HI S.B. 961.

12. Idaho

13. Illinois

Commission on Electronic Commerce. In April 1996, Illinois Attorney General Jim Ryan announced the formation of a Commission on Electronic Commerce and Crime, which is charged with the task of drafting digital signature legislation for Illinois. The Commission has been meeting since July 1996, and is working on draft digital signature legislation to be introduced in the Illinois General Assembly in January 1998. Titled the "Illinois Electronic Commerce Security Act," it is designed to facilitate electronic commerce by:

- Ensuring that electronic records and electronic signatures of all types meet the writing and signature requirements within the State of Illinois;

- Designating a class of "secure" electronic records and "secure" electronic signatures that provide a heightened degree of legal protection; and

- Specifying when digital signatures will qualify as "secure" signatures, as well as the rules that govern the activities of the various parties to a digitally signed transaction.

1997 Illinois House Bill 276. This Bill, introduced January 29, 1997, and engrossed April 18, 1997, allows for the use of digital signatures in any communication between a state agency and the comptroller in which a signature is required or used. It provides that the use of a digital signature will have the same force and effect as the use of a manual signature if the digital signature is unique to the person using it, is capable of verification, is under the sole control of the person using it, is linked to the data in such a manner that if the data is changed, the digital signature is invalidated, and conforms to regulations adopted by the comptroller.
    LEXIS: 1997 IL H.B. 276.

1997 Illinios Senate Bill 516. This Bill, introduced February 6, 1997, and enrolled on May 8, 1997, is essentially the same as House Bill 276.
    LEXIS: 1997 IL S.B. 516.

14. Indiana

Electronic Digital Signature Act; Senate Bill 5 a. Enacted June 5, 1997, this Bill applies only to transactions with the State, and provides that a digital signature on a document received by or filed with the state is effective if: (1) it is unique to the person using it; (2) it is capable of verification; (3) it is under the sole control of the person using it; (4) it is linked to data in such a manner that if the data are changed, the digital signature is invalidated; and (5) it conforms to regulations adopted by the State Board of Accounts. It also provides that the State Board of Accounts is responsible for implementing and administering a method used by the state to conduct authenticated electronic transactions using digital signatures, and requires the State Board of Accounts to seek the advice of public and private entities in adopting administrative rules.
1997 IN S.B. 5 a.

Electronic Digital Signature Act; 1997 House Bill 1945. Digital signature legislation was introduced in the House on January 27, 1997, and enrolled on May 6, 1997. The bill applies only to transactions with the State, and provides that a digital signature on a document received by or filed with the state is effective if: (1) it is unique to the person using it; (2) it is capable of verification; (3) it is under the sole control of the person using it; (4) it is linked to data in such a manner that if the data are changed, the digital signature is invalidated; and (5) it conforms to regulations adopted by the State Board of Accounts. It also provides that the State Board of Accounts is responsible for implementing and administering a method used by the state to conduct authenticated electronic transactions using digital signatures, and requires the State Board of Accounts to seek the advice of public and private entities in adopting administrative rules.

15. Iowa

Code of Iowa Section 48A.13 (1995). Iowa permits electronic signatures for voter registration forms once "the state voter registration commission shall prescribe by rule the technological requirements for guaranteeing the security and integrity of electronic signatures."
Iowa has also just begun investigating legislation relating to digital signatures. However, no draft legislation has yet been prepared.

16. Kansas

Kansas Digital Signature Act; 1997 Kansas House Bill 2059. The Kansas Digital Signature Act was enacted on May 15, 1997. The Act simply provides that a digital signature may be accepted as a substitute for, and, if accepted, shall have the same force and effect as, in other form of signature. It defines a digital signature as a computer created electronic identifier that is (1) intended by the party using it to have the force and effect of a signature; (2) unique to the party using it; (3) capable of verification; (4) under the sole control of the party using it; and (5) linked to data in such a manner that it is invalidated if the data is changed.

LEXIS: 1997 KS H.B. 2059.

17. Kentucky

Kentucky Electronic Signatures web site.

18. Louisiana

West's Louisiana Revised Statutes Annotated Section 40:2144 (1995). Louisiana has adopted legislation similar to that of Connecticut for electronic signatures. It provides for the use of "alphanumeric or similar codes, fingerprints, or other identifying methods" for medical records, subject to guidelines promulgated by the Department of Health and Hospitals.

Louisiana 1997 House Bill 294. Introduced on March 31, 1997, and engrossed April 16, 1997, this bill provides for the admissability into evidence of specific bank records that contain signatures created and stored by digital or electronic means.

LEXIS: 1997 LA H.B. 294.

Louisiana 1997 House Bill 1929. On April 16, 1997, this Bill was reported favorably from the House Committee on Health and Welfare. This bill redefines "vital records" to include electronic records and defines "signature" to include a written or electronic signature.

LEXIS: 1997 LA H.B. 1929.

Louisiana 1997 Senate Bill 609. On May 5, 1997, this Bill was amended on the House floor. This Bill relates to vital statistics and redefines "vital records." The Bill defines "signature" and "sign(ed)" to include written or electronic signatures.

LEXIS: 1997 LA S.B. 609.

19. Maine

1997 Maine Senate Bill 473. Introduced on March 11, 1997, this Bill amends the provisions of the main motor vehicle code to authorize the use of the digital image of the applicant's signature.

LEXIS: 1997 ME S.B. 473.

20. Maryland

Maryland Digital Signature Act; 1997 Maryland House Bill 1015. Introduced on February 3, 1997, this Bill provides for the licensing and regulation of Certification Authorities. It also provides that the Secretary of State shall be a certification authority, and shall adopt regulations for licensing, audits, investigations, duties, etc., of certification authorities. It generally takes a Utah-based approach to digital signature legislation.

LEXIS: 1997 MD H.B. 1015.

Maryland Digital Signature Act; 1997 Maryland Senate Bill 822. Introduced on February 10, 1997, this Bill is substantially similar to Maryland House Bill 1015.

LEXIS: 1997 MD S.B. 822.

1997 Maryland House Bill 1386. Introduced on February 24, 1997, this Bill establishes a task force on digital signature law for purposes of studying and making recommendations on digital signature law in the state. The task force is charged with addressing issues of:

(a) The extent to which digital signature technology should be available or mandated
(b) Qualifications for a certification authority
(c) Alternatives for the standard of care in safeguarding private keys
(d) Alternatives to the degree and scope of regulation of a certification authority

(e) Alternatives for assuring the financial responsibility of a certification authority

(f) Coordination with digital signature law in other states.

LEXIS: 1997 MD H.B.1386.

21. Massachusetts

Massachusetts is drafting legislation that takes a minimalist approach that equates all electronic signatures (including digital signatures) with traditional ink and pen technology for purposes of evidence admissibility and weight.

22. Michigan

Michigan Digital Signature Act; 1997 Michigan Senate Bill 204. Introduced on February 19, 1997, this Bill provides for the licensing and regulation of certification authorities, specifies the duties of certification authorities and subscribers, specifies the effect of using a digital signature, and addresses the recognition and liability of repositories.

LEXIS: 1997 MD S.B. 204.

23. Minnesota

Electronic Signature Legislation. Minnesota has enacted "electronic signature" legislation that allows for facsimile and digitized signatures in limited situations, such as use by the Department of Administration Organization (Chapter 16B.05), use on orders relating to workers' compensation (Chapter 176.281), service of papers relating to workers' compensation matters (Chapter 176.285), use on electronically filed tax returns (Chapter 289A.07), and use on motor fuels tax reports filed with the State (Chapter 296.041).

Minnesota Electronic Authentication Act; 1997 Minnesota Senate Bill 173. A Utah/Washington-style digital signature statute, titled the Minnesota Electronic Authentication Act, was enacted in Minnesota on May 19, 1997. It provides for licensure of certification authorities, performance audits and investigations, requirements for and obligations of certification authorities, controls of private keys, suspension, revocation, and expiration of certificates, recommended reliance limits and liability, presumptions in adjudication of disputes, and standards for recognition of repositories. It authorizes the Secretary of State to issue rules governing licensing of certification authorities, financial responsibility, and recordkeeping requirements. The bill was amended and passed by the Judiciary Committee on March 24, and by the Government Operations Committee on 4/11

1997 Minnesota Senate Bill 1905.   Enacted May 30, 1997, Article 3 of this Bill is devoted to information technology issues. It provides for the use of digital signatures in accordance with procedures approved by the Commissioner. It also establishes an Office of Technology to provide leadership and direction for information and communications technology policy in Minnesota.
LEXIS: 1997 MN S.B. 1905.

Minnesota Electronic Authentication Act; 1997 Minnesota H.F. 56.   This Bill is the same as 1997 Minnesota Senate Bill 173.

1997 Minnesota Senate Bill 240.   Provides for the electronic conduct of state business; authorizes the Commissioner of Administration to approve the use of electronic approvals and digital signatures in conduct of state business. Introduced 1/30/97 and sent to the House Committee on Government Operations on April 30, 1997.

1997 Minnesota House Bill 871.   Introduced on February 20, this Bill provides for the electronic conduct of state business and authorized the Commissioner of Administration to approve digital signatures. It is limited to use by personnel of the Department of Administration in accordance with the Commissioner's delegated authority and instructions. Essentially the same as Senate Bill 240.
LEXIS: 1997 MN H.B. 871 and 1997 S.B. 240.

24. Mississippi

Digital Signature Act of 1997; 1997 Mississippi H.B. 752.   On March 17, 1997, Mississippi enacted the Digital Signature Act of 1997.

The legislation authorizes the Secretary of State to:

- Serve as the certification authority to verify the digital signature of any public entity in Mississippi
- License private certification authorities on a showing that they —
  - possess proficiency in encryption technology
  - possess sufficient working capital
  - maintain an office or registered agent in the state

Under the Bill, digital signatures "verified by a licensed certification authority" shall have the same force and effect as a written signature. The use of digital signatures is optional.

1997 Mississippi Senate Bill 2904. Introduced 1/21/97: authorizes the use of digital signature for document certification, requires Secretary of State to license providers of certification services, and to certify digital signatures for public entities in Mississippi.

25. Missouri

26. Montana

1997 Montana House Bill 468. Introduced 2/6/97, amended 2/18/97: authorizes Secretary of State to develop and implement a statewide electronic filing system. In the event of its development and implementation, requires the Secretary to promulgate rules on access, security, and integrity of electronic filing.

LEXIS: 1997 MT H.B. 468.

27. Nebraska

1997 Nebraska Legislative Bill 286. A limited digital signature statute was introduced in the State legislature on January 14, 1997. It uses the term "digital signature" to refer to an electronic identifier, created by a computer, intended by the party using it to have the same force and effect as the use of a manual signature. It authorizes the use of digital signatures on communications with State agencies, and provides that the digital signature shall have the same force and effect as a manual signature if: (1) it is unique to the person using it; (2) it is capable of verification; (3) it is under the sole control of the person using it; (4) it is linked to data in such a manner that if the data is changed, the digital signature is invalidated; and (5) it conforms to regulations adopted by the Secretary of State. The Secretary of State is required to promulgate regulations on or before September 1, 1998, on the use of digital signatures.

1997 Nebraska Legislative Bill 42. Introduced on January 9, 1997, the Bill authorizes the use of digital signatures (and provides that they will have the same force and effect as the use of a manual signature) provided that the digital signature is (1) unique to the person using it; (2) capable of verification; (3) under the sole control of the person using it; (4) is linked to data in such a manner that if the data is changed, the digital signature is invalidated; and (5) conforms to rules and regulations adopted by the Secretary of State.
  LEXIS: 1997 NE L.B. 42.

1997 Nebraska Legislative Resolution 262. Introduced on May 22, 1997, this resolution provides for a study of the issues surrounding the enactment of digital signature legislation, including the policy issues presented by L.B. 42 and L.B. 286.
  LEXIS: 1997 NE L.R. 262.

28. Nevada

1997 Nevada Senate Bill 42. Enacted April 26, 1997, this Bill authorizes the State Controller to provide by regulation for the use of electronic signatures in financial transactions "pertaining to this state."
  LEXIS: 1997 NV S.B. 42.

29. New Hampshire

1997 New Hampshire House Bill 190. Introduced on January 9, 1997, this Bill authorizes the use of electronic signatures and provides that they will have the same force and effect as a written signature. It also authorizes the Secretary of State to issue certificates for the purpose of verifying digital signatures.
  LEXIS: 1997 NH H.B. 190.

New Hampshire Digital Signature Act; 1997 New Hampshire Senate Bill 207. Introduced on January 23, 1997, and passed by the First House with amendments on April 24, 1997, this Bill requires the Secretary of State to issue regulations for the certification and regulation of certification authorities and provides that the Secretary of State will be a certification authority.

LEXIS: 1997 NH S.N. 207.

30. New Jersey

31. New Mexico

1996 NM H.B. 516. On March 4, 1996, New Mexico enacted the Electronic Authentication of Documents Act. The Act describes as its purpose to "provide a centralized, public, electronic registry for authenticating electronic documents by means of a public and private key system; promote commerce; and facilitate electronic information and document transactions." An "office of electronic documentation" is established under the secretary of the state to maintain a register of public keys. The Secretary of State is required to adopt regulations to accomplish the purposes of the Act, and may contract with a private, public, or quasi-public organization to provide services under the Act. The Act took effect July 1, 1996, and is codified at NMSA Sections 14-15-1 to 14-15-6.

32. New York

Digital Signatures Act; 1997 New York S.B. 2238 and A.B. 6813. A Utah/Washington-style digital signature statute, titled the Digital Signatures Act, was introduced in the New York State Senate on February 5, 1997 and in the New York General Assembly on March 4, 1997. It was sent to the Judiciary Committee.

33. North Carolina

Electronic Commerce Commission; 1997 North Carolina House Bill 290. Introduced on February 20, 1997, this Bill establishes a legislative study commission on electronic commerce to determine the best means of developing electronic commerce in the state. Issues the Commission is to address include evaluating the feasibility and desirability of authorizing the use of digital signatures, reviewing digital signature legislation in other states, and determining whether or not it is in the public interest to regulate the practices of certification authorities, etc.

LEXIS: 1997 NC H.B. 290.

Information Technology Commission; 1997 North Carolina House Bill 1047. Introduced on April 21, 1997, this Bill establishes a legislative study commission on information technology to review current information technology that impacts public policy. The goals and objectives of the Commission are to develop electronic commerce in the state and coordinate the use of information technology by state agencies. Issues the Commission is to address include evaluating the feasibility and desirability of authorizing the use of digital signatures to facilitate the development of electronic commerce, reviewing digital signature legislation in other states, and determining whether or not it is in the public interest to regulate the practices of certification authorities, etc.

LEXIS: 1997 NC H.B. 1047.

North Carolina 1997 House Bill 925. Introduced on April 10, 1997, as part of an act to protect the privacy of health information, this legislation defines "electronic signature" to mean "Digital or electronic signatures in conformity with applicable provisions of the Uniform Commercial Code recommended by the National Conference of Commissioners on Uniform State Laws and the American Law Institute, Electronic Information and Digital Signature Guidelines established by the organizations set forth in g.s. 132a-4-1(d), the Digital Signature Guidelines recommended by the American Bar Association Science and Technology Committee Section, Committee on Information Security, or other electronic signature guidelines authorized by federal or state law.

LEXIS: 1997 NC H.B. 925.

North Carolina 1997 Senate Bill 1005. (Similar to House Bill 925) Introduced on April 21, 1997, as part of an act to protect the privacy of health information, this legislation defines "electronic signature" to mean "Digital or electronic signatures in conformity with applicable provisions of the Uniform Commercial Code recommended by the National Conference of Commissioners on Uniform State Laws and the American Law Institute, Electronic Information and Digital Signature Guidelines established by the organizations set forth in g.s. 132a-4-1(d), the Digital Signature Guidelines recommended by the American Bar Association Science and Technology Committee Section, Committee on Information Security, or other electronic signature guidelines authorized by federal or state law.

LEXIS: 1997 NC H.B. 1005.

34. North Dakota

1997 North Dakota Senate Concurrent Resolution 4024. This resolution directs the legislative council to study the development of an electronic mail and records management policy for governmental entities. The resolution recognizes that official business may be conducted electronically using digital signatures.

LEXIS: 1997 ND S.C.R. 4024.

35. Ohio

1997 Ohio House Bill 243. This Bill allows the use of electronic signatures or authorizations for medical records. The legislation is primarily intended to facilitate in-hospital verifications of medical reports, diagnoses, and similar administrative signatures.

36. Oklahoma

Electronic Signature Act; 1997 Oklahoma House Bill 1690. Enacted on April 15, 1997, the Bill creates a task force on Electronic Signature Technology, and requires submission of a report to the House Science and Technology Committee by December 1, 1997.

LEXIS: 1997 OK H.B. 1690.

37. Oregon

Electronic Signature Act; 1997 Oregon House Bill 3046. Introduced on March 7, 1997, and engrossed on May 6, 1997 this Bill authorizes the use of electronic signatures and provides that they have the same force and effect as a written signature. It also authorizes the Department of Consumer and Business Services to issue certificates for the purpose of verifying digital signatures, and to take other actions necessary to achieve the purposes of the Act including the suspension or revocation of certificates issued by the Department of Consumer and Business Services. The Department of Consumer and Business Services is also authorized to register certification authorities (called "authentication authorities") to ensure the integrity of digital signatures.

LEXIS: 1997 OR H.B. 3046.

38. Pennsylvania

39. Rhode Island

Electronic Signatures and Records Act; 1997 Rhode Island House Bill 6118. Introduced on February 4, 1997, and substituted on April 29, 1997, this Bill authorizes the use of electronic signatures in written communications between state departments and/or public agencies.

LEXIS: 1997 RI H.B. 6118.

Digital Signature Act; 1997 Rhode Island Senate Bill 612. Introduced on February 11, 1997, this Bill provides for the licensing and regulation of certification authorities by the Secretary of State, and provides that the Secretary of State shall be a certification authority. It also specifies the obligations of certification authorities and subscribers, and specifies the effect of using a digital signature.

LEXIS: 1997 RI S.B. 612.

40. South Carolina

41. South Dakota

42. Tennessee

Tennessee 1997 Senate Bill 1090. On April 16, 1997, this Bill was introduced to the Senate Committee on the Judiciary. This Bill authorizes courts to implement procedures for the use of electronic signatures in signing of pleadings, court orders, judgment orders, or other court documents.

LEXIS: 1997 TN S.B. 1090.

Tennessee 1997 House Bill 1718. On April 23, 1997, this Bill was introduced to the House Committee on the Judicary. This Bill authorizes courts to implement procedures for use of electronic signatures in signing of pleadings, court orders, judgment orders, or other court documents.

LEXIS: 1997 TN H.B. 1718.

43. Texas

Texas H.B. 984. Enacted on June 1, 1997, this Statute amends the Business & Commerce Code to establish the equivalence of written and digital signatures and allow digital signatures to authenticate written electronic communications sent to state agencies, subject to compliance with rules adopted by the Comptroller, State Auditor, and the Attorney General. It uses the term "digital signature" to refer to an electronic identifier, created by a computer, intended by the party using it to have the same force and effect as the use of a manual signature. It provides that a written electronic communication sent from or received in the state of Texas is considered signed if a digital signature is transmitted with the communication. However, a digital signature may be used on communications with state agencies only if it conforms to regulations adopted by the Department of Information Resources. The regulations are to consider factors that may affect the reliability of a digital signature, including whether a digital signature is: (1) unique to the person using it; (2) capable of verification; (3) under the sole control of the person using it; and (4) transmitted in a manner that will invalidate the digital signature if data in the communication or digital signature is changed.

LEXIS: 1997 TX H.B. 984.

Texas S.B. 748. A limited digital signature statute was introduced in the State legislature on February 26, 1997. It is essentially the same as H.B. 984, except that it is limited to communications sent from or received by a State agency.

Texas S.B. 787. A limited digital signature statute was introduced in the State legislature on March 3, 1997. It is similar to S.B. 984, in that it is limited to communications sent from or received by a State agency. It also sets forth the same requirements for a digital signature as H.B. 984 and S.B. 748.

1997 Texas Senate Bill 645.   This Bill was enrolled on May 28, 1997. It authorizes the state comptroller to establish procedures for using a digital signature under certain conditions. It also provides that a digital signature has the same legal force and effect for all purposes as a manual signature for purposes of state agency transactions.
   LEXIS: 1997 TX S.B. 645.

1997 Texas Senate Bill 370.   This Bill was engrossed on April 21, 1997, and Recommended as Substituted from Committee on May 13, 1997. It authorizes the Department of Transportation to accept license applications that are transmitted with a digital signature, provided that the digital signature meets the requirements of applicable rules, is unique to the person using it, is capable of independent verification, is under the sole control of the person using it, and is linked to the data such that if the data is changed the signature is invalidated.
   LEXIS: 1997 TX S.B. 370.

44. Utah

The Utah Digital Signature Act, Utah Code Annotated & sect; & sect; 46-3-101 to -504 (1995).   A copy of this Act and related commentary can be found at www.state.ut.us. This legislation was the first to authorize commercial use of digital signatures. It governs the use of public-private key pair encryption and certification authorities and was designed to comport with various international and national standards that are already in place. Certification authorities are to be licensed by the Utah Department of Commerce. The legislation also protects the subscriber's private key as property, and therefore its theft or unauthorized use is subject to criminal and civil liability.

1996 Utah Senate Bill 73.   This Bill was signed by the Governor on March 8, 1996. It makes some minor technical amendments to Sections 46-3-103 and 46-3-301 of the Utah Digital Signature Act.

1996 Utah Senate Bill 188.   This Bill was signed by the Governor on March 12, 1996. It is the first set of substantial amendments to the Utah Digital Signature Act. The Act is concerned with notarization and authentication. Among other things, it defines certain terms; outlines the role of the Division of Corporations and Commercial Code; provides certification requirements, procedures, and duties; provides for performance audits and investigations; outlines enforcement responsibilities; provides for warranties and obligations of certification authorities; specifies control of the private key; provides for suspension, revocation, and expiration of certificates; gives recommended reliance limits and liability; provides for collection on suitable guaranty; specifies signature requirements and presumptions in adjudications; recognizes repositories and their liabilities; and provides exemptions to auditing requirements.

Utah is continuing to draft its administrative rules to implement its digital signature program. It has also recently selected a vendor to develop a repository and to provide digital signature software and certification authority services for the state. Utah anticipates that it will begin implementing certification authority licensing and start using digital signatures by August 1997.

1997 Utah House Bill 95. Introduced on February 4, 1997, this Bill contains provisions regarding to notary publics. The Bill provides that a notary's acknowledgment on an electronic message or document is considered complete without the imprint of the notary's official seal if the message has been digitally signed in the presence of a notary, and the notary signs the acknowledgement with a digital signature.

LEXIS: 1997 UT H.B. 95.

45. Vermont

1997 House Bill 60. House Bill 60 was introduced by Representative Keenan on January 14, 1997, to establish a digital mechanism to authorize the signing and authentication of documents. The proposed legislation takes an approach similar to the Utah and Washington models, in that it provides for the licensing and regulation of certification authorities. It also provides that the Secretary of State will be a certification authority.

46. Virginia

Virginia Senate Bill 923. Enacted on April 19, 1997, this is a limited digital signature statute. It uses the term "digital signature" to refer to an electronic identifier, created by a computer, intended by the party using it to have the same force and effect as the use of a manual signature. It provides legal recognition for digital signatures; allows digital signatures to serve in place of notarized or acknowledged signatures when filing documents with executive agencies of the Commonwealth; and requires the Council on Information Management to promulgate regulations on or before September 1, 1998, on the use of digital signatures. (to be codified as chap. 39, Section 59.1-467 et seq. Virginia Statutes)

1996 Virginia House Joint Resolution 195. This Bill relates to digital signatures and issues related to electronic commerce. It establishes a joint committee to study digital signature issues and to determine whether Virginia should adopt legislation that would facilitate the development of electronic commerce in Virginia. It passed the Senate on February 29, 1996, and the House concurred in the Senate amendments on March 4, 1996.

1997 Virginia House Bill 2138. Approved on April 2, 1997, this Bill established the Joint Commission on Technology and Science (JCOTS). The new Commission is, in addition to its many other duties, responsible for studying and promoting all aspects of technology and science in the Commonwealth (including digital signatures, cryptography, etc.). The bill amended the Code of Virginia by adding into Title 30 a chapter numbered "11," consisting of sections numbered 30-85 through 30-88.

47. Washington

Digital Signature Act; 1996 Washington Senate Bill 6423. This Bill was signed by the Governor on March 29, 1996. It creates the Washington Digital Signature Act. It declares an intent to facilitate commerce by means of reliable electronic messages, to minimize the incidence of forged digital signatures and fraud in electronic commerce, to implement legally the general import of relevant standards, and to establish in coordination with multiple states uniform rules regarding the authentication and reliability of electronic messages. The Washington bill is modeled after the Utah statute. Washington is in the process of amending its digital signature legislation.

1997 Washington Senate Bill 5308. 1997 Washington Senate Bill 5308 was approved on April 8, 1997, and signed by the governor on April 15, 1997. It amends existing digital signature law to provide that the Secretary of State is a certification authority, and that certificates issued by the Secretary have the same effect as a certificate issued by a licensed certification authority. It grants the Secretary discretionary authority to adopt rules to govern certification authorities, and repositories, suspension and revocation of licenses, recordkeeping, etc. It also makes a number of other minor changes and corrections to the Washington Digital Signature Act.

LEXIS: 1997 WA S.B. 5308.

State of Washington Digital Signature Web Site

48. West Virginia

49. Wisconsin

50. Wyoming

Wyoming Statutes 9-1-306. Wyoming enacted limited digital signature legislation in 1996. Codified at Wyoming Statutes 9-1-306, it authorizes the use of digital signatures for documents filed electronically with the Secretary of State. It also extends civil and criminal penalties applicable to fraudulent manual or facsimile signatures to electronic signatures. It also authorizes rulemaking by the Secretary of State.

51. National Conference of Commissioners on Uniform State Law (NCCUSL)

In July 1996, NCCUSL voted to establish a drafting committee on electronic contracting to draft a uniform statute relating to the use of electronic communications and records in contractual transactions. The fundamental premise of this project is to draft such revisions to general contract law as are necessary or desirable to support transaction processes utilizing existing and future electronic or computerized technologies. The drafting committee held its first drafting committee meeting on May 2-3, 1997, and the next meeting is scheduled for September 19-21,

1997. A copy of the drafting committeee's draft statute is available at the NCCUSL web site.

Federal Legislation & Regulations

52. U.S. Food and Drug Administration

Regulations on Electronic Records; Electronic Signatures — 21 CFR Part 11 (March 20, 1997). The U.S. Food and Drug Administration released new regulations on March 20, 1997, that set forth the criteria for acceptance by FDA of electronic records, electronic signatures, and handwritten signatures executed to electronic records as equivalent to paper records and handwritten signatures executed on paper. These regulations, which apply to all FDA program areas, are intended to permit the widest possible use of electronic technology, compatible with FDA's responsibility to promote and protect public health. The use of electronic records as well as their submission to FDA is voluntary.

53. Federal Key Escrow Legislation (draft)

Electronic Data Security Act of 1997 (March 12, 1997, draft). The first draft of the Clinton Administration's proposed key recovery (or key escrow) legislation has recently been made public. Titled the "Electronic Data Security Act of 1997," the March 12, 1997, draft legislation seeks to "enable the development of a key management infrastructure for public-key-based encryption . . . that will assure that individuals and businesses can transmit and receive information electronically with confidence in the information's confidentiality, integrity, availability, and authenticity, and that will promote lawful government access."

The Act authorizes the Secretary of Commerce to register certification authorities and key recovery agents. Certification authorities registered under the Act may issue public key certificates certifying a public key that can be used for encryption only if the person to whom the certificate is issued stores information with a key recovery agent sufficient to allow the recovery of the plain text of such person's encrypted data and communications. Key recovery agents will be required to disclose key recovery information to a government agency acting pursuant to a duly authorized warrant or court order, and to a law enforcement or national security government agency merely "upon receipt of written authorization in a form to be specified by the attorney general." The draft bill specifies no further standards for the release of keys and prohibits notice to the person whose key has been revealed.

International

54. United Nations Commission on International Trade Law (UNCITRAL)

Model Digital Signature Legislation. Beginning in February 1997, UNCITRAL has begun the task of drafting model international digital signature legislation. Meetings were held at the United Nations from February 18-28, 1997. See the Report titled "Planning of Future Work on Electronic Commerce: Digital Signatures, Certification Authorities and Related Legal Issues" issued by the United Nations Secretariat on December 31, 1996. A report summarizing the results of the February 18-28, 1997, meetings was issued by the secretariat on March 12, 1997.

55. European Union

Study on the Legal Aspects of Digital Signatures. In mid-1996 the Commission of the European Communities DG XV issued an invitation to tender for a Study on the Legal Aspects of Digital Signatures, which should give an overview of national and EU policies, existing and envisaged rules and regulations, as well as practices concerning digital signatures in the Member States and the EU's main trading partners.

56. Organization for Economic Co-operation and Development (OECD)

Guidelines for Cryptography Policy. "The OECD has adopted Guidelines for Cryptography Policy, setting out principles to guide countries in formulating their own policies and legislation relating to the use of cryptography. The Recommendation which came before the governing body of the OECD, the Council, on Thursday 27 March, is a non-binding agreement that identifies the basic issues that countries should consider in drawing up cryptography policies at the national and international level. The Recommendation culminates one year of intensive talks to draft the Guidelines."

The Guidelines recognize the commercial importance of cryptography, noting that it "can be an effective tool for the secure use of information technology by insuring confidentiality, integrity and availability of data and by providing authentication and nonrepudiation mechanisms for that data." They also recognize that the failure to utilize cryptographic methods can adversely affect the protection of privacy, intellectual property, business and financial information, public safety and national security, and the operation of electronic commerce.

The Guidelines do not, however, endorse the key escrow or key recovery position sought by the U.S. Government. Instead, they let countries decide on their own whether to require government access to decoding "keys." Moreover, they recommend that member countries remove, or avoid creating, unjustified obstacles to international trade and the development of information and communications networks.

The Organisation for Economic Co-operation and Development is an international organization with 29 Member countries from North America, Europe and the Asia-Pacific area. Based in Paris, France, it is a forum permitting governments of the industrialized democracies to study and formulate economic and social policies. Its sole function is direct cooperation among the governments of its Member countries.

57. Canada

Survey of Legal Issues Relating to the Security of Electronic Information.

58. Denmark

59. France

France's Proposed Statutory Trusted Third Party Rules for Encryption. This is Article 12 of France's proposed telecommunications law (translation), posted by Steptoe & Johnson.

60. Germany

The final draft of the German digital signature law was approved by the federal cabinet and submitted to the lower house of the federal parliament ("Bundesrat") by Chancellor Helmut Kohl on December 20, 1996. Together with the final draft of the "Multimedia Law" (of which the digital signature law constitutes Article 3), the draft law will be debated in parliament during 1997, with the government's aim being to have it enacted as law by August 1, 1997.

(translation and commentary by Christopher Kuner)

61. Italy

Proposed Italian digital signature legislation.

62. Japan

Certification Authority Guidelines (Alpha Version). Prepared by the Electronic Commerce Promotion Council of Japan (ECOM) and released on April 7, 1997.

63. Malaysia

Digital Signature Bill 1997.

64. United Kingdom

Licensing of Trusted Third Parties for the Provision of Encryption Services — Public Consultation Paper on Detailed Proposals for Legislation (March 1997). The UK government has issued a blueprint of its key recovery/digital signature/encryption legislative plans. The report is a "Public Consultation Paper on Licensing of Trusted Third Parties for the Provision of Encryption Services." It is intended as a prelude to the introduction of legislation. It sets out the UK government's policy proposals for the mandatory licensing and regulation of Trusted Third Parties (TTPs) to provide a range of information security services to their clients. Comments are invited until May 30, 1997.

APPENDIX V

Pointers to Pertinent Web Sites

This is a list of the URLs listed in the text of the book, plus some addtional pointers. This list is available online at: www.commerce.net/press/uds

General Internet Statistics Pointers

- GLG Consulting's Facts, Figures and Forecasts
  http://www.glgc.com/fff.html

- Netcraft's Web Server Growth http://www.netcraft.co.uk/survey/

- Network Wizards' Internet grow statistics
  http://www.nw.com/zone/WWW/top.html

- NUA's Internet Survey Summary http://www.nua.ie/surveys/

Security and Cryptography Resources

- Counterpane's Crypto Links
  http://www.counterpane.com/hotlist.html

- WWW Virtual Library's Crypto Page
  http://world.std.com/~franl/crypto/

- Yahoo!'s Security and Encryption Page
  http://www.yahoo.com/Computers_and_Internet/Security_
  and_Encryption/

Case Studies

Identification/Authentication

- Commonwealth of Mass. http://www.state.ma.us/itd/legal
- GE Corporate Research http://www.crd.ge.com
- GTE http://www.gte.com
- Hewlett Packard http://www.hp.com
- Qspace http://www.qspace.com
- Stein Rowe http://www.steinroe.com
- U.S. Government http://www.gsa.gov/fsi
- USWeb http://www.usweb.com

Securing Communication

- Ultramar Diamond Shamrock http://www.diasham.com
- Mellon Bank http://www.mellon.com
- PrimeHost http://www.primehost.com
- Wells Fargo Bank http://www.wellsfargo.com

Application Integration

- CyberCash http://www.cybercash.com
- E-Stamp http://www.estamp.com
- NetDox http://www.netdox.com
- Open Market http://www.openmarket.com
- U.S. Postal Service http://www.usps.gov

Other Public Key Systems

- Pretty Good Privacy http://www.pgp.com
- Certicom http://www.certicom.com

Legal Sites

- IETF PKIX Working Group
  http://www.ietf.org/html.charters/pkix-charter.html
- McBride Baker & Coles' Digital Signature Legislation Summary
  http://www.mbc.com/ds_sum.html
- EPIC Crypto Policy Page
  http://www.epic.org/crypto/export_controls/
- U.S. Encryption Policy Resource Page http://www.crypto.com
- Entrust CPS Guide http://www.entrust.com/downloads/cps.pdf
- VeriSign's CPS http://www.verisign.com/repository/CPS
- American Bar Association
  http://www.abanet.org/scitech/home.html

Understanding Digital Signatures Home Page
http://www.mcgraw-hill.com

Products and Services

- Atalla http://www.atalla.com
- BBN http://www.bbn.com
- Certco http://www.certco.com
- Cylink http://www.cylink.com
- Entrust http://www.entrust.com
- GTE CyberTrust http://www.cybertrust.gte.com
- IBM http://ww.internet.ibm.com/commercepoint/registry
- Netscape http://www.netscape.com
- VeriSign http://www.verisign.com
- VeriSign's Digital ID Center http://digitalid.verisign.com
- xCert http://www.xcert.com/

Applications and Toolkits

- E-Stamp http://www.estamp.com
- Harbinger http://www.harbinger.com
- Premenos http://www.premenos.com
- RSA Data Security http://www.rsa.com
- Terisa Systems http://www.terisa.com
- S/MIME Mailers
    - Baltimore Technologies Ltd.'s SecureMail
      http://www.baltimore.ie/mailsecure.htm
    - ConnectSoft's E-mail Connection http://www.connectsoft.com
    - FrontierTech's Intranet Genie http://www.frontiertech.com
    - Microsoft's Internet Explorer http://www.microsoft.com/ie/
    - Netscape's Communicator
      http://home.netscape.com/comprod/products/communicator/
    - OpenSoft's ExpressMail
      http://www.opensoft.com/products/expressmail/
    - WorldTalk's Secure Messenger http://www.deming.com/sm.htm
- SET Vendor Status Chart http://www.visa.com/cgi-bin/vee/nt/ecomm/set/vendor.html
- WebCompare's List of Web Servers http://www.webcompare.com

APPENDIX VI

U.S. Government

7th and D Sts, SW
Washington, DC
www.gsa.gov/fsi

Background   Government is beginning to use the recent advances in information technology to lower costs; increase efficiency and productivity; and collect, use, and analyze far more information, much of it personal. Furthermore, new electronic government applications—particularly those focused on service-to-the-citizen programs—present non-traditional challenges and vulnerabilities regarding accuracy, authentication, privacy, and security. These challenges and vulnerabilities are both technical and policy related. Prominent among these today is the appropriate role of the federal government in privacy and security. The American people want trustworthy, readily available information and computer systems that are user-friendly, secure, and protective of individual privacy. Public acceptance and reliance on electronic information and data require:

- striking the proper balance between an individual's personal privacy and the government's need for information,
- providing a high degree of security against unauthorized access or use, and
- maintaining the accuracy of the information stored or processed.

The Paperless Federal Transactions for the Public pilot project is a public key infrastructure initiative utilizing a hardware token for digital signature and encryption in support of federal standards. The Federal Information Security Infrastructure Program Management Office (SIPMO) was chartered by the Government Information Technology Service (GITS) working group to coordinate, develop, and launch pilot programs in support of the Vice President's vision for secure paperless transactions across the National Information Infrastructure (NII). Under joint General Services Administration (GSA)/Department of Defense (DOD) leadership, the SIPMO put together an interagency task group, the Federal Security Infrastructure Program (FSIP), tasked with developing a paperless pilot. The decision was made to concentrate on real-time World Wide Web (WWW) transactions using a hardware token and two-way authentication of certificates capable of supporting the basic security services of a public key infrastructure (PKI) (authentication, integrity, access confidentiality, and nonrepudiation) in a web environment.

Problem The electronic business of government requires security services to be viable. In the traditional data security model, there are five basic security services offered to end users and their applications: authentication, access control; (limiting access to the resources of an AIS [Automated Information System] only to authorized users, programs, processes, or other systems), data integrity, nonrepudiation, and confidentiality (privacy).

Why Public Key Certificates? As a practical matter, these services cannot be delivered in a networked world without a public key infrastructure. It is the essential enabling technology for accomplishing business objectives in a secure fashion. The majority of the security effort needs to be addressed at the agency level, but a government-wide infrastructure is needed to facilitate those agency actions. The broad introduction and application of this technology requires a security infrastructure having the service integrity and assurances required to support the distribution and verification of public key certificates. The infrastructure must incorporate the necessary policies, personnel, software, and information processing resources required to generate, issue, and revoke certificates, and provide for archiving, adjudication, and directory services. These are critical to the success of an electronic government.

How the Application Works The Paperless Federal Transactions for the Public project, based on Vice President Gore's vision, is as follows:

> Imagine this: A business woman walks into a post office, presents a picture ID, and is given a "public key." Using this key card, she electronically signs a federal contract and transmits it over the National Information Infrastructure to a contracting agency. This transaction is valid, secure and paperless.

It establishes a Federal Public Key Infrastructure pilot initially focused on World Wide Web technology. The developed security infrastructure will permit federal agencies to deploy WWW applications accessible to citizens using standard security services (identification, authentication, access control, integrity, confidentiality, and nonrepudiation). In this pilot the FSI will be the Certification Authority (CA) to support transition to a business environment in which government-to-citizen transactions are paperless, electronic, and private. To ensure the privacy of citizens' electronic transactions, the services will be used by both citizens and participating federal agencies.

Under the pilot, each participant will be issued a hardware token that resembles a 3.5" floppy diskette, which contains a certificate identifying the individual and a public/private key pair unique to the individual. With this token, the participant will be able to access a secure server, then exchange certificates in order to verify each other's identity. Once identity verification is complete, an encrypted connection is established and the digitally signed data is exchanged.

In order to make this pilot a reality, the SIPMO developed a plug-and-play concept and approached industry to participate in providing products that meet federal standards for digital signature and encryption. Several companies signed up and worked with each other and the SIPMO to solve interoperability problems. Four key participants were: Atalla (a Tandem Company), CygnaCom Solutions, Fischer International, and Frontier Technologies. Additional industry partnerships were established with Banyan Vines, Information Security Corporation, SAIC, and Trusted Information Systems to provide unique related hardware and software solutions.

As a result, the SIPMO can now demonstrate PKI security services utilizing the Fischer SmartDisk, the Frontier secure web browser, and the Atalla WebSafe.

Pilot participants include:

- The Department of Transportation Federal Transit Administration will use secure web access to process grants for state and local transit agencies.

- The Department of Transportation Office of Motor Carriers will use certificate-based access control to provide access to commercial license records.

- The GSA Federal Acquisition Services for Technology will accept proposals for rapid procurement services online.

- The GSA Federal Telecommunications Service will distribute post-FTS 2000 solicitations.

- The Government Printing Office will accept secure transactions to place Commerce Business Daily announcements.

■ The National Security Telecommunications and Information Systems Security Committee will use the secure web for creating a "virtual" meeting place for members to exchange information.

Issues   Adherence to a set of Federal Standards (DES, DSS, SHA)—FIPS 186 makes it mandatory to use the DSA signature algorithm within the federal government. Current commercial trends support the RSA algorithm in most off-the-shelf products. This limits the applications that can be used and/or increases applications cost to implement a DSA solution.

Online validation: The pilot will use online validation to provide near real-time validation of certificates. The certificate is considered invalid unless checked for validity. Current commercial models use certificate revocation lists, which require significant effort to maintain, manage, and distribute in a timely manner. The certificate is considered valid until instructed otherwise.

Use of hardware tokens to protect private signature key: One requirement in the federal government, in relation to obligation of funds, is that the private key for signature be under the sole control of the owner. One implementation of that requirement is the use of hardware tokens to provide key generation capability so that the private key exists only on the token. With the current state of technology, this drives user costs up and makes it difficult to find applications that support hardware tokens.

Positive ID proofing: Users will be required to fill out X.509 certificate request forms containing the user's name and present it to the CA Registrar. The Registrar, acting on behalf of the CA, will require two predetermined proof-of-identity documents, one of which must contain a picture. Upon successful identity proofing of the individual, the Registrar will issue a certificate binding the individual's identity to their public key. This method of registration is necessary for a high assurance system; however, it requires a significant infrastructure to implement on a large scale.

Benefits

Standardization of federal guidelines for entity identification and registration (proofing) and streamlining of token paradigms for rapid deployment with legacy systems are two key benefits. This pilot will help to prototype secure federal transactions with new-age approaches (WWW) and engineer and test secure web server to web client confidentiality and integrity.

INDEX

295